St Kilda

St Kilda

GEORGE SETON

Introduction by
Charles W. J. Withers

ORIGIN

This edition published in 2019 by
Birlinn Origin, an imprint of
Birlinn Limited
West Newington House
10 Newington Road
Edinburgh
EH9 1QS

www.birlinn.co.uk

2

ISBN 978 1 912476 46 6

British Library Cataloguing-in-Publication Data
A catalogue record for this book is available from the British Library

Typeset by Hewer Text UK Ltd, Edinburgh
Printed and bound by Clays Ltd, Elcograf S.p.A.

Contents

List of Illustrations

Introduction

Charles W. J. Withers

St Kilda, or, more properly, the St Kilda group of islands – Hirta, Soay and Borerary – is the remains of an ancient volcano and lies about forty miles north-west of the Hebridean island of North Uist. Only Hirta is and has been habitable and it is this island that has, since the late seventeenth century at least, been known as 'St Kilda'. The island was finally abandoned in August 1930: at that moment, Scotland shrank, never again to have the same geographical extent. For such a small and isolated island, St Kilda has had an extensive and, even, a remarkable literature associated with it. It is, of course, the island's very remoteness and the seeming strangeness of the inhabitants' lives and customs that has been the source of fascination for so many.

George Seton's account of the island was written nearly 200 years after St Kilda was effectively brought to the attention of the outside world through the writings of Martin Martin, a Skye man and correspondent for London's Royal Society, in his *Voyage to St Kilda* (1698) and his 1703 *A Description of the Western Isles of Scotland*. Seton's work is more noteworthy, however, than just being a later addition to the St Kilda 'canon' established by Martin. Seton offers not just his own commentary on St Kilda and its inhabitants, but a commentary on others' writings about the island. To be sure, Seton draws more from some than others. He treats Martin's work, for example, as, rightly, a reliable and intesting source in its own terms as well as the basis for comparison with conditions as Seton himself saw them. He did not see them himself for very long: his only direct experience of the island was as a passenger on board the *Dunara Castle* on its maiden voyage in 1877. Yet the overall benefit to the modern reader is two-fold: we are afforded an account of the island through the eyes of a late Victorian social commentator, and we are given a sense of how St Kilda has been differently seen and understood through the ages.

Seton's own commentary is of further value for his attention to that apparatus of record keeping so typical of his time – to the census returns on population and the numbers of inhabited houses and the occupational status of the inhabitants, and, in an important section in the book, to the registers of death kept by an incumbent minister between 1830 and 1844. Seton's interest in the certainty of numbers perhaps reflects his position as an advocate. To this statistical testimony, Seton adds the voices of St Kilda migrants with whom he has corresponded and the memories of some St Kildans recalling life there in the 1820s, including men like Donald MacKinnon, precentor in the Harris parish church and a native of the island, as well as the evidence arising from his own visit.

Something of the contemporary academic literature then appearing on St Kilda's customs and antiquities is also cited. Seton was on the General Council of the University of Edinburgh in the year he visited the island, a position, like the fact of his being a Fellow of the Royal Society of Edinburgh (from 1872), which would have afforded ready access to academics and to their writings. In the final chapter, the island and its future are shown to be the subject of considerable public debate. We should not, of course, judge the remarks of Seton and others in this context knowing them to be, in the event, fruitless: at the time of their writing, the abandonment of St Kilda by its inhabitants was fifty years into the future. Even so, Seton's remarks in this respect have an added poignancy in the fact that, as he notes at the end of his detailed account, one of the plans being publicly debated in the 1870s was indeed the total removal of the island's population.

Introduction

To many, Scots as much as others, St Kilda was the source of so much attention because it was imagined to be a sort of ethnological showcase, the people there understood to exemplify that state of cultural and social development once evident in all Scots or, at least, in all Hebrideans and Highlanders. Although Seton cautions against such a reading in strict terms, his view of the island and of its inhabitants is, nevertheless, informed by a belief that Scotland's Outer Isles were, in the late nineteenth century, the past on Scotland's doorstep, inhabited as he puts its, 'by an interesting race of people, who still exhibit the purest vestiges of Celtic manners and customs'. In these terms, St Kilda offered an even 'purer' and more ancient Scotland, distant as it was from the rest of the country.

Like many commentators at this period, however, Seton's view of what those manners and customs represented was profoundly ambivalent. On one level, he was, with others, interested in them much as contemporary social anthropologists comment upon native peoples: as unusual, even exotic, hard to comprehend on 'our' terms but, nonetheless, worth reporting upon. On another level and at the same moment, he was concerned that Gaelic – the medium through which St Kildans lived their lives – was a barrier to social development and to their capacity for moral advance. Seton's view that the speaking of Gaelic on St Kilda was a 'curse', something 'much to be regretted', was felt by many at this time. It was an attitude with deep roots. Alexander Buchan, who was, as Seton notes, sent to the island in the early eighteenth century by the Society in Scotland for the Propagation of Christian Knowledge (as one of its very first schoolmasters), was directed to 'Be diligent not only to teach them to read English but also to write and lay it on such as profit by you to do all they can for the edification of others and teach them their duty to their superiors'. But it was not an attitude shared by all in Seton's day. His aside in this respect (on p. 188) – 'Professor Blackie notwithstanding' – is interesting, referring as it does to the Professor of Celtic at the University of Edinburgh who was, at this time, actively campaigning for Highlanders' land rights and the continued use of Gaelic as a living language.

Seton begins his discussion of others' published accounts of St Kilda with a detailed description of the location of the island. Like those commentators before him, he is, as it were, trying to 'get a fix' on the island, trying to secure it as an object of study. More is known now of Martin Martin and of his 'discovery' of St Kilda than was the case in Seton's day, but Seton gets the main facts right concerning Martin and the evidence of this early and valuable testimony surfaces throughout Seton's text as the later author compares circumstances in his time with Martin's. Whilst Martin represents the first detailed account of the island, it should, with Seton's and the others, be seen as just that: a textual description. As the several different maps of St Kilda suggest (see plate section), textual description was not accurate physical measurement. In these terms, the island only takes its 'correct' shape in Seton's time despite having figured in people's geographical imaginations for more than two centuries.

Seton's chronology of visitors and commentators shows a heightening of interest in the island from the later eighteenth century apparent in MacAulay (1758), Brougham (1799) and, in 1803, in that Enlightenment polymath and 'man of letters', Sir George Stewart Mackenzie. Such an interest at that time is consistent with that more general attention shown in the Highlands and Islands by topographers and painters. Thereafter, and particularly after the visit in 1815 by the geologist MacCulloch, the number of travellers increased sharply. Between 1830 and 1858 the island had seven separate visitations, from clergymen and natural historians each keen to enumerate and monitor their different flocks. To judge by what Seton tells us about the numbers of visiting parties in the 1870s, the islanders might have been forgiven for feeling tired at such consistent scrutiny by outsiders. Who, indeed, would have been the stranger? One can only wonder what the islanders themselves thought as they were visited and reported upon, subjected to statistical enquiry, mapped and, from the later nineteenth century, photographed.

Seton's account is illuminating not just in terms of what he tells us, but how he does so. The rather romanticised, if not also senti-mentalised, descriptions of the physical environment, notably of the sheer scale and grandeur of the sea cliffs, are typical of much late Victorian rhetoric.

Despite the northerly position of the island and the effects of the sea air, the island's arable agriculture, if limited in extent, produced barley and potatoes and a little oats. In the eyes of earlier commentators, such agriculture was sufficient for the inhabitant's needs and care seems to have been taken to manure the grounds with seaware. To judge from Seton's comments, however, there had been a reduction in the extent of cultivated land during the first half of the nineteenth century and both he and others remark upon the difference between the neatly laid-out 'gardens' and the diminishing returns from a soil that was never put to grass and allowed to 'rest'. Pastoralism was dominated by sheep, held on the main island and on the smaller outlying islands. Since we have to take given numbers as correct in the absence of other evidence, it seems likely that the flock size maintained had changed little – at around two thousand sheep overall – between Martin's day and Seton's. As the latter notes, sheep were not held in common but as individual flocks on which, then, different levels of income and of rental would be expected. The agricultural landscape of the island was also remarkable for the large numbers of 'dome-shaped stone buildings' as Seton terms them, the small storage facilities, known as 'cleits', created by the islanders for their local produce.

Notable in this respect were the products stemming from the St Kildans' dependence upon sea-birds. So close had this relation-ship come by Seton's day that he felt compelled to observe how 'The devotion of the islanders to the more profitable pursuit of fowling induces them to neglect farming operations'. As he later notes, the terms of an 1869 Act for the Preservation of Sea-Birds did not extend to St Kilda since, as the Act realised, 'the necessi-ties of the inhabitants' depended upon them. Drawing in part upon others' earlier remarks, Seton offers a wonderfully vivid description of the noise arising from the myriads of sea-birds on the island and, even, how the whole landscape and the islanders themselves would at times be covered in feathers. The cries of the different sea-birds come in for attention and we are given detailed lists of the given local names for the birds and of the scientific names together with – and here Seton again draws from Martin – the calendar of the birds' migratory movements. Descriptions of several species follow, notably of the Great Auk and of evidence for its extinction, and of the Fulmar, which, in its aggressive territorial behaviour to others, Seton likens to the political aggrandisement of contemporary Germany.

Considerable attention is also paid to the feats of the islanders, men and women, in catching the sea-birds (women concentrated upon catching puffin), and to what we might think of as 'the culture' of St Kildan cragsmen where the climbing ropes were seen as objects of status and as heirlooms and where failure on Stack Briorach, the rock stack between Soay and St Kilda, might condemn a man to bachelorhood. Dependent as they were upon sea-birds for their oil, flesh and eggs, it is hard to avoid the feeling that the islanders had a keen sense of the dramatic and of the theatrical in regard to their activities on the cliffs. Seton certainly alludes to such a sense in noting that, as part of his visit in July 1877, 'one of the principal features in the programme was, of course, a practical display of the prowess of the cragsmen'. It is clear that the performance that then followed was at the prior arrangement of their minister and was designed more to entertain the passengers on board the *Dunara Castle* than from any immediate need on behalf of the islanders. It certainly thrilled Seton – 'It is difficult, by means of verbal narration, to convey anything like an adequate idea of the sensation produced by the wonderful performance which I have endeavoured to describe' – and was judged better than other contemporary 'extreme entertainers' in doing so.

Of course, we should not think of nineteenth-century St Kilda as, simply, some sort of exhibition site for the ethnologically curious. It is clear that the island and its inhabitants were not the isolated or unknowing species they were sometimes made out to be. Trade with other parts of Scotland was well established. The island's principal exports were feathers, fulmar oil, cloth, cattle, cheese and barley. Seton, citing others, several times observes how more might be made by the islanders of the export of fulmar oil, potentially for medicinal purposes. Lists of imports for various dates show an understandable need for the more 'luxury' goods of tobacco, tea and whisky. The St Kildans should be understood as a community which, whilst it might have been 'lax' in Seton's eyes in regard to matters of formal education, was otherwise highly moral and self-regulating.

The picture we should hold of the island and of its inhabitants, then, is of a population fitted for its environment and with limited but important connections with the outside world through trade, the arrival of the estate factor and the infrequent movement of individuals to Lewis or to Glasgow and beyond. This idea of 'fittedness' to environment even had, in Seton's mind, a directly Darwinian sense: in his description of the 'St Kilda cragsman', he interestingly observes that 'The great toes of the cragsmen are widely separated from the others, from the circumstance of their frequently resting their entire weight on that part of the foot in climbing'.

By the same token, we should not think of the community that was St Kilda in the nineteenth century as unchanging. Returns from the land were never guaranteed to cover everyone's daily needs and harvest shortage would mean reduced circumstances for all. It is clear from the evidence of the census that the population was declining from at least 1851 – the first year the island was officially enumerated in this source despite the first census having been begun fifty years before – and that the number of inhabited houses also fell between 1851 and 1871. Most occupied persons were enumerated, simply, as 'cottars and cragsmen', and nearly all the inhabitants in Seton's time were St Kildans by birth. The fact that many persons of both sexes were unmarried was common in the nineteenth-century Highlands. It resulted from the prolonged absence of many persons from their native parish engaging in circuits of labour migration to the farms and towns of the Scottish Lowlands. This had the effect of altering the sex-ratios within Highland populations. And as Seton makes abundantly clear, population numbers and the age structure of St Kilda could be quickly altered from the effects of disease.

Quite why Seton should pay the attention he does to the diseases of the islanders is unclear. He had no formal medical training. Nevertheless, what was clearly a source of fascination for him is also of interest to the modern reader and, indeed, valuable to the population historian. Bearing in mind that we are not necessarily given medically accurate descriptions as to the cause of death, Seton's summary tables on the nature of mortality and the age at death are alike remarkable for the evidence relating to infant mortality, and, especially, to the 'eight-day sickness'. This was, very largely, the result of 'lockjaw' or *trismus nascentium*, as it is also termed here. This is better known now as tetanus and the form of *trismus* identified here was so called because it killed within two weeks of birth – hence the local name of 'eight-day sickness' – and was different from *trismus traumaticus*, or tetanus arising from blood poisoning after a wound. It was not always easily distinguishable, however, from those other forms of tetanus associated with infants and with childbirth, *trismus neonatorum* and *trismus uteri* respectively.

Seton's comparative analysis of the infant mortality on St Kilda with other parts of the Hebrides, with urban Scotland, and, finally, with figures in a Dublin institution, is highly instructive. What he offers is a comparative geography of mortality for one section of the population. 'The pestilential lanes of our great cities', Seton writes, quoting from contemporary medical opinion, 'present no picture so dark as this'. Commentators on Glasgow at this time, for example, might have disagreed: Scotland's 'shock city' then had staggeringly high rates of infant mortality, especially from typhus, scarlet fever and whooping cough. In 1870s Glasgow, it was the small houses and over-crowding which produced the high infant death rate. For many authorities upon whom Seton drew, the same explanation applied to St Kilda. Other explanations – the mode of dressing the umbilical cord (which might explain deaths attributed to *trismus neonatorum* had such clinical distinctions been given), the use of birds' excrement as fuel, and 'the indoor manufacture of manure' – should be discounted, although Seton is persuaded by one commentator's view that the high death rate was due to diet, reliance upon the meat of sea-birds and the effects upon the mother's milk. Dysentery on the island was likewise attributed to the effects of eating too much dried fish.

Seton ends with what he calls the 'Western Question': a discussion of the proposals then circulating in the popular press as to what to do about the island and its inhabitants. As one might expect an advocate to do, he carefully assesses the options presented: temporary removal of the inhabitants; total permanent removal; keep things as they are but try to improve the St Kildans' circumstances. He draws parallels with the island communities of Pitcairn and Tristan da Cunha, but throughout stresses the attachment of St Kildans to their native place and is, as a result, persuaded by those arguing for the third option.

We will never know exactly what 'the clergy, and lawyers, and doctors, and civil engineers, and artists, and merchants, and travellers – the passengers of the *Dunara Castle* who spent that Monday in July last [1877] upon the island of St Kilda' thought of the island and its inhabitants. Nor will we ever know what the inhabitants thought of their visitors. But in Seton's *St Kilda* we have a splendid guide to how the island has been thought of, not just by one man on that late Victorian summer's day, but by all those travellers drawn, like Martin Martin and the many others, by the island's enduring fascination.

Preface

One of the earliest writers on St Kilda concludes his account with an apology for what some of his readers might regard as prolixity, and justifies his narrative by asserting that 'the St Kildans may be ranked among the greatest curiosities of the moral world'. Concurring in that opinion, the author has long turned his attention to the vital and social statistics of the remote islanders; and the large amount of public interest in their lonely rock which has been aroused by the recent appearance of numerous letters and articles in the columns of the Scottish press has induced him to compile the present volume. Upwards of twelve years ago, he prepared a lecture on St Kilda, which he delivered in various parts of the country; and since that time, he has collected a number of additional facts bearing upon its history and circumstances, and has, moreover, visited the island during the past summer. In referring to the rare appearance of strangers on its distant shores towards the beginning of the present century, Dr Macculloch says that every *avatär* of that nature was well remembered, and that he who had no other means of reaching the temple of fame had only to find his way to St Kilda, in order to be recorded in its archives. Even in these later days of rapid locomotion and increased intercourse, the visitors to the island are comparatively few and far between; and for one that has landed on its rocky coast, probably tens of thousands have accomplished the hackneyed 'Swiss round', or even penetrated the wilds of Norway.

With the exception of the incidental notices of Macculloch, Wilson, and one or two later writers, nearly all the accounts of St

Kilda were published before the end of last century; and hitherto no work has appeared which embraces anything like a detailed description of the island and its primitive inhabitants. Besides a careful persual of all the known literature on the subject – most of which is comparatively scarce – the author has examined the various official documents relative to St Kilda in the custody of the Registrar-General, and has been favoured with a number of notes and verbal statements by several friends who have visited the island during the last twenty years, of whom he must specially mention Captain F. W. L. Thomas, RN, formerly engaged on the Admiralty survey. He has also been furnished by Mrs McVean of Killin, a native of St Kilda, with an interesting series of reminiscences.

For some of his most attractive illustrations, the author is indebted to the sketch-books of Mr Alexander Carlyle Bell (kindly lent to him by Lord Young) and of the Rev. Eric J. Findlater of Lochearnhead; while the groups of women and children are from photographs taken by Captain Thomas in 1860.

St Bennet's, Edinburgh,
15th December 1877

The Hebrides or Western Isles

As distinguished from the mainland, which is itself but the northern extremity of an extensive island, the islands of Scotland, territorially, constitute a pretty considerable portion of that kingdom. In point of population, however, they are comparatively insignificant. At the census of 1871, their inhabitants amounted to only 161,909 persons – 74,332 males and 87,577 females – being a decrease of about 3000 since the previous census of 1861. At the same period, the proportion of the population on the mainland was upwards of 95 per cent, while the insular population was under 5 per cent. At the census of 1851, the returns relative to the islands were believed to be somewhat imperfect; and accordingly, both in 1861 and 1871, an effort was made to get the omissions supplied. A circular was issued by the Registrar-General to the registrar of every parish or district to which islands were known to be attached, with the view of ascertaining their names, and whether or not they were inhabited. A complete list was thus obtained of all the islands, other than bare rocks, which were either inhabited by man or capable of affording pasturage to cattle or sheep – the word 'island' having been defined to be 'any piece of solid land, surrounded by water, which affords sufficient vegetation to support one or more sheep, or which is inhabited by man'. All mere rocks which are the resort of wildfowl were accordingly excluded, and the following proved to be the result in 1861:

Inhabited islands	186[1]
Uninhabited	602
Total	788

Some of the uninhabited islands are of great extent, and furnish pasturage to from three to four hundred sheep. Others, again, are so small as not to be more than sufficient for the sustenance of a single sheep, which is removed, when fattened, to make way for a leaner member of the flock. No fewer than 749 of these 788 islands belong to the six counties of Shetland, Orkney, Sutherland, Ross and Cromarty, Inverness, and Argyll; while the remaining thirty-nine pertain to the counties of Caithness, Bute, Forfar, Perth, Clackmannan, Fife, Haddington, Edinburgh, Linlithgow, Renfrew, Ayr and Kirkcudbright. Three of these counties – viz., Shetland, Orkney and Bute – are entirely made up of separate islands. Two of the smaller islands belonging to the county of Bute,

> With verdant link
> Close the fair entrance to the Clyde[2]

and constitute the parish of Cumbraes, a former minister of which had so exalted a notion of the importance of his little territory, that, after first invoking God's blessing on his own people, he was in the habit of devoutly remembering, in his prayers, 'the adjacent islands of Great Britain and Ireland!'

The most populous of the inhabited islands is Lewis, of which the greater part is in the county of Ross – the remaining portion (Harris) pertaining to Inverness-shire. At the last census its inhabitants amounted to 25,947 – 12,372 males, and 13,575 females. The least populous islands, at the same date, were Bound-Skerries, in Shetland, inhabited by two males; and Cramond, in the county of Edinburgh, of which a male and a female constituted the entire

---

1 In 1871 the inhabited islands amounted to 190.
2 'Lord of the Isles', v. 13.

population. At the census of 1851, it would appear that the island of Inchcolm, in the Firth of Forth, was tenanted by a solitary man, and Little Papa, in Shetland, by a solitary woman!

The male inhabitants of these islands are exposed to no little danger, in consequence of their only road or highway being across the channels which separate island from island, or from the mainland, through most of which fierce currents flow. The deaths from drowning are, accordingly, very numerous, and help to make the proportion of the sexes even more unequal than on the mainland, where the 'lords of creation' are in a decided minority.[3] In 1871, the proportion of females on the mainland was 109.19 to every 100 males; while in the islands the proportion was as high as 117.82. This striking difference is, to a great extent, accounted for by the fact of an exceptionally large proportion of the insular males being engaged in the whale, seal and other fishings, or connected with the merchant shipping – such avocations necessarily implying long and frequent absence from their homes.

In the earliest period of our written history, these islands were peopled by the Celtic race. A large number of them, however, bear names given by the Northmen, by whom they were seized, partly for the purposes of commerce, but principally as naval stations, from which they could make inroads on the mainland. In their ships, or 'sea-horses', they braved the dangers of the deep, and succeeded in effecting permanent settlements in various parts of the kingdom – the Jutes and Saxons on the south coast of England, the Danes on the east coast and in the Lowlands of Scotland, and the Norwegians in Shetland and Orkney from which they extended their power over the Hebrides. The Western Islands, however, were gradually recovered by the mainland population; but the Northmen held their ground in Caithness, Orkney and Shetland, where their language has latterly given way to English – Gaelic being spoken in the Western Isles. The impress

---

3 There is a line of cottages in Stornoway called 'The Widows' Row', from the circumstance of all the occupants having lost their husbands in a single storm.

of the Northmen, however, is still very perceptible. In the words of the lamented author of *A Summer in Skye*:

> Old Norwegian castles, perched on the bold headlands, yet moulder in hearing of the surge . . . Hill and dale wear ancient names that sigh to the Norway pine. The inhabitant of Mull or Skye perusing the 'Burnt Njal' is struck most of all by the names of localities – because they are almost identical with the names of localities in his own neighbourhood . . . The Norseman found the Hebrides convenient stepping-stones, or resting places, on his way to the richer southern lands . . . Doubtless, in course of time, he looked on the daughter of the Celt, and saw that she was fair, and a mixed race was the result of alliances. To this day in the islands the Norse element is distinctly visible – not only in old castles and the names of places, but in the faces and entire mental build of the people . . . The Hebrideans are a mixed race; in them the Norseman and the Celt are combined, and here and there is a dash of Spanish blood which makes brown the cheek and darkens the eye . . . The Islesman is a Highlander of the Highlanders; modern life took longer in reaching him; and his weeping climate, his misty wreaths and vapours, and the silence of his moory environments, naturally continued to act upon and to shape his character.

It is necessary, however, to speak with considerable caution on the subject of race, as supposed to be indicated by complexion or physique. Broadly stated, the Celt may be described as being generally characterised by black hair and a dark complexion, and the Norseman by the opposite attributes. But we must bear in mind that Tacitus and other early writers refer to the *rutilae comae* of the Caledonians; and we all know that both *Bane* and *Roy* – indicating white and red – are very common epithets among the Highlanders proper; a red-haired, blue-eyed Celt being by no means rare. Complicated alliances necessarily affect and modify their results; and not unfrequently a remote influence is strikingly displayed many generations after it first began to operate. Not a few remarkable examples of this have occurred in our historic families; and doubtless the same effects would be observed among the humbler classes, if their pedigrees could be established.

The Hebrides, or Western Islands, consist of an elongated group flanking nearly the whole west coast of Scotland. Anciently called Hebrides, Aebudae, etc., they at one time comprehended the various islands and islets in the Firth of Clyde, the isle of Rathlin off the north-east corner of Ireland, and even the Isle of Man on the Cumberland coast. The modern Hebrides, however, only include the islands and islets extending from 55° 35′ to 58° 37′ N lat., and lying westward of the peninsula of Kintyre on the south, and of the mainland of Scotland in the middle and on the north. They may be classified under five divisions—

1st, The Islay and Jura group ⎫	
2nd, The Mull group ⎬	Inner Hebrides
3rd, The Skye group ⎭	
4th, The Long Island group ⎫	Outer Hebrides
5th, The St Kilda group ⎭	

The estimated area of the Hebrides, measured on the plane, is about 3000 square miles,[4] or 1,920,000 imperial acres, thus constituting nearly a tenth part of Scotland. When Dr Walker published his *Economical History of the Hebrides* in 1812, the arable land in the Western Isles was estimated at only one-eightieth part of the uncultivated ground; but the proportion is, no doubt, now considerably larger.

In addition to the St Kilda group, the Outer Hebrides (or the 'Long Island'), include Lewis, Harris, North and South Uist, Benbecula and Barra, and are inhabited by an interesting race of people, who still exhibit the purest vestiges of Celtic manners and

4 Equal to about 3600 square miles, if measured over the undulations of their superficies.

customs. With regard to the physical characteristics of these islands, while Harris and Barra are entirely mountainous – the former consisting of two extensive ranges – in Lewis there are four principal groups of mountains, of which one is a ramification of one of the Harris ranges. North Uist presents two ranges of inferior elevation, while South Uist chiefly consists of one extended group. The loftiest of these mountains are Hecla, or Eachcla, in South Uist, and Clisheim in Harris, of which the latter was recently ascertained to be 2430 feet in height, many of the Lewis mountains being only a little inferior. Speaking generally, the Outer Hebrides are greatly indented by lochs and creeks.[5] Beaches and sands are of comparatively rare occurrence; and although on the eastern coasts there are several excellent harbours, very few are to be found on the west, except in Lewis. One of the most characteristic features of the Outer Hebrides is the large number of lakes, more particularly in North Uist, and in the lower parts of South Uist, Benbecula and Lewis. In the eastern portion of North Uist, it is said to be difficult to determine whether land or water predominates; and Macculloch, speaking of Benbecula, says 'The sea is here all islands, and the land all lakes.' Some of these lakes are of considerable extent, the largest being Loch Langavat, in Lewis, which is upwards of ten miles in length, and singularly tortuous.

The leading characteristics of the scenery are ruggedness, sterility and gloom. The total absence of wood, the bleak and dismal aspect of the mountains, the endless tracts of shell-sand hillocks, and the dark and sullen waters of the lakes, complete the picture of desolation which these wild regions present. The climate is moist and variable; the clouds exhibiting every diversity of form and elevation, and producing the most magical effects upon the landscape. The temperature is by no means low (about 40° in

5 Although covering only ten square miles, Lochmaddy in North Uist has a coastline which, measuring the various islands, creeks and bays, has been estimated to ramify over no less than 300 miles.

spring and 52° in autumn), open weather being the normal condition of the atmosphere. Snow seldom lies for any length of time, and frost is rarely intense or of long duration. Ozone has been ascertained to be more abundant in the Hebrides than in any other part of the world. Spring commences about the end of March, and is usually accompanied by easterly winds and dry weather, but the green livery of the succeeding season does not appear till towards the beginning of June. July and August constitute the Hebridean summer, during which the wide and sandy stretches of the western shores are carpeted with daisies, buttercups, sea-pinks and milk-white clover. From September to the middle of October there is usually a continuance of dry weather, after which westerly gales begin to blow, getting more boisterous as the season advances, and being generally accompanied by very heavy rain. Of rare occurrence in summer, thunder is frequently heard in the coldest period of the year; and the violent tempests which then prevail afford undeniable evidence of their severity in the unroofed houses and stranded boats of the inhabitants. But although the first impression of the scenery of the Outer Hebrides, even under the favourable influence of a summer's sun, is apt to be associated with dreariness and gloom, after a little while the peculiar character of the surroundings undergoes a gradual transformation, and the dullest features of the landscape seem to present a beauty of their own. The barest mountain displays its picturesque scars and 'corries'; the loneliest lake is enlivened by its weeds and water-lilies; and even the varied outlines of the arid sandhills contrive to excite our admiration. At one moment the glorious orb of day shines forth with dazzling lustre, and the peaks of the mountains stand out sharp and clear against an azure sky, while the sea is smooth as a mirror, gently and silently laving the golden sand; at another, the black clouds gather from the west, and veil every eminence in mist, the wind drives furiously from shore to shore, and the mighty deep is troubled, tossing its long line of breakers to the heavens. Doubtless the due appreciation of every aspect of nature depends largely upon temperament and association; and many a dweller in the plains, with their grassy slopes and luxuriant foliage, would fail to discover any form of comeliness in these lonely western lands. But as Macgillivray says—

> What can be more delightful, than a midnight walk by moon-light along the sea-beach of some secluded isle, the glassy sea sending from its surface a long stream of dancing and dazzling light – no sound to be heard save the small ripple of the idle wavelet, or the scream of the seabird watching the fry that swarms along the shores! In the short nights of summer, the melancholy song of the throstle has scarcely ceased on the hill-side, when the merry carol of the lark commences, and the plover and snipe sound their shrill pipe. Again, how glorious is the scene which presents itself from the summit of one of the loftier hills, when the great ocean is seen glowing with the last splendour of the setting sun, and the lofty isles of St Kilda rear their giant heads, amid the purple blaze, on the extreme verge of the horizon!

The scenery of Scotland and of Switzerland present some remarkable contrasts. Every observant traveller in the Western Islands will readily acknowledge that the beauty of our rugged shores is greatly enhanced by the sea and its surroundings. Grand as are the snow-clad peaks of the Alps, the absence of the ocean in the land of William Tell cannot fail to be regarded as a serious want by anyone who has been accustomed to watch the various aspects of that wondrous element. Independently of the pictur-esque effects of the sea, its important influence on the commer-cial as well as on the political and intellectual character of certain nations – Greece, Italy, Spain and England – has been noticed by various historians. Goethe suggests that 'perhaps it is the sight of the sea from youth upward that gives English and Spanish poets such an advantage over those of inland countries'; and other writers have remarked upon the impression of the illimit-able which is derived from the majesty of the ocean. In his interesting little volume on Iona, the Duke of Argyll makes some very pertinent remarks on the characteristics of marine scenery. That of the Hebrides, he says

> is altogether peculiar; and by those whose notions of beauty or of fertility are derived from countries which abound in corn and wine and oil, the charms of that scenery can perhaps never be understood. And yet these charms are founded on a wonderful combination of the three greatest powers in nature – the sky, the sea, the mountains.[6] But these stand in very different relations to the early memories of our races. As regards the sky, there is no speech or nation where its voice is not heard; there is no corner of the world where the sweet influences which it sheds do not form, consciously or unconsciously, an intimate part of the life of men. But it is not so with the ocean. There are millions who have never seen it, and can have no conception of the aspect of the most wonderful object upon earth . . . To eyes that have been accustomed to rest upon the boundless fields of ocean, there is nothing in nature like it. The inexhaustible fountain of all the fertility and exuberance of earth – the type of all vastness and of all power – it responds also with infinite subtlety of expression to every change in the face of heaven. There is nothing like its awfulness when in commotion. There is nothing like its restfulness when it is at rest. There is nothing like the joyfulness of its reflected lights, or the tenderness of the colouring which it throws in sunshine from its deeps and shallows. I am sorry for those who have never listened to, and therefore can never understand, the immense conversation of the sea.

A single word about the inhabitants of the Western Isles. The author of *Land of Lorne* tells the Princess Louise of the destitution and hard lives of the Hebrideans, notwithstanding which he says

---

6 'Earth, ocean, air, beloved brotherhood!' – Shelley.

that 'though all the powers of earth seem leagued against them, these people are as fresh and wholesome-hearted, as generous and guileless, as any men or women you will meet with in your earthly pilgrimage'. He quotes the favourable estimates of the accomplished writer of *Tales of the West Highlands*, and of the large-hearted Norman Macleod, relative to their good feeling and intelligence, and speaks of the 'quaint thoughts and dreams with which they cheer their otherwise melancholy firesides' – pronouncing them 'a race apart'. Solemn in aspect, and with faces rarely illumined by a smile, the denizens of the Outer Hebrides are indisposed to be gay and sportive. Unlike those of more brilliant nations, 'their visions are steady rather than fitful', and by them the world and the things thereof are always contemplated under a sober and unchanging light. Essentially a home-loving people, they show little inclination to find their way to distant lands – and their hospitality to strangers has long been proverbial. Even in the humblest of huts the visitor is asked to partake of *something* – a glass of luscious milk, or, at least, a draught of sparkling water; and 'the smile that sweetens such gifts is like Christ's, turning water into wine'. They have, of course, their weak points – a slow and listless demeanour, a want of life and energy, a tendency to huddle together and to neglect ablution, an unwillingness to change old ways; and Mr Buchanan does not hesitate to acknowledge that 'they must inevitably sink and perish' in the race with the Southron. But with all their faults, they are devout and spiritual; 'the voices of winds and waters are in their hearts, and they passionately believe in God'. As Alexander Smith says—

> The Celt is the most melancholy of men. He has turned everything to superstitious uses, and every object of nature, even the unreasoning dreams of sleep, are mirrors which flash back death upon him . . . In his usual avocations, the Islesman rubs clothes with death as he would with an acquaintance. Gathering wild-fowl, he hangs, like a spider on its thread, over a precipice

on which the sea is beating a hundred feet beneath. In his crazy boat he adventures into whirlpool and foam. He is among the hills when the snow comes down, making everything unfamiliar, and stifling the strayed wanderer. Thus death is ever near him, and that consciousness turns everything to omen.

Published Accounts of St Kilda

Not the least interesting of the Western Hebrides is the lonely island of St Kilda, which lies in the midst of the wide Atlantic,

Nature's last limit, hemmed with oceans round –[1]

in lat. 57° 48' 35" N, long. 8° 35' 30" W, between forty and fifty miles to the west of North Uist and Harris,[2] which are themselves about fifty miles from the mainland. From Shillay island, which is situated at the north-west entrance to the Sound of Harris, the course for St Kilda is WNW ¾ N; the compass course being NW by W. Lowestoft Ness (1° 46' E long.), on the east coast of Suffolk, and the island of St Kilda (8° 35' W long.) lie 10° of longitude apart; consequently the sun rises and sets on the east coast of

1 Mallet's 'Amyntor and Theodora', canto i, line 352.
2 The statements relative to the distance of St Kilda are somewhat different. Thus—
76 nautical miles from Dunvegan, Skye – Sands' *Life in St Kilda*
70 miles from Barra Head Lighthouse – Otter's *Sailing Directions for the Hebrides*
c. 60 miles from island of Pabbay, erroneously said to be 'the nearest land to St Kilda'
– Rev. Dr McDonald's *Second Journal*
c. 55 miles from Ardavoran Head, the northern extremity of North Uist – Note on Ainslie's *Map of Scotland*
52 miles west of Harris – Johnston's *General Gazetteer*, 1877
50¼ miles west of Shillay island (c. half a mile NW of Pabbay) – Johnston's *Royal Atlas*
c. 45 miles from Hougray Point, the western extremity of North Uist – Letter from Mr Alex. Grigor, Examiner of Registers, 27th November 1861
40 miles from Griminish Point, the north-western extremity of North Uist – Black's *Map of Scotland*, compiled by Bartholomew
34 miles from Monach islands, the nearest land to St Kilda – Otter, *ut supra.*

England thirty-nine minutes before it rises and sets on St Kilda. At one time belonging to North Uist,[3] St Kilda now forms a part of the parish of Harris – the southern portion of Lewis, in the county of Inverness – the northern and larger portion, as already stated, pertaining to Ross-shire. The parish of Harris includes six other inhabited islands besides St Kilda, ranging in population, at the census of 1871, from 6 to 421.

The notices of St Kilda in the pages of Fordun, Boethius, Buchanan, Camden and Sir Robert Moray (to be afterwards referred to), besides being very brief, are merely statements at second hand. The earliest account of the island, from personal observation, is contained in the work of Martin,[4] a factor of the Macleod family, who visited St Kilda along with the Rev. John Campbell, minister of Harris, in the summer of 1697 – ten years before the union of England and Scotland. The following is the title of his somewhat scarce and curious work:

A late Voyage to St Kilda, the remotest of all the Hebrides or Western Isles of Scotland, with a History of the Island, Natural, Moral and Topographical. Wherein is an Account of their Customs, Religion, Fish, Fowl, etc. As also a Relation of a late Impostor there, pretended to be sent by St John Baptist. By M. Martin, Gent., London: Printed for D. Brown and T. Goodwin: At the Black Swan and Bible without Temple Bar; and at the Queen's Head against St Dunstan's Church in Fleet Street. MDCXCVIII.

It appears from the preface that the said voyage was undertaken in an open boat, 'to the almost manifest hazard of the author's life'; and the adventurous crew reached their destination after a prolonged passage. He also informs us that, besides his liberal education at the university, he had the advantage of seeing

3 *Fasti Eccles. Scot.*, iii, 140.
4 Martin appears to have been at least three weeks on the island.

foreign places, and the honour of conversing with some of the Royal Society, who raised his natural curiosity to survey the Isles of Scotland more exactly than any other. This probably refers to a communication which he made to the Royal Society, entitled 'Several Observations on the North Islands of Scotland', in which he is described as 'Martin Martin'.[5] He is similarly described in the index to Gough's *British Topography*. He took the degree of Master of Arts at the University of Edinburgh; and in 1681 subscribed his name to the usual forms of oath as 'Martinus Martin'. Gough says that he was a native of one of the Western Islands, where he lived as a factor; the authority for which statement was no doubt derived from the preface to the edition of Buchan's *Description of St Kilda*, published in 1773, to be afterwards referred to. The *Voyage to St Kilda* passed through four editions, of which the latest was published in 1753; and it again appeared in the volume embracing Donald Monro's 'Description of the Western Isles', published at Edinburgh in 1774.

In the year 1703 Martin published a larger work, entitled *A Description of the Western Islands of Scotland*, which contains a short account of St Kilda, and of a visit of a native of that island to Glasgow. The following note is endorsed on the title-page of the copy in the Advocates' Library:

This very Book accompanied Mr Samuel Johnson and me in our Tour to the Hebrides in autumn 1773, Mr Johnson told me that he had read Martin when he was very young. Martin was a native of the isle of Sky, where a number of his relations still remain. His book is a very imperfect performance; and he is erroneous as to many particulars, even some concerning his own island. Yet as it is the only Book upon the subject, it is very generally known. I have seen a second edition of it.[6] I

5 *Philosophical Transactions*, vol. xix, October 1697, No. VI.
6 Published in 1716.

cannot but have a kindness for him, notwithstanding his defects.

James Boswell

16 April 1774

In his *Life* of the great lexicographer, Boswell also mentions Johnson's early perusal of Martin's work, with which he was then much pleased, having been particularly struck by the St Kilda man's quaint notion that the High Church of Glasgow had been hollowed out of a rock! At a later period, however (1778), when speaking of the inelegant style of books written towards the beginning of the eighteenth century, the Doctor said: 'No man now writes so ill as Martin's' *Account of the Hebrides* is written. A man could not write so ill, if he should try.' In common with Macculloch, he elsewhere laments the fact of Martin having failed more fully to record the 'uncouth customs' and 'wild opinions' which no longer prevail in the Western Islands.

> The mode of life which was familiar to himself, he did not suppose unknown to others, nor imagined that he could give pleasure by telling that of which it was, in his little country, impossible to be ignorant. What he has neglected cannot now be performed. In nations where there is hardly the use of letters, what is once out of sight is lost for ever.[7]

In the year 1705, at the desire of the Society for Propagating Christian Knowledge, the Rev. Alexander Buchan was sent to St Kilda, where he remained till his death in 1730. His *Description of St Kilda, the most remote Western Isle of Scotland*, was published several years after his death. The earliest edition, with a short introduction, printed at Edinburgh for the author, and 'sold by his Daughter', bears the date 1741; but most of his statements appear to have been taken verbatim from Martin's work. A later

---

7 *Journey to the Western Islands in 1773*, p. 145.

edition, with a preface by his daughter, Jean Buchan (one of thirteen children), was published in 1773, and reprinted at Glasgow in the second volume of the *Miscellanea Scotica*, in 1818. She mentions that she was sent from St Kilda to school in Glasgow when about fifteen years of age, and was shipwrecked upon the Mull of Kintyre; nevertheless, she adds:

> I went to Glasgow for my education, where I continued for some time; from thence I went to Edinburgh, where I had the misfortune to be beat by a horse on the street and broke my jaw-bone, which has rendered me incapable of earning my bread by the needle, to which I was brought up. I had also another misfortune to get my arm broke, and not being carefully sett, is mighty uneasy to me.

Buchan's wife survived him, in very destitute circumstances, till her sixty-sixth year. The following entry occurs in the parish register of Findo Gask, Perthshire, under the disbursements of the kirk session – '1731, 15th August. To Katharin Campbell, relict to Mr Alexander Buchan, Minister of the Gospell at St Kilda, eighteen shillings.'

A small anonymous volume, published in London in 1751, entitled *A Voyage to Scotland, the Orkneys, and the Western Isles of Scotland*, contains a few pages relative to St Kilda, which, in the opinion of the author, of all the Western Islands, 'deserves the most notice, as it abounds more with singularities'. After referring to the abundance of horses, cows, sheep, etc., he pronounces the solan goose to be 'the main support of the inhabitants', which then consisted of about thirty families. He also alludes to the fulmar, to the genius of the natives for poetry and music, their wonderful feats in fowling, and their morality, and hospitality to strangers.

The next work relating to St Kilda is that of the Rev. Kenneth Macaulay, who paid a visit to the island in June 1758. It was published six years afterwards, under the following title—

A Voyage to and History of St Kilda. Containing a Description of this remarkable Island; the Manners and Customs of the Inhabitants; the Religious and Pagan Antiquities there found; with many other curious and interesting Particulars. By the Rev. Mr Kenneth Macaulay, Minister of Ardnamurchan, Missionary to the Island from the Society for Propagating Christian Knowledge. London, 1764.[8]

Macaulay's volume embraces considerably more than twice the amount of matter contained in Martin. The authorship, however, is strongly questioned by both Dr Johnson and his biographer. Boswell states that he had been told the book was written by Dr John McPherson of Skye, from the materials collected by Macaulay; and the truth of this allegation is confirmed in a note by Mr Croker, in his edition of Boswell. Although Dr Johnson complimented the Rev. Kenneth by describing the book as 'a very pretty piece of topography', he privately said to Boswell, 'There is a combination in it of which Macaulay is not capable.' Macaulay graduated at King's College, Aberdeen, in 1742, and was ordained assistant and successor to his father, Aulay Macaulay, minister of Harris (who died 1758), in 1751. He was translated to Ardnamurchan in 1760, and twelve years later to Cawdor, where he was visited by Dr Johnson and Boswell on their northern tour. He died in 1779, at the age of fifty-six.[9] Kenneth's eldest brother John, successively minister of Barra, South Uist and Inveraray, was father of Zachary Macaulay, and grandfather of Lord Macaulay, who was consequently the grand-nephew of the historian of St Kilda.

In the *Travels in the Western Hebrides from 1782 to 1790*, published in 1793, by the Rev. John Lane Buchanan, AM, missionary minister to the isles from the Church of Scotland, we find a chapter on St Kilda, extending to about thirty pages. Although the work bears the name of Buchanan, it is said to have been written from his

8 Another edition was published at Dublin in 1765.
9 *Fasti Eccles. Scot.*, vol. iii.

notes by Dr William Thomson.[10] The professed author acknowledges, in his preface, that what he has written 'will give offence to
many petty tyrants'; and assures his readers, in language worthy of
the Far West, that he has been 'actuated by motives of humanity
and of duty to the common Parent and Lord of all mankind!' He
describes the tacksman of St Kilda, 'for some time a charity-
schoolmaster in that place,' as one who, 'having forgot his former
insignificance, has assumed all the turbulent pride of a purse-proud
pedagogue, to keep the inhabitants under'.

In the first volume of his *Life and Times*, published in 1871,
Lord Brougham gives an amusing account of a visit which he paid
to St Kilda, along with two friends,[11] in August 1799, when in his
twenty-second year. It is embraced in a long letter, written at
Stornoway, to his kinsman Lord (William) Robertson, an occu-
pant of the Scottish Bench; and some of the statements which it
contains will be afterwards referred to.

There is an interesting notice of the hydrography, scenery, and
geology of St Kilda in the second volume of *A Description of the
Western Islands of Scotland*, by John Macculloch, MD, published in
1819; and the third volume of the same work contains an engraving of the island. The later publication of the same author[12] (vol.
iii pp. 168–197) embraces some curious particulars relative to St
Kilda, which he appears to have visited in the year 1815, I feel
called upon to say a word on behalf of Macculloch. In his *Land of
Lorne*, Mr Buchanan speaks of him as—

the author of a very clever but otherwise worthless book on
the Highlands . . . a writer who, with all his great ability, lacked

---

10 See Chambers' *Lives of Eminent Scotsmen*, iv, 353.
11 John Joseph Henry, nephew of Lord Moira, who afterwards married the Duke of
Leinster's daughter; and Charles Stuart, eldest son of Sir Charles Stuart, and grandson
of John, third Earl of Bute.
12 *The Highlands and Western Isles of Scotland*; containing Descriptions of their Scenery
and Antiquities, etc., founded on a series of annual journeys between the years 1811
and 1821, in Letters to Sir Walter Scott, Bart. 4 vols. 8vo. London, 1824.

the two great gifts of spiritual imagination and human insight. He was a foolish scholar; and his book would be worthless on the ground of its pedantry alone. His remarks on landscape are sometimes singularly astute, but he never seems to be greatly moved . . . His book is amusing, and nothing more . . . Yet his letters were addressed to Walter Scott, who was doubtless much edified by their familiarity and endless verbiage.

A later writer, who, I suspect, has only dipped into his pages, and who evidently has never even heard of his earlier work, summarily declares that 'he might as well not have gone near St Kilda, for all the information he has given on the subject'; and that although geology was his speciality, he makes no allusion to it in the account of his visit to the island! These are severe criticisms. The doctor's writings have, no doubt, a perceptible flavour of the pedant, and perhaps he does not entirely apprehend the Highland character; but I venture to think that he must have been a man who, on the whole, observed accurately, besides appreciating and describing with considerable humour the pride, solemnity, and caution of the Celt. Dr Macculloch, who was of Scottish extraction, was born at Guernsey in 1773, and died at Penzance in 1835, in consequence of an amputation rendered necessary by an accident.

In 1838, a little work was published by Mr McPhun of Glasgow, entitled, 'Sketches of the Island of St Kilda . . . taken down, for the greater part, from the oral narration of the Rev. N. Mackenzie, clergyman of the island, by L. Maclean, author of "Adam and Eve", "Historical Account of Iona", etc.'[13] It contains

---

13 In his work on our first parents, the learned author endeavours to prove that Gaelic was the language of Paradise – a circumstance which has much more recently been chronicled in a clever *jeu d'esprit*, by the minister of a rural parish in Perthshire, of which the following is the second stanza—

> When Eve, all fresh in beauty's charms,
> First met fond Adam's view,
> The first word that he'll spoke till her
> Was '*Cumar achum dhu*'

some curious anecdotes illustrative of the dangers to which the fowlers are exposed, and other interesting details.

Probably the best account of St Kilda is embraced in the second volume of *A Voyage round the Coasts of Scotland and the Isles*, published in 1842, by James Wilson, the well-known writer on ornithology, and brother of the better-known Christopher North, who visited St Kilda, along with Sir Thomas Dick Lauder, secretary to the Board of Fisheries, in August 1841. A portion of this account is contained in a letter addressed to the secretary of the Society for Propagating Christian Knowledge, and published, with three interesting engravings, in the Appendix to the Report of that Society's proceedings for 1841.

There are also several other shorter notices of St Kilda, of which I may mention the article in the *Edinburgh Encyclopaedia*, by an intelligent eyewitness; the *Journals* of the Rev John McDonald of Urquhart, who visited the island on four different occasions, between 1822 and 1830, at the request of the Society for Propagating Christian Knowledge;[14] the incidental account by Mr Thomas S. Muir of Leith, who touched at St Kilda in 1858, in his excellent work on the *Characteristics of Old Church Architecture, etc., in the Mainland and Western Islands of Scotland*; a short sketch of a visit to the island in June 1860, published in *Macmillan's Magazine* for June 1861, under the title of 'The Falcon among the Fulmars; or, Six Hours at St Kilda', by John E. Morgan, MA Oxon., at that time tutor in the family of the late Mr Rainy of Raasay; 'A Visit to St Kilda in 1873', by Dr R. Angus Smith, described in two papers in *Good Words* for 1875; 'A Visit to St Kilda', by a Lady (Lady Baillie of Polkemmet), embraced in the January number of the *Church of Scotland Missionary Record* for the same year; a little volume, published in 1876 (and a second edition in 1877), entitled *Out of the World; or, Life in St Kilda*, by J. Sands, Ormiston, Tranent, with illustrations etched on copper by the

14 Embraced in the *Apostle of the North – the Life and Labours of the Rev. Dr McDonald*, by the Rev. J. Kennedy, Dingwall, 1866.

author;[15] and a pamphlet of thirty pages, bearing the name of 'St Kilda and its Inhabitants' (recently issued under the auspices of the Highland and Agricultural Society of Scotland), by Mr John Macdiarmid, who accompanied HMS *Flirt* to the island, with a supply of seeds and provisions, towards the beginning of May 1877.

15 The same writer also contributed three papers, entitled 'Life in St Kilda', to Chambers' 'Journal' for May 1877, besides a short notice of the island, accompanied by several illustrations, in the 'Graphic' of 7 April of the same year.

History and Ownership

Very little seems to have been ascertained respecting the early history of St Kilda, by which name the island has been known for less than three centuries. Its ancient appellation was Hirt, Hirth, Hirta or Hyrtha, a contraction of *h-lar-tir*, the Gaelic for 'west land' or 'west country',[1] and not a corruption of *Förd*, the Norse word for 'earth' or 'land', as indicated by Macaulay in a very elaborate argument.[2] Hirt is pronounced 'Hirst' by the inhabitants, who have a proverb indicative of the great distance of their abode from the centre of Scotland – viz., 'From Hirst to Perst' (i.e. Perth). The island is referred to under its old designation by Fordun, Camden, and other early writers, and also in Scott's *Lord of the Isles*,[3] where 'grey Morag' thus commences her address to 'bright Edith' of Lorn, in praise of the heir of mighty Somerled—

---

1 *Proceedings of the Society of Scottish Antiquries*, x, 706.
2 Boethius and Bishop Lesley, to be afterwards referred to, derive the name of Hirtha from that of a sheep peculiar to the island.
3 Canto i., stanza viii. An earlier poet than the 'author of Waverley' – to wit, David Mallet or Malloch, who died more than 100 years ago – adopted St Kilda as the scene of a touching, but somewhat improbable, episode in the latter part of the reign of Charles II, which he describes in a poem of three cantos, entitled 'Amyntor and Theodora; or the Hermit'. Originally intended for the stage, it was afterwards altered to its present form, and is now known to a very limited number of readers. It contains a few interesting allusions to the scenery of the island, the simple lives of the natives, and the transmigrations of the birds.

'Daughter,' she said, 'these seas behold,
Round twice a hundred islands rolled,
From Hirt, that hears their northern roar,
To the green Ilay's fertile shore.'

The 'father of Scottish history', whose work was completed towards the end of the fourteenth century, after enumerating the most important of the Hebrides, speaks of 'Insula de Irte, quae sub Circio [north-west] constat esse, et in margine mundi; ultra quam, in illis finibus non reperitur terra.' In connection with the island of Lewis, he elsewhere describes 'Hirth' as 'omnium insularum fortissima; juxta quam est insula quaedam [Soa?] viginti milliarium longa [!], in qua dicitur oves inesse sylvestres, quae nequaquam, praeter a venatoribus, capiuntur.'[4]

After an allusion to the Isle of Man (Mona), Boethius says: 'Ab ea, quae prima est, ad Hirtha, quae Hebridum est postrema, intercapedinem septuaginta septem ac trecentorum millium passnum interesse. Nomen huic insula ab ovibus, quas prisca lingua Hierth vocamus, inditum est.'[5] Then follows a short notice of the sheep, the annual visit of the steward and priest, and other particulars, which are substantially repeated by Buchanan in connection with the following passage:

Sexaginta fere ultra hanc (Haskeir) millia ad occidentem aestivum recedit Hirta, frugum, pecorum, ac maxime ovium ferax; procerioresque gignit quam ulla aliarum insularum ... Tota insula non superat longitudinem mille passuum, totidem prope lata: nec ab ulla aliarum insularum videri pars ejus ulla potest, praeter tres montes in littore attollentes, qui ex locis editioribus cermmtur. In iis montibus sunt oves eximiae pulchritudinis; sed ob violentiam aestus marini vix cuiquam est ad eos aditus.[6]

---

4 Fordun's *Scotichronicon*, lib. i, cap. vi, and lib. ii, cap. x.
5 *Scotorum Historia*, 1574 (originally published in 1527), fol. 8.
6 *Rerum Scoticarum Historiae*, lib. i, cap. xli.

In his description of the Western Islands, Bishop Lesley says

> Omnium ultima est Hirtha, in polaris quidem elevationis sexagesimo tertio gradu constituta ... Accipit autem Hirtha nomen ab ove quadam, qui Hirth appellant, qua illa, et ea quidem sola insula abundat. Haec caprum altitudine, cornuum quidem longitudine bubalum superat, magnitudine vero exaequat.

After speaking of the islands of Skye, Lewis and Uist, Camden informs us that 'all the rest, save onely Hyrtha, are of small account, being either very stonie, or else inaccessible by reason of craggy cliffes, and skarce clad with any green sord'.[7]

In the *Description of the Western Isles of Scotland, called Hybrides*, by Mr Donald Monro, High Dean of Isles, 'who travelled through most of them in 1594', is a short reference to St Kilda, under the name Hirta, which he describes as being situated 'to the west-north-west' of the isle of Haysker, stating (in addition to some curious particulars, to be afterwards referred to), that 'the streams of the sea are starke and very eivil entring.' Eighteen years later (1612), a similar and still briefer notice of the island appears in John Monipennie's *Abridgment of the Scots Chronicles*, to which is annexed a 'true description' of Scotland, including its cities, castles, rivers, islands, etc. 'This Hirta', he says, 'is the last and farther isle in Albion; so that betwixt the Isle of Man, being the first isle in Albion, and this isle, there is (as stated by Boethius) 377 miles.' Both of these works are reprinted in the first and second volumes of *Miscellanea Scotica*, published at Glasgow in 1818. The same collection (vol. ii) contains a very brief 'Account of Hirta and Rona, given to Sir Robert Sibbald by the Lord Register, Sir George MacKenzie of Tarbat, afterwards Earl of Cromartie' (*c.* 1680). 'Of all the isles about Scotland,' says the writer, 'the island of Hirta lyeth furthest into the sea, is very mountainous, and not accessible but by climbing.'

---

7 *Brittania*, 1610, p. 216.

The tenth volume of the *Philosophical Transactions* of the Royal Society (No. 137, February 1678) contains a short paper by Sir Robert Moray, one of His Majesty's Council for the Kingdom of Scotland, entitled, 'A Description of the Island Hirta', in which he refers to the great difficulty of landing at Borrera, which he calls Burra, and erroneously indicates its position as *six* miles northward of Hirta. He also mentions the seal-hunting expeditions of the islanders in Soa, and their still more hazardous attempts to scale the heights of 'Stacka Donna' in search of sea-fowl, besides a few other curious particulars.[8]

According to Martin, the present name of the island was derived from one Kilder, who lived on the lonely rock, and after whom the well, near the village, called 'Toubir-Kilda', was also named.[9] Macaulay occupies several pages with speculations relative to the origin of the name, in the course of which he discusses the rival claims of a certain female saint called Kilda, who flourished during the infancy of the Saxon Church; of an old British writer named Gildas, who does not, however, appear to have been dignified with the title of 'Saint'; and of the ancient clergy of the kingdom, the Culdees, Keledei, or Gille-Dee – i.e. 'servants or ministers of God' – one of whose disciples, he conjectures, may have found his way to Hirt, and given the name of his fraternity, in a corrupted form, both to the well and the island. Mr James Wilson adopts the same view, adding that—

the Celtic term *kil*, or rather *cille*, is applied to a place of sepulture, or it may be also (like the Latin *cella*) to the cell or chapel

---

8 Moray was the son of Sir Mungo Moray, or Murray, of Craigie, a cadet of the family of Abercairney. In early life he entered the French service, and afterwards became a devoted adherent of both Charles I and II, by the latter of whom he was appointed Justice-Clerk in 1651. He was the first President of the Royal Society (1662), and died June 1673. Both Bishop Burnet and Wodrow record his numerous virtues and splendid talents. Their high estimate, however, is somewhat abated by the fact that Sir Robert contributed another paper to the *Transactions of the Royal Society* relative to the development of barnacles into sea-birds!

9 No further information is given in Bishop Forbes' *Kalendars of Scotish Saints*.

of a devotee; and then, by a kind of misty and imaginative personation, the prefix 'Saint' is added; thus investing with something of a spiritual character the wild and rocky region of the fulmar and gannet.

With regard to the colonization of St Kilda, Martin simply states that 'the inhabitants of this isle are originally descended of those of the adjacent isles, Lewis, Harries, South and North Vist and Skiy.' Macaulay, on the other hand, thinks it probable that Hirta was at first peopled by 'pyrates, exiles or malefactors who fled from justice'. He also refers to the supposed Irish origin of the inhabitants, according to which theory, a Hibernian rover, named Macquin,[10] was the first settler in St Kilda, along with a small colony of his countrymen. The prevailing belief, however, appears to be that the first inhabitants of St Kilda – like the Outer Hebrideans generally – were a compound of Celt and Northman; and this view is assuredly confirmed by the physical aspect of the present inhabitants, as well as by many of the names of places, etc., in the island.[11] There is a curious tradition to the effect that the people of Harris and Uist were both desirous of possessing the remote island; that an agreement was made that two boats (or *currachs*), with an equal number of rowers, from Harris and Uist respectively, should start at the same time for the island, and that the party which first touched its shores should be the acknowledged lords of St Kilda. A close and exciting race was the resuit. On nearing the wished-for land, the Uist men (Macdonalds?) had got a few strokes ahead, and would, in all probability, have gained the coveted prize, had not Colla Macleod, the leader of the Harris

10 In 1861 there were seventy-two Macquiens or Macqueens in North Uist, and twenty-two in Lewis and Harris. At the same date, there were 4 in St Kilda, and eight in 1871. The name in Gaelic is MacChuinn = 'son of Conn'.
11 E.g. 'Osterveaul', a hill on the east side of the island, from the Norse Austr-fell = 'east fell' or 'east hill'; Soay, one of the adjacent islands, from the Norse *Saud-ey* = 'sheep isle'; and fulmar, the bird peculiar to St Kilda, from the Norse *Fúl-mar* = 'stinking maw' or 'gull' – See *Proceedings of Society of Scottish Antiquaries*, xi, 472.

crew, chopped off his left hand at the wrist, and tossed it ashore over the heads of the adverse party! By this plucky act the Macleods are said to have become the possessors of St Kilda.

The version of this story in Euphemia Macrimmon's state-ment[12] is somewhat different, being to the following effect:

There were two brothers, one named Colla Ciotach, the other Gilespeig Og or Young Archibald. Each of them had a boat, and both were racing to St Kilda, for he who got there first was to be the proprietor. When they neared St Kilda, Coll saw that his brother would arrive there first; so Coll cut off his hand, and threw it on the east point, which the boats pass as they come into the harbour, and he cried to his brother, 'This [the hand] is before you'; and the point is called Gob Cholla, or Coll's point, to this day; and there is also a well not far from the point called also Tobar Cholla, or Coll's Well.

Passing, however, from unsupported tradition to authentic history, it would appear that the fourteenth century is the earliest date to which the name of Hirta can be traced. According to Macaulay, in a charter granted (before the year 1380 ?) by John, Lord of the Isles, and confirmed by Robert II, the island of St Kilda, under the name of Hirt, was made over to his son Reginald, along with certain other places. In the course of two or three generations St Kilda was transferred by one of Reginald's successors – the predecessor of Clan Ranald – to the Macdonalds of Sleat; and again, at a later period, by the Macdonalds to the Macleods, by whom it has now been possessed for upwards of three hundred years.[13] On the other hand, it appears from the 'Fragment of a Manuscript History of the Macdonalds,

12 Embraced in Miss Anne Kennedy's letter to Captain Thomas, RN, 9th April 1862 – *Proceedings of Society of Antiquaries*, x, 702.
13 In alluding to the question of early ownership, Macaulay says 'So contradictory are the accounts given, and so slender the historical evidences on every side, that any judicious person will choose to leave that matter undetermined.'

written in the reign of Charles II'[14] that the grant, which included 'North Uist, Benbecula, the one half of South Uist, Boysdale, Canna, Slate and Knoydart', was made to Reginald's elder brother Godfrey; and that, in the words of the manuscript, 'it was he gave Boysdale to MacNeill of Barra, and gifted Hirta or St Kilda to the Laird of Harris.' According to that statement, seeing that Godfrey is said to have died before the close of the fourteenth century, the Macleods may have been the possessors of St Kilda for nearly five hundred years.

In the account of the family of Macleod of that Ilk in Douglas's *Baronage of Scotland*, reference is made to a grant in the time of Alexander III (1249–86) of the lands of Harris, etc. by Paul, son of Boke, sheriff of Skye, to Leod, son of King Olaus, by Christina, daughter of Farquhar, Earl of Ross, and brother of Magnus, last king of Man and the Isles, which Leod is regarded as the ancestor of the Macleods of Lewis and Harris. Of this grant, however, it is to be feared there is no legal evidence. Somewhere about a hundred years later (1372) we find, in the Register of the Great Seal, a charter of confirmation by Robert II to Reginald de Insulis, son of John of the Isles, of various lands and islands, including 'insula de Herc [Harris] cum omnibus aliis minutis insulis ad dictas insulas pertinentibus'. In 1475, the lands of Harris, etc. were forfeited by John, Lord of the Isles; and although restored by James III the following year, they were again finally forfeited in 1493. There can be no doubt, however, that for several centuries the lands of Harris were held by a family known as Macleod of Glenelg, Harris or Dunvegan. The first that seems to have been styled 'of Harris' was William McLoyd of Glenelg, who appears on record between 1449 and 1478. Twenty years later (1498), James IV granted in heritage to Alexander Makloide,[15]

---

14 Printed in *Collectanea de Rebus Albanicis*, i, 298 (Iona Club, 1839.)

15 Styled *crottach*, or 'humpbacked', whose elaborate monument at Rodel, in Harris, is referred to in the Diary kept by Scott during his voyage to the Scottish islands in 1814. Sir Walter makes the date of the inscription a hundred years older than it really is – viz., M.CCCC.XXVIII. Instead of M.CCCCC.XXVIII. In a heel-ball rubbing which I took at Rodel last July, five c's are quite apparent.

son and heir of the deceased William John Makelodeson of Dunbegane, the lands commonly called Ardmanach in Herag of Lewis, with the small isles belonging to them, and other lands, which were formerly held by William Makcloid of John, Lord of the Isles. In 1547, Queen Mary granted to Archibald, Earl of Argyll, the ward of all the lands that belonged to the deceased Alexander McCloid of Dunvegane, including, of course, the lands of Harris;[16] and in 1588, Alexander's grandson William appears as the heir of his father, Tormod, 'in terris de Herre nuncupatis Ardmannach de Lewes cum totis minutis insulis pertinentibus ad terras Ardmannach de Lewes'.[17]

Through the courtesy of Macleod of Macleod, the proprietor of St Kilda, I have had access to his charter-chest, the earliest writs in which pertain to the very end of the fifteenth century. The descriptive clause in all the deeds relating to Harris makes no special mention of St Kilda. It usually runs as follows: 'All and whole the lands of Harries, called Ardmeanach of Lewes, with the whole small islands thereto belonging.' The name of the remote island first occurs in a Precept from Chancery, dated 6th January 1776, for infefting Norman Macleod of Macleod as heir to his grandfather, Norman Macleod of Macleod, in all and whole the lands of Harries called Ardmeanach of Lewes, with the small islands thereto belonging, excepting, amongst others, the island of St Kilda, in the parish of Kilbryde called Harris, which was sold by the said grandfather of the grantee to the deceased John Macleod, younger of Macleod, his eldest son.

Unlike that of many Highland families, the pedigree of the Macleods seems to be unusually well vouched. The author of a detailed account of the Mackenzies in Mr Fraser's recent work on the Earls of Cromartie,[18] informs us that the origin of that family

---

16 *Origines Parochiales Scotiae*, ii, 376.

17 *Abridgement of Retours* – Inverness, vol. i.

18 *History of the Family of Mackenzie*, by Sir George Mackenzie, First Earl of Cromartie, ii, 462.

is not so remote, *ut caput inter nubila condat*. The word *nubila* is irresistibly suggestive of the name borne by the Lairds of Harris, and their extensive possessions in Skye might reasonably be supposed to indicate the possibility of a *myst*erious origin! Joking apart, however, it appears to be generally believed that the Macleods spring from a Scandinavian source[19] – deriving their descent from Leod, son of King Olaus, already referred to, from whom, according to some writers, the island of Lewis or Leodhus (the habitation of Leod) received its name.[20] Some of Leod's descendants are said to have obtained settlements in the west of England, Wales and Ireland, where they assumed the surnames of Lloyd and Floyd. In later times, besides the entire island of Lewis and Harris, the Scotch Macleods possessed the greater part of Skye, and a considerable portion of the western coast of Inverness-shire.

It appears from the 'Twelfth Detailed Annual Report of the Registrar-General' that, in the year 1863, Macleod occupied the thirtieth place in the list of the most common surnames in Scotland. At that date, the clan amounted to upwards of 14,000 persons, of whom more than 5000 were in Ross and Cromarty, and the rest chiefly in Inverness-shire. They were, however, surpassed by four other 'Macs' – viz, the Macdonalds, their ancient rivals (36,000), who were only beaten by the Smiths; the Mackenzies (21,000); the Mackays (18,000); and the Macleans (16,000). The only other 'Macs' among the fifty most common Scottish surnames were Mackintosh (11,000), and Macgregor (10,000).

---

19 Dr McLauchlan, however, thinks it questionable whether they are primarily a Scandinavian race, notwithstanding the number of Scandinavian names 'in their older genealogies' – *Celtic Gleanings*, p. 79.

20 From the tenth to the thirteenth century, the Hebrides were overrun by Danes and Norwegians, till in 1266 – three years after the battle of Largs – they were united to Scotland by Alexander III.

For a different theory regarding the origin of the Macleods, see a communciation by Captain F. W. L. Thomas, RN – *Proceedings of Society of Scottish Antiquaries*, xi, 507.

In 1861 the Macleods were slightly more numerous in Harris than the Macdonalds, by whom, however, they were quite eclipsed in North and South Uist. The comparatively small strength of the former clan, however, is of little consequence, so long as the 'Fairy Flag' at Dunvegan retains its magical power. According to Pennant,[21] the first time it was produced was in an unequal engagement with the Clan Ranald, 'to whose sight the Macleods were multiplied tenfold!' In alluding to these two distinguished clans, the author of *A Summer in Skye* says that

> both are of great antiquity, and it is as difficult to discover the source of either in history as it is to discover the source of the Nile in the deserts of Central Africa ... The two families intermarried often, and quarrelled oftener. They put wedding-rings on each other's fingers, and dirks into each other's hearts. Of the two, Macleod had the darker origin; and around his name there lingers a darker poetry. Macdonald sits in his castle in sunny Sleat with a southern outlook – Macleod retains his old eyrie at Dunvegan, with its drawbridge and dungeons ... The rocks and mountains around him wear his name even as of old did his clansmen.

At the time of Martin's visit, in 1697, St Kilda 'belonged in property to the Laird of MackLeod (Roderick Macleod of Macleod), head of one of the ancientest families of Scotland;' and, some sixty years later, Macaulay informs us that the proprietor was Norman Macleod of Macleod, whose ancestors were then said to have possessed it for at least two hundred years. In 1779, Norman's grandson, General Macleod of Macleod – the grandfather of the present Macleod of Macleod – sold 'the Herries and St Kilda' to Captain Alexander Macleod, 'late of the *Mansfield* Indiaman', for the small sum of £15,000. By feu-charter, dated 26 April, 1804, Alexander Hume, formerly Alexander Macleod of Harris, son of

---

21 *Tour in Scotland*, ii, 340.

the aforesaid Captain Alexander Macleod, in consideration of the sum of £1350, disposed to Colonel Donald Macleod of Achagoyle 'all and whole the island of St Kilda, being a part and portion of the lands and estate of Harries, which are parts of the lands of Ardmeanach of Lewes and of the barony of Dunvegan, together with the following smaller islands, being pertinents of the said island of St Kilda, or contiguous thereto – viz. Borora, Soa and Duun, with the several insular rocks adjacent to the said islands on which the sea-fowl are in use to breed, with the sea fishings', etc. Colonel Donald Macleod, son of a former minister of St Kilda (?), was father of Sir John Macpherson Macleod, KCSI, by whom St Kilda was sold, for £3,000, to the present Macleod of Macleod, in 1871.

Speaking of St Kilda a hundred years earlier, Boswell told Johnson that he thought of buying it. The Doctor at once replied,

> Pray do, sir. We will go and pass a winter amid the blasts there. We shall have fine fish, and we will take some dried tongues with us, and some books. We will have a strong-built vessel, and some Orkney men to navigate her. We must build a tolerable house; but we may carry with us a wooden house ready made, and requiring nothing but to be put up. Consider, sir, by buying St Kilda, you may keep the people from falling into worse hands. We must give them a clergyman, and he shall be one of Beattie's choosing. He shall be educated at Marischal College. I'll be your chancellor, or what you please.
>
> Boswell: Are you serious, sir, in advising me to buy St Kilda? for if you should advise me to go to Japan, I believe I should do it.
>
> Johnson: Why yes, sir, I am serious.
>
> Boswell: Why then, I'll see what can be done.

The contemplated purchase, however, was never effected.

Local Incidents Since
the Beginning of the
Seventeenth Century

It will not be considered strange that I should be unable to refer to many events in the history of the distant isle. From a letter addressed by Sir Roderick Macleod, alias 'Rory More', to Lord Binning, and dated 'Dunvegane, 18th of June 1615',[1] it appears that a raid was made on St Kilda towards the beginning of that year, by a certain Coll Macgillespick, son of Sir James Macdonald (of the family of Colonsay), and father of Alister Macdonald, lieutenant to the Marquis of Montrose during the civil wars. The adventurous invader was popularly called 'Coll Keitach', or Left-handed Coll, from which his son Alister took the designation of 'McColl Keitach', abridged to 'Colkitto'. After referring to an accident which he met with at Stirling, in the month of April, during a visit to the south of Scotland, Sir Roderick informs his correspondent that,

> in the mean tyme of my absence, Coill Makgillespick and his companie come [from Islay] to the north illes, and stopped the first night at the yle of Carnis [Canna?], and thereafter passed directlie to North Wyest, Donald Gorme his lands, where he

---

1 *Gregory's Manuscript Collections*, iii, 285 – Library of the Society of Scottish Antiquaries. The latter portion of the letter, which is not embraced in the text, will be found in *Pitcairn's Criminal Trials*, iii, 19.

was rescat [received], and his men enterteaned; and Mackintoshe's dochtor, Donald Gorme's wyff, beeing for the tyme in that countrey, togidder with young Donald Gorme, Makkenyee's good-brother, send to the said Coill, being scant of vivers, four horse lead [load] of meat, in the witche there wes two swyne, one salted and one unsalted; and the said Coill and his companie wes perswaded, moved, and requested by the said Donald Gorme's wyff and young Donald and clann Neill vaine, the special tenants of North Wyest, to pass to a yle of myne called Zirta,[2] a day and a night sailing from the rest of the north yles, far out in the ocean sea, and to that effect directed two of the tenants of North Wyest to be there guyd and pylat there, for they wer unknowen thameselves there. And coming to the ylle, they slew all the bestiall of the ylle, both cowes, and horses and sheep, and took away all the spoolyee of the yle, onlie reserved the lyves of the enhabitants thereof And when all wes done, they returned to North Wyest againe, where they randered there guyde and pyllats againe, and gave to the enhabitants thereof all and whole the spoyle of my yle. And afore my comeing to the yles, the said Coill Makgillespick passed away south to Ila againe.

The letter concludes with a commendation of Lord Binning 'to God's most holie tuition', and is signed to 'Zor lo. homble servitor at powar, Sr Rorie Makcleud'.[3]

---

2 i.e. 'Yirta', indicating the pronunciation of the name.
3 Upwards of a hundred years before the occurrence of Coll's raid, a short Act was passed in the Parliament held at Edinburgh on the 11th day of March 1503 (15 James IV), which provides that 'all our Soveraine Lordis lieges beand under his obeysance, and in special the *Iles*, be ruled be our Soveraine Lordis awn Lawes, and the commoun Lawes of the Realme, and be name uther Lawes.' Owing to its physical peculiarities, however, it is to be feared that many a long day is likely to elapse before St Kilda will enjoy the benefit of the legal protection provided in the statute of the chivalrous monarch. So far as I am aware, it is not under the ken of the Poor Law authorities; and its inhabitants, as afterwards stated, were officially enumerated, for the first time, in the year 1851. 'Out of sight, out of mind', may be applied, with a considerable amount of truth, to the remote island.

It is not a little singular that, twenty-six years later (1641), the same Coll Macgillespick again found his way to St Kilda, in the capacity of a refugee, 'having made himself obnoxious to the law'. In briefly alluding to the circumstance, Macaulay speaks of him as 'Colonel' instead of 'Coll' Macdonald. The event, however, is more fully described by Buchan, who informs us that

Coll Macdonald alias Ketoch being defeat in battle, losing his right hand, and his army, which he had raised for the Popish interest, routed, was forced with a few to flee for his life; and getting his foot in a vessel, comes to land in St Kilda, whom, when the inhabitants saw, they run away from him and his men into a cave in some remote corner of the island, where they thought they might be most safe from him, whom they thought to be an enemy come to destroy them; but he sending some few of his men after them, told them of his friendly designs, and he himself, advancing gradually, enforces what his men had said, by telling them he had no hostile design against them, and that though he had, he was not in condition to effect it, since he wanted the right hand (showing them the stump); so pulling out his mull, and giving them a snuff, with which, and some other significations of kindness, they came to be delivered of their former fears; so that he lived in safety and quietness with them for the space of three quarters of a year.

It further appears that on his finding that the inhabitants were not properly instructed in the Lord's Prayer, Decalogue and Creed, Coll rebuked the priest, whom his flock wished to depose; but when the matter was referred to Coll for his adjudication, he solemnly declared that he had never heard of a priest being deposed for ignorance![4]

4 This curious incident recalls a good story of an Inverness-shire shepherd, who, on the occasion of one of the half-yearly visits of his spiritual father, complained of his inability to remember his 'Pater Nosters'. In reply to the priest's interrogation, Donald

In alluding to the hospitality of the natives of St Kilda, Martin mentions the wreck of 'a company of French and Spaniards' at Rokol[5] in the year 1686. It appears that they came in a pinnace to St Kilda, where they were plentifully supplied with barley-bread, butter, cheese, solan geese, eggs, etc.

> Both seamen and inhabitants were barbarians one to another, the inhabitants speaking only the Irish tongue, to which the French and Spaniards were altogether strangers. Upon their landing, they pointed to the west, naming Rokol to the inhabitants; and after that they pointed downward with their finger, signifying the sinking and perishing of their vessel; and they showed them Rokol in the sea-map, far west off St Kilda. This, and much more, the masters of these ships told to a priest in the west island, who understood French.

The author further states that the pinnace which carried the seamen from Rokol was so low that the crew added a foot of canvas all round, and began to work at it on Sunday, much to the annoyance of the inhabitants, who plucked the hatchets and other instruments out of their hands, and did not restore them till Monday morning.

The same year (1686) there was an earthquake on the island of Borrera, which lasted only a few minutes, and 'was very amazing to the poor people, who never felt any such commotion before or since'.[6]

---

admitted that, like most of his avocation, he knew every member of his flock by head-mark; on which the priest advised him to place his sheep in a row, and associate with each of them a word of the prayer – the first in order representing 'Pater', the second 'noster', and so on to the end; assuring him, at the same time, that his memory would be greatly assisted by such a mode of procedure. At his next visit, Donald lost no time in giving a specimen of the result, repeating the words as follows: 'Pater noster, qui es in coelo . . . nomen tuum,' etc. 'Wrong,' said the priest, 'you've missed out a word.' 'Na, na! your reverence,' rejoined Donald, ' "sanctifetur" "dee'd last Christmas!'

5 Now known as Rockall, a rocky islet about 200 miles nearly due west of St Kilda.
6 Martin's *Voyage to St Kilda*, pp. 43, 153.

About the year 1695, 'a cock-boat came from a ship for water, being favoured with a perfect calm'. The crew discovered an endless number of eggs upon one of the adjacent islets; and, having secured a liberal supply, one of the seamen was

so careful as to put them into his breeches, which he put off on purpose for this use! Some of the inhabitants of St Kilda happened to be in the isle that day. A parcel of them were spectators of this diversion, and were offended at it, being done without their consent; therefore they devised an expedient which at once robbed the seamen of their eggs and breeches. They found a few loose stones in the superficies of the rock, some of which they let fall down perpendicularly above the seamen, the terror of which obliged them quickly to remove, abandoning both breeches and eggs for their safety; and those tarpaulin breeches were no small ornament there, where all wore girded plaids![7]

Towards the end of the seventeenth century, a native of St Kilda, called Roderick, pretended to have been commissioned by John the Baptist 'with new revelations and discoveries'. Immediately after landing, on 1 June 1697, Martin and his companion, the minister of Harris, proceeded to examine the inhabitants regarding the doings of the false prophet; and one and all of them expressed their abhorrence of the miserable delusions and immoral deeds which he had practised for several years. Martin describes him as 'a comely, well-proportioned fellow, red-haired, and exceeding all the inhabitants of St Kilda in strength, climbing, etc.'; and although, like the rest, 'illiterate', he had the reputation of being a poet, and of being endowed with the faculty of second-sight. Besides a very

---

7 Martin's *Voyage to St Kilda*, p. 38. This curious incident will probably remind some readers of the successful and more fatal expedient adopted by the Norwegians at Kringelen, in the year 1612, which proved so destructive to George Sinclair and his Scottish followers in the course of their endeavour to assist Gustavus Adolphus against the King of Denmark.

strict fast on Fridays, he imposed a number of extraordinary penances upon the simple-minded inhabitants; commanded every family to slaughter a sheep upon the threshold of their houses; forbade the use of the Lord's Prayer, Creed and Ten Commandments; and privately taught the women a 'devout hymn', assuring them that if they fully complied with the new revelation they would be carried to heaven upon white horses! His villainous designs were at length discovered by the ground-officer's wife, and ultimately his influence entirely disappeared. In due course he was carried off by Martin and the minister of Harris to that island, and afterwards removed to Skye, where he made a public confession of his false teaching and wicked acts.[8]

About the year 1724 a 'contagious distemper' swept away the greater part of the inhabitants of St Kilda. According to Macaulay, the distemper in question was smallpox, by which one of the islanders was seized during a visit to Harris, where he died. 'Unluckily one of his friends carried his clothes away next year, and these, it is thought, communicated the infection at Hirta.' He further informs us that very few escaped the visitation, only four adults surviving out of twenty-four families, with the burden of twenty-six orphans. Their lives appear to have been providentially spared, in consequence of their having gone to one of the adjacent islands for the purpose of catching gannets; and owing to the 'universal confusion and mortality' which ensued at home, and their boat having been brought back to St Kilda before the distemper assumed an epidemic form, the fowlers were obliged to be absent from about the middle of August till the following Whitsunday. Macaulay states that smallpox had never previously visited St Kilda; and up to the publication of his work in 1764 the disease had not again appeared in the island.

The most painfully interesting event connected with the history of St Kilda is doubtless the story of Lady Grange's enforced

8 *Voyage to St Kilda*, pp. 135–158. See also Martin's other work on the Western Islands, p. 289; and Macaulay's *History of St Kilda*, p. 202.

confinement on the lonely rock. It is embraced in a comparatively recent communication to the Society of Scottish Antiquaries by Dr David Laing, who enumerates the principal accounts of the abduction.[9] Rachel Cheisley, daughter of the assassin of Sir George Lockhart of Carnwath, Lord President of the Court of Session, and sister of Major Cheisley of Dalry, near Edinburgh, married, about the year 1709, the Hon. James Erskine of Grange, second son of Charles, tenth Earl of Mar, who in 1707 was raised to the Scottish bench under the title of Lord Grange, and became Lord Justice-Clerk three years afterwards. After a matrimonial career of upwards of twenty years, resulting in a family of eight children, they agreed to live apart; and shortly afterwards, on the plea that she might prove a dangerous spy upon his proceedings, Lord Grange resolved upon his wife's removal from Edinburgh. As usually happens in such cases, there appear to have been faults upon both sides; and as, in those primitive days, discordant couples were unable to resort to the peaceful procedure of the Divorce Court, the suspicious husband took the law into his own hands, and, with the aid of a party of Highlanders, he succeeded in getting the poor woman carried off in a most brutal manner, a little before midnight of 22 January, 1732. It is generally believed that the notorious Lord Lovat was a party to the transaction, although he boldly denies having been concerned in it, in a curious letter from which an extract was given by Dr Laing. She was transported, by successive night journeys, to the island of Hesker, near Skye, where she was detained for two years. In 1734 she was conveyed to the still more remote island of St Kilda, and after spending about eight years in that desolate region, was removed, through the instrumentality of her friends, to Assynt, in the county of Sutherland, and thence to the island of Skye, where she ended her unhappy life in May 1745. Dr Laing's paper was illustrated by several autographs, of which the most curious is a letter

9 *Proceedings of the Society*, x, 722, and (revised) xi, 595. Dr Macculloch professes to have heard five versions of the story – *Letters*, iii, 196.

addressed by the unfortunate woman to the Lord Advocate (Charles Erskine), afterwards Lord Tinwald and Lord Justice-Clerk, dated 'St Kilda, Jan. 20, 1738', in which she gives an account of her treatment. A facsimile of a portion of the letter, embracing the date and signature, accompanies Dr Laing's original communication.[10] At a still more recent date (14 May, 1877), Dr Laing favoured the Society of Antiquaries with a notice of another original letter, addressed by Lady Grange to her husband, in July 1730, in which she meekly says: 'Since you are angry with me, and will not live with me, I promise that if you'll allow me a hundred pounds yearly . . . and if you'll drop the process of separation you have raised against me . . . I will retire and live by myself for five years from the date hereof.'

Mr John Lane Buchanan erroneously asserts that Lady Grange terminated her miserable life at St Kilda. He states that a poor old woman told him that when she served her there 'her whole time was devoted to weeping, and wrapping up letters round pieces of cork, bound up with yarn, to try if any favourable wave would waft them to some Christian, to inform some humane person where she resided, in expectation of carrying tidings to her friends at Edinburgh.' He also mentions that her detention at St Kilda would never have been heard of had Lady Grange not prevailed on the minister's wife to go to Glenelg for the purpose of posting a letter concealed under her clothes, which thus found its way to her friends.

A more recent writer (Mr L. Maclean) informs us that on the occasion of his visit to St Kilda in 1838, he inspected the ruins of the hut occupied by Lady Grange, accompanied by the grandson of Finlay McDonald, who attended her in her exile. It measured about twenty feet by ten, and, like the rest of the cottages, was divided in the centre by a partition of rude loose stone.

---

10 The letter is actually addressed to Erskine as Solicitor-General, from which office (unknown to his correspondent) he was promoted to that of Lord Advocate in January, 1737.

In one of these apartments sat Finlay McDonald every night for seven years, and Lady Grange in the other – for she never slept at night . . . She had acquired the Gaelic tolerably well, and took pleasure in listening to the native tales and romances of Finlay. Through the day she slept, except when she took a solitary ramble to converse with grief and the roaring ocean. Finlay had made for her a seat of twisted straw – a luxury in St Kilda. This seat she carried with her when she went, leaving twelve shillings with Finlay in lieu of it.

Contrary to the statement of Mr Maclean, which he makes on the authority of his guide, Mr Sands says that she never learned Gaelic. He adds that the house in which she lived was demolished a few years ago, that it belonged to the steward, and was exactly like the existing old cottages, but a little larger.

A dearth happened to prevail during the whole time she remained on the island; but she got an ample share of what little food there was. The best turf was provided for her fire, and the spot where it was got is still called the Lady's Pool.

My friend Captain Thomas has recently sent me a poetical 'Epistle from Lady Grange (under the name of "Matilda") to Edward D—, Esq., written during her confinement in the island of St Kilda', and published in Edinburgh in 1799. In the 'advertisement' prefixed to the poem – which extends to nearly 350 lines – the author states that the 'hint' on which the epistle is founded occurs in the reference to Lady Grange's exile in Boswell's *Journal of a Tour to the Hebrides*, and that 'the additional circumstances introduced are mere fictions of the imagination'. The general tone of the epistle is very warm and passionate. The simple and guileless maidens of St Kilda remind the unhappy exile of the bright scenes of her childhood; and in the pathetic allusions to her later career, she introduces the 'unpitying father', the 'reluctant wife', and the 'fell tyrant', to whose tender mercies she had been heartlessly consigned. The following allusion to her sea-girt prison, and the avocations of the islanders, occurs towards the middle of the poem. The 'rocky plain', the 'straggling ivy', and the 'cormorant's downy nest', are good examples of the 'fictions of the imagination'.

> Far from the crimes and follies that I trace,
> Kind Nature holds me 'midst her favourite race.
> – Escaped the severed world by happy stealth,
> A skiff their navy, and a rock their wealth,
> Rough as the stormy element they brave,
> Fearless they ride upon the heaving wave.
> For them the ocean rears her finny store,
> And rustling legions cloud the darkening shore:
> Pure from the rock the dimpling fountains play,
> And wind and glitter to the orient ray;
> Nor haughty Wealth, with proud contemptuous sneer,
> Nor Poverty, the child of Wealth, is here.
>
> When now the morning trembles o'er the main,
> Brown Labour calls them to the rocky plain;
> With patient toil each tills his little spot,
> And Freedom pours contentment on their lot.
> O'er the steep rock, with straggling ivy drest,
> Clambering, they seek the cormorant's downy nest.
> As up the fractured crevices they wind,
> They mark their dwindled partners far behind.
> When the sun, sinking in the western deep,
> Resigns the world to night and balmy sleep,
> O'er the high cliff their dangerous trade they urge,
> Below, tremendous roars the boiling surge;
> As pendent from the straining cord they play,
> I mark their slow-descending form decay.
> The solan birds are hushed in deep repose,
> Fearless of danger from their hovering foes.

The sentinel betrayed, no signals fly,
And the death-fated squadrons gasp and die.
Till scared, the remnant start with hollow croak,
And, wildly wheeling, mourn their plundered rock.

When gathering clouds the blackening sky deform,
And sweeping whirlwinds swell the heaving storm,
While far at sea their solitary skiff,
The faithful matrons climb the shelving cliff;
With tears of love and anguish heaven implore,
To guide the labouring bark to Kilda's shore.
Each marks her shroudless husband, pale, aghast,
Rise from the deep, and ride the driving blast.

– The storm is hushed, the prospering breezes play,
They mark the whitening canvas far away:
With faithful hearts (the only wealth they boast),
They hail the storm-tossed nation to the coast.
Up springs the jovial dance, the festive lay,
And night repays the labours of the day.

After the departure of Lady Grange about the year 1742, a wide
gap seems to occur in the annals of St Kilda; at least I am unable
to record any event of the smallest importance during the long
period of eighty-five years. The day after my return from St Kilda
(3 July, 1877) I had an interview at Obbe with Donald McKinnon,
precentor in the parish church of Harris, who is a native of St
Kilda, and whose brother still resides on the island. He is an intelligent man of about sixty years of age, and, *inter alia*, he related the
two following incidents:

Somewhere about fifty years ago (1827), the 'Laird of Islay' landed
at St Kilda from his yacht, and falling in love with a girl called
Marion Morison, promised to return, for the purpose of marrying
her, in the course of a year. This he duly did in a vessel carrying a

few small guns, the sight of which so alarmed the inhabitants that they took refuge among the rocks, and the faithful suitor, like 'Young Mivins' of 'Bon Gualtier', was obliged to depart, a disappointed bachelor! The girl composed a 'Lament' in commemoration of the event, the tune of which the precentor hummed. He heard her sing the air, and distinctly remembers her appearance, and her 'long, flowing hair'. A somewhat similar occurrence is said to have taken place very recently; and at the present moment, something more than a *tendresse* is believed to exist between the latest male sojourner in St Kilda, and one of its comely, fair-haired maidens, whose name I must forbear to disclose.

About Christmas 1839, the *Charlotte* of Hull, Captain John Bremman (?), was wrecked on the islet of 'Rockhall', about 200 miles due west of St Kilda, to which reference has already been made in connection with a previous catastrophe of the same kind. Eighteen of the crew found their way in a boat to a cave in the west bay of St Kilda, where they remained for two days and nights, and were ultimately discovered by a herd-boy who happened to notice the boat in the neighbourhood of the cave from the summit of an adjacent cliff. McKinnon descended with the aid of a rope, and brought up the mariners one by one, after which they were taken round by the natives, in their own boat, to the village on the east bay, where they were clothed, housed and fed by the islanders. After remaining on St Kilda for eleven days, McKinnon accompanied them in their boat to the island of Pabbay, in the Sound of Harris, whence they went to Portree. They left their boat with McKinnon, who sold it for about nine pounds, and returned to St Kilda in another. The captain promised to see that the St Kildans[11] should be liberally remunerated

11 Although most writers on St Kilda describe the inhabitants as St Kildians or St Kildeans, I have advisedly adopted the spelling in the text – following the analogous cases of Spartans and Romans, from Sparta and Roma. I have occasionally met with St Kildaites, but never with St Kildese, which the phraseology of a celebrated southern island might seem to justify – Malta – Malese.

for their hospitality and assistance, but they never received a farthing! This is probably the same event which is referred to by Mrs McVean of Killin, in her *Reminiscences of St Kilda*.[12] She states that

> a party of English sailors were once shipwrecked on the uninhabited part of the island, where they remained for a whole day and night without discovering that it was peopled. At last they saw a woman coming across the hill to the glen in which they were; and as soon as she observed the strangers, she rushed away in the greatest alarm. She did not fail, however, to send some men to ascertain who they were, when it was discovered that one of the poor fellows had broken his leg, and was in great pain. He was carried, as gently as possible, to the nearest hut and lowered into one of the odious wall-beds. The poor sailor afterwards told the minister that 'he thought the savages were lowering him into a well!' Fortunately, Mr McKenzie was able to set the broken limb, having previously had a good deal of experience in surgical cases, connected with accidents in fowling expeditions.

Mrs McVean alludes to the impression produced upon the islanders by the first appearance of a steamboat.[13] Greatly alarmed by the unwonted sight, they rushed into the manse to inform the minister that 'a ship on fire' was approaching their shores! Their terror and amazement was not a little increased by the music of a brass band on board the vessel; and when the passengers landed, all the inhabitants fled to the rocks, except a few of the bravest of

12 Mrs McVean, wife of the Rev. C. A. McVean of Killin, is a daughter of the Rev. Neil McKenzie, formerly minister of St Kilda, where she passed the first eleven years of her life.
13 Probably the *Vulcan* of Glasgow, in which Mr Maclean and the party specified in his Sketches of St Kilda, visited the island in July, 1838. The party included the Rev. Dr Dickson of Edinburgh, and the Rev. Dr Macleod of Glasgow.

the male sex, who anxiously watched the movements of the strangers.

During the last twenty years,[14] the remote island has been occasionally visited by government steamers, private yachts and other vessels. In July 1860, the Duke of Athole and Mr Hall Maxwell accompanied Captain (afterwards Admiral) Otter in HMS *Porcupine*, and remained two days on the island. It is said that the duke partook of the 'brew' made from the flesh of the fulmar, and that he slept on the floor of one of the cottages, which is still pointed out as his place of shelter. About a fortnight after the duke's sojourn, Captain and Mrs Thomas visited St Kilda in the same vessel, and were three days on shore. Shortly after the departure of the *Porcupine*, Mr John E. Morgan, author of the article in *Macmillan's Magazine* already referred to, touched at St Kilda in the *Falcon* cutter yacht of twenty-five tons, and, along with a friend, spent six hours on the island.

In June 1861 (and in the same month ten years later), the census of St Kilda was taken by Mr Alexander Grigor, lately Examiner of Registers for the Northern District of Scotland. On the former occasion he was conveyed to the island in the *Porcupine*, and in 1871 in the *Jackal* gunboat.

In the summer of 1863, Mrs Thomas again accompanied Captain Otter to St Kilda in the gunboat *Seagull*, and spent about twenty hours on shore. Not many weeks before their visit, an event occurred which spread a painful gloom over the little island. In the year 1861, a fine large boat, fully equipped, and which cost about £60, was sent to St Kilda, with the view

14 The following is a list of earlier visits to St Kilda, most of which have already been incidentally mentioned: Martin, 1697; Buchan, 1705; Macaulay, 1758; Lord Brougham, 1799; Sir George Stewart Mackenzie of Coul, *c.* 1803; Macculloch, 1815; Rev. John McDonald of Urquhart, 1822, 1824, 1827 and 1830; Sir Thomas Dyke Acland, *c.* 1837; Mr Maclean and party, 1838; Mr John Macgillivray, the naturalist, 1840; Mr James Wilson, 1842; Rev. Dr McLauchlan of Edinburgh, 1854; and Mr Thomas S. Muir, 1858.

of encouraging the inhabitants to extend their fishing operations. This boat was named the *Dargavel*, in honour of Mr Hall Maxwell's visit to the island the previous year. Early in April 1863, the boat left St Kilda in a favourable wind, with seven men and one woman on board, and when last seen from the heights of the island, was careering onward at a rapid speed. Towards night the wind changed to the south, blowing very hard, and it was supposed that the little craft must have gone out of its course, several miles to the north of the Sound of Harris. Nothing more was known regarding the lamentable occurrence, except the loss of the boat and all its occupants, as was supposed to be clearly indicated by certain articles of clothing cast ashore at Maelsta, on the west coast of Lewis. The sad intelligence was conveyed to the islanders by three London smacks, about a month after the disappearance of the boat; and it is unnecessary to add that the sorrow produced among the surviving friends by the announcement was of no ordinary kind. Mr Sands mentions that the three skippers came on shore, where they played 'quoits' with flat stones, and mocked the poor natives when they gave expression to their grief. The catechist (Mr Kennedy) did not think of noting the names of the smacks; but the islanders assert that the crews belonged to London, and that one of their number could speak Gaelic. Towards the end of May, some of the clothes of the missing men, 'torn as if in a scuffle', were brought to St Kilda by the factor (Mr McRaild), who informed the inhabitants that they 'had been found in a cave in Lewis'; and on the occasion of his first visit, Mr Sands heard some of the St Kildans express their belief that the lost crew had been murdered. At the time of the occurrence, however, Sir John Macleod, then proprietor of the island, caused an investigation to be made in Lewis, but without eliciting any information. Three of the seven men were married, and besides their widows, left seven children. The other four were skilful fowlers, in the prime of life, and were survived by mothers, sisters and other dependent relatives. The boat contained cloth, salt-fish and other native produce to the value of upwards of £80, as well as some money in notes, which the owners wished to exchange for gold. The solitary female passenger was Betty Scott, wife of Malcolm McDonald, and a native of Lochinver, in Sutherlandshire, who went to the island as servant to the Rev. Neil Mackenzie. With the exception of Mr Kennedy, the catechist, she was the only islander who could speak English; and being in other respects intelligent and superior, was sometimes called the 'Queen of St Kilda'. Unlike the Orcadians, the St Kildans are not good sailors, and the want of nautical skill was probably the chief cause of the disaster. A crew of about the same number visited the 'Long Island' the previous year in the same boat, and were nearly lost in the neighbourhood of Balranald, North Uist. On that occasion also they had a good deal of produce, which they sold to advantage.

A remarkable circumstance connected with the loss of the *Dargavel* has lately caused a considerable amount of excitement both in St Kilda and the 'Long Island'. Towards the end of 1875 a letter was received by the minister of Harris from a firm in the Transvaal Republic, in which it was stated that Donald McKinnon, supposed to be one of the missing crew, had recently died of fever, at Pilgrim's Rest, Lydenburg goldfields, leaving property amounting to about £40, which it appears has been lodged in a bank at Stornoway. If the deceased was really the Donald McKinnon of the *Dargavel*, it certainly seems strange that he should never have written to acquaint his father and other relatives in St Kilda of his fate. On the assumption that he actually survived till 1875, it is of course quite possible that others of the crew may be still alive; and possibly the question relative to the identification of the deceased may require to be settled by the law courts. It is, however, reported that it has now been proved, to the satisfaction of the authorities in South Africa, that the Donald McKinnon who died at Pilgrim's Rest was a native of Lewis, and not of St Kilda.

On the night of 7 April, 1864, after beating about for several days in very dense fog, the ship *Janet Cowan* of Greenock, 831 tons burthen – Captain James McKirdy – on her passage from Calcutta to Dundee with a cargo of jute, was wrecked on the rocks of St Kilda. Encouraged by the calmness of their captain, the entire crew contrived to leave the disabled vessel in their boats; but owing to the darkness of the night, and the heaviness of the surf, they were compelled to lie off the island till the following morning. At daybreak only the poop of the vessel was to be seen; and as no landing-place could be discovered near the wreck, the crew rowed round the island, and about ten o'clock found a point on the north-east side, where they managed to land and to haul up their boats. None of the inhabitants being visible, they resolved to traverse the island in detached parties in hopes of finding some of the natives, which they succeeded in doing in the course of the day. They afterwards made more than one attempt to recover something from the wreck, but all that could be saved was a cask containing a few pieces of meat, from the forward part of the ship. The gale continued for several days, and on the tenth the captain observed from one of the cliffs that only the bow remained upon the rocks. After being seven days on the island, although it was still blowing fresh, feeling that he and his crew were proving a heavy burden on the supplies of the islanders, Captain McKirdy resolved to make an attempt to reach the mainland; and having procured the loan of an open fishing-boat, the shipwrecked mariners embarked, at 5 a.m. on 14 April, some in the borrowed boat, and the rest in one of the ship's boats, and steered for Lewis, the wind being from the south. When about half-way across, as the ship's boat seemed likely to be swamped by the heavy sea which they encountered, the captain was obliged to take the entire crew into the fishing-boat, and to cut adrift the other, which was being towed astern. About 7 p.m. they succeeded in reaching the island of Scarp, off the north-west coast of Harris; and re-embarking next day, they proceeded to West Loch Tarbert in Harris, where they left the St Kilda boat, and made their way to Greenock, via Stornoway. In the course of the summer the owners of the vessel sent the inhabitants a supply of meal, flour and woollen neckerchiefs, along with a purse of nine pounds, contributed by the captain and crew, besides paying the cost of taking back the fishing-boat to the island.

Among recent visitors to St Kilda, I may mention Mr Bouverie Primrose, secretary to the Board for Manufactures, etc.; Mr Walker of Bowland, Chairman of the Board of Supervision; the Rev. Eric J. Findlater of Lochearnhead, on three different occasions; Captain Macdonald of the Fishery cruiser *Vigilant*; the Commissioners of Northern Lighthouses in the *Pharos*; Sir William and Lady Baillie of Polkemmet, with the late Mr Baird of Cambusdoon, in August 1874; Sir Patrick-Keith Murray in his yacht *Crusader*, in July 1875; Dr Murchison of Harris, on two occasions, during the same year; Lord and Lady Macdonald, in the yacht *Lady of the Isles*, accompanied by Miss Macleod of Macleod, the Rev Archibald McNeill, minister of Sleat, and Mr Macdonald, Tormore, on 15 June, 1877; and the pleasant party, of which I had the good fortune to form one, in the SS *Dunara Castle*, 245 tons, on 2 July, 1877.[15] Probably the longest sojourner in St Kilda, with the exception of Lady Grange and the various ministers and catechists, is Mr John Sands of Ormiston, who first spent seven weeks on the island in 1875 – from 3 June to 19 July,

15 Our party numbered about forty, and, besides three ladies, included the following gentlemen: Captain Macdonald of Waternish; Major James Colquhoun, Arroquhar, and a younger brother; Dr George Keith and son, Edinburgh; Mr Bulkeley, procurator-fiscal, Lochmaddy; Captain Macdonald of the *Vigilant*, Dr Messer, Helensburgh; Rev. John Macrae, minister of North Uist; Dr Mackenzie, Old Calabar; and Mr Thomas Ormerod, Brighouse. Miss Macleod of Macleod accompanied us on our return. We spent four hours (10 till 2) on shore, and then sailed round the island. Although the sea was somewhat heavy outside, we had no difficulty in landing; and the weather was most propitious throughout. The captain (McEwan) and Mr Donald, the clerk of the steamer, did everything in their power to insure an enjoyable expedition. A graphic account of the entire cruise of the *Dunara* from Glasgow and back appeared in a series of nine articles in the *Ayr Observer*, between 24 July and 2 October, from the pen of Mr W. M. Wilson, who formed one of the party.

when he was taken off in the yacht *Crusader*, and, secondly, eight months in 1876–77 – from 21 June to 22 February, when he got a passage in the gunboat *Jackal*, as afterwards mentioned. Towards the beginning of the present year, the captain and eight of the crew of the Austrian barque *Peti Dubrovacki*, 880 tons, en route from Glasgow to New York, spent about five weeks in St Kilda, at the close of Mr Sands's second sojourn. On 17 January, Mr Sands was startled by the appearance of a boat in the bay. Accompanied by some of the natives, he hastened to the shore, and at a certain point of the rocks where there seemed to be less surf than elsewhere, the islanders threw ropes to the occupants of the boat, who, however, declined to be drawn ashore. Putting about his craft, the captain made for the shore in front of the village, and the foreigners forthwith leapt into the water and swam to land, where they were received by the natives. In the course of a few minutes the boat was dashed to pieces on the rocks. The disabled vessel lay on her beam-ends, about eight miles west of St Kilda. She was not visible the day following, and doubtless went to the bottom with the seven members of the crew who had remained on board. The rescued mariners were billeted among the islanders, the minister taking charge of the captain, and were most hospitably treated. An attachment is said to have sprung up between one of the foreigners and a damsel of St Kilda, and although neither understood the language of the other, they both fully comprehended the signs and tokens of love. The scene at parting was of the most affecting character. On 30 January, a life-buoy belonging to the lost ship, with a small sail and bottle containing a letter attached to it, was launched from the island, in the hope of its reaching some civilised portion of the kingdom. With the aid of the Gulf Stream it drifted to Birsay in Orkney, and was forwarded to Lloyd's agent in Stromness on 8 February.[16] On 17 February – a month after

---

16 A canoe hewn out of a log by Mr Sands, with a sail and two bottles containing letters attached, was despatched on 5 February, the wind being in the north-west. It

the shipwreck – the Austrian skipper made a bargain with the natives to be taken along with Mr Sands, in their own boat, to Harris. While they were patiently awaiting the advent of settled weather, HMS *Jackal* appeared in the bay, on the morning of the 22nd, having been despatched in consequence of the tidings received at Stromness; and the Austrians and Mr Sands were forthwith conveyed to Greenock. Within ten days of their arrival, the Austro-Hungarian vice-consul at Glasgow published the following letter from the captain of the lost barque; and a subsequent representation to his government resulted in the transmission of £100 from Vienna to the Board of Trade, for behoof of the 'warmhearted islanders'.

Captain Chersonaz, on behalf of himself and the other surivors of the ill-fated vessel *Peti Dubrovacki*, lately wrecked near the island of St Kilda, wishes to express, in this the only way that lies in his power, his warmest thanks to the inhabitants of that island for the gallant manner in which they afforded immediate assistance to them in their distressed condition, and for the generous hospitality displayed towards them. Even when provisions became scarce, the natives shared what they had, and did everything in their power to make their enforced stay comfortable.

Captain Chersonaz also begs to acknowledge, with deepest gratitude, the humanity and promptitude of the government in despatching the steamer *Jackal* to their rescue; and desires to convey to the commander, officers and crew of that steamer his keen sense of the very kind and hospitable treatment he and his companions received at their hands whilst on board. This was all the more welcome in consequence of the destitute

---

was found on a sandbank at Poolewe in Ross-shire on the 27th of the same month, when the letters were posted by the finder. Lastly, a small ship, containing a letter, was sent off in December, and nine months afterwards – September 1877 – was picked up by a boy at Sortland, Verbracle, Norway, from which the letter was forwarded to its address in Edinburgh.

condition in which they were found, having lost everything with the exception of the clothes they had on.

Signed Basilio Chersonaz
Late captain of the Austro-Hungarian barque
Peti Dubrovacki.

The facts relative to the ecclesiastical history of St Kilda will be found in a subsequent chapter.

Natural Features of the Island

The geographical position of St Kilda, and its distance from various points in the Outer Hebrides, have already been referred to. Its remote and remarkable situation is thus described by Mallet, in the opening lines of his 'Amyntor and Theodora'—

> Far in the watery waste, where his broad wave
> From world to world the vast Atlantic rolls
> On from the piny shores of Labrador
> To frozen Thule east, her airy height
> Aloft to heaven remotest Kilda lifts,
> Last of the sea-girt Hebrides that guard,
> In filial train, Britannias parent coast.

Unfortunately, St Kilda has not yet found a place among the trustworthy sheets of the Ordnance Survey. In the ordinary maps of Scotland, its position is indicated by a *note* in that portion of the Atlantic called by the old geographers *Oceanus Deucaledonius*, owing to the scale not being sufficiently large to embrace the remote island. So far as I am aware, its earliest occurrence in a map is in the *True and exact hydrographical Description of the Sea-coast and Isles of Scotland, made in a voyage round the same by that great and mighty prince James the 5th*, published at Paris in 1583, and at Edinburgh, by John Adair, FRS, in 1688.[1] It

---

1 Adair (from whom the author happens to be paternally descended) held the office of Geographer for Scotland, and had a hired vessel for several summers along the western coast – See Chambers' *Domestic Annals of Scotland*, ii, 484.

there appears as 'St Kildar', and is incorrectly placed a little to the north-west of West Loch Tarbert.[2] Macculloch compares its shape to that of a 'leg of mutton'; and if the map of the island which he gives in the third volume of his earlier work is anything like a correct representation, it no doubt bears a considerable resemblance to that familiar object. He explains, however, that his plan merely conveys 'a general notion of the form of the island', besides illustrating the hydrographical details of his narrative. Mr Wilson's *Voyage* also contains a map of St Kilda, furnished by Sir George Mackenzie of Coul, which indicates a much more compact configuration, and bears a general resemblance to the map given by Martin. It appears that Sir George measured a short base on Mullach-More, and took angles from its extremities of all the principal points in sight, filling up the remainder by the eye; but he regarded his plan as only approximately and not absolutely correct. The three maps have been reproduced for the purpose of comparison. It will be observed that Macculloch's map gives no indication of the west bay, and that the north-east portion of the island, embracing Conagher, presents a very different appearance from what is indicated in the two other plans. Both Martin and Macculloch represent the adjacent islet of Soa as almost circular, while in Sir George Mackenzie's map its length is nearly three times greater than its breadth. The extent of St Kilda is considerably understated by Martin, who makes it only two miles long by one broad, and five miles in circumference. In point of fact, however, the island is about three miles long from east to west, by two miles broad, the circumference being somewhere about seven miles. According to Macdonald,[3] if we include the adjacent islands, the group comprehends nearly 3,000 acres of superficial extent; while in Johnston's *General Gazetteer* the area is given as 4,000 acres, or upwards of six square miles.

2 St Kilda also appears as 'S. Kilder', in much the same position, in a map bearing the date of 1610, in Speed's *Theatre of the Empire of Great Britaine*. In the accompanying letterpress, however, the island is referred to under the name of 'Hirta'.
3 *Agriculture of the Hebrides*, p. 815. In the same work, the sea-coast of St Kilda, at high-water mark, is stated to be equal to twenty English miles.

Except at the east or village bay, the island is almost entirely surrounded by stupendous cliffs, rising like walls of adamant out of the dark Atlantic. These cliffs are indented by numerous caves and fissures of very remarkable aspect, many of them bearing descriptive names, such as Géo-na-h-àirde, or 'the Creek of the Eminence', and Géo-nan-plaideachan, or 'the Creek of the Blankets', where the natives lie all night, watching the arrival of the fulmar, covered with thick blankets to protect them from the ocean's spray.

The number of hills, or rather *tops*, is variously stated by different writers, of whom some enumerate as many as six. The more important, however, are four in number – viz., Conagher, or Conna-ghàir, the name being descriptive of the increasing noise (*gàir*) of the surrounding waves; *Mullàchscail*, or 'Bald Top'; Mullàch-geal, or 'White Top'; and Mullàch-osterveaul, or 'East Top', sometimes written Mullàch-Oshival, or 'the Top of Oswald'. The highest of these is Conagher, which is stated in the Admiralty Chart to be 1220 feet above the level of the sea, consisting of one gigantic precipice (according to Mr Sands the loftiest in Britain[4]), and constituting the summit of the uneven ridge which forms the island. While Martin pretty accurately describes it as 200 fathoms high, Macaulay has the audacity to state that its height exceeds 5,000 feet, styling it the 'Teneriffe of Britain!' 'I made a shift', he says, 'to take its height with some degree of exactness, and found it no less than 900 fathoms. Had I never seen the immense mass' (he adds), 'I should very probably dispute the

4 Macculloch makes Conagher 1,380 feet, and Sir George Mackenzie nearly a hundred feet higher.

  Colonel Bayly of the Ordnance Survey Office informs me that the cliff, called the Kaim, at the western extremity of the ridge on the island of Foula, in Shetland, is exactly the same height at Conagher – viz. 1,220 feet; but it is not quite perpendicular, having a break in its face. It appears that in consequence of numerous accidents, the practice of fowling was abandoned in Foula about twenty years ago, fishing being now the principal occupation of the inhabitants. The island is from six to seven miles in circumference; and at the last census the population amounted to 257–125 males and 132 females.

credibility of the account now given, just as much as any one else may do after perusing this account.' In referring to this grave statement, Wilson sensibly remarks: 'Our having seen it is our chief reason for not only disputing but denying the point in question.' 'Not many yards beneath the summit of Conagher,' says Macculloch, 'the hill is cut almost abruptly down to the water – a dizzy height to the spectator who looks down upon the almost inaudible waves dashing below. At the foot of this fearful precipice some lower rocky points project, which in any other situation would attract notice, but are lost in the overpowering vicinity of the cliffs that tower above them.'

On reaching the summit of the same mountain [says Morgan], a startling prospect opened before us. Behind, the moss-grown sides of the hill gradually terminated in the richer hues of the village pastures; before, in outstretched majesty, the wide Atlantic foamed and eddied at our feet – one step beneath our feet – but what a step! Eight hundred feet – without a break – without one resting-place – steep, mural precipices, adamantine ramparts of this sea-girt isle. To obtain a good view of the cliffs, we lay down on a large flat slab of rock, and looked over its side. A plumb-line suspended from the spot would have alighted in the sea . . . These cliffs vary considerably, both in height and abruptness, ranging from about 1,200 to 400 feet – here cold and bare, there padded with narrow moss-clad terraces, rising one above the other, their sides decked with yellow primroses.

It is not easy to convey anything like a correct or adequate conception of the magnificent and fantastic outlines presented by the rugged promontories and beetling headlands of St Kilda and the adjacent islets. The vast variety of form and colour which delighted the party on board the *Dunara Castle* on the afternoon of 2 July will not soon be forgotten. Being in water of forty fathoms, we were able to keep very close to the shore; but the rate at which we steamed round the island – although probably not exceeding nine knots an hour – was not sufficiently slow to enable the most rapid observer fully to realise the grandeur of the remarkable scene. I almost feel disposed to summarise my impressions by quoting part of an American author's description of Inspiration Point in the Yosemite Valley. 'In all my life,' he says, 'let it lead me where it may, I think I shall see nothing else so grand, so awful, so sublime, so beautiful . . . It was only yesterday evening – I cannot write of it yet. How long I sat there on the rocks I never shall know. I brought the picture away with me. I have only to shut my eyes, and I see it as I saw it in that hour of hours!'

The first object that presented itself, as we left the crescent-shaped bay, was the Dune, a long craggy islet, separated from Mullách-geal by a narrow rocky channel, nearly dry at low water, and forming the southern horn of the bay. Although not particularly lofty, its jagged peaks exhibit a very striking appearance; and, like the remarkable rock in the Shevroy range of mountains in Madras, it has been compared to a vast cathedral, with a central tower and flanking spires, the resemblance being increased by a lofty opening, not unlike an arched doorway, through which the ocean flows.

Rather more than a mile and a quarter south-east of the extremity of the Dune is the bare, flat-topped, and inaccessible islet of Levinish, of which the summit is about 200 feet above the level of the sea. Martin considerably underestimates the height of Levinish, but his description of its form and position appears to be tolerably correct. He mentions that it has a spring of fresh water, and that, by an ancient custom, it belonged to the crew of the steward's galley; but it is not easy to conjecture what practical benefit could have been derived from an inaccessible rock. About 150 yards NNE from the northern end of Levinish is the only dangerous rock – a low-water one – in the neighbourhood of the St Kilda group. It is, however, generally visible, except in very smooth water.[5]

5 Otter's *Sailing Directions for the West of Scotland*, part i, p. 15.

After coasting along the southern side of the island, with a continuous line of rocky battlements of nearly two miles in length, we reached the little island of 'Soa', or 'the sheep island',[6] at the western extremity of St Kilda, and near the southern entrance to the west bay. About a mile in length, and with an average breadth of a quarter of a mile, its greatest height is 1,031 feet; and on every side, except at the south 'nose,' where the natives effect a landing in moderate weather, the cliffs are steep and lofty. Like the well-known table-rock of the Quirang in Skye, it has a grassy top, which affords goods pasturage to a large flock of sheep. When viewed from a certain quarter, Soa is thought to resemble a tiger couching for its prey. It is separated from St Kilda by a narrow passage or sound, about 400 yards in width, from which rise three lofty needles or 'stacks', of very peculiar form, one of which is perforated by an arched opening. They are respectively named Stack Biorrach, or 'the Pointed Stack', (from four to five hundred feet high, and regarded by the fowlers as the most difficult rock to climb), Stack Soa and Stack Donadh, or the bad stack, from the circumstance of its sea-birds not being very numerous. At the northern extremity of Soa is another small but highly picturesque rock, bearing the name of Plasta. One of the former, from a particular point of view, 'presented the appearance of a gigantic nondescript animal trying to wade across to Soa; while another assumed at times a somewhat complex aspect, presenting as it were alternately the character of an old beggar-woman, a Scotch preacher, and an Egyptian sphynx!'[7] Having rounded Soa and the western extremity of St Kilda, we shaped our course in the direction of Borrera – called by Mallet 'the lesser isle' – situated about three and a half miles to the north of the principal island, between the two remarkable rocks Stack an Armin, or 'the Hero's Rock', and Stack Lii

6 According to some authorities, Soa (pronounced 'Soay') means 'good', being so named from its abundant produce of sea-fowl.
7 Wilson's *Voyage*, ii, 66.

(Leathad), or 'the Sloping Stack'. About a mile and a quarter long, by a quarter of a mile broad, its formation is somewhat similar to Salisbury Crags, with a verdurous slope towards the east, but without any water; while its dark and precipitous cliffs face westwards, and reach the height of 1072 feet. With its adjoining stacks, it forms a highly picturesque group of rocky islets; in the opinion of Macculloch, 'far eclipsing St Kilda in the landscape, by their more elevated and decided characters'. Stack Lii is a huge insular mass, about the height of the Bass Rock, nearly one-third of a mile from the west side of Borrera, and tenanted by myriads of solan geese. From Harris, to the naked eye, it appears like a ship under sail leaning to the northward. It is described by Wilson as exhibiting on one side 'a sharpish edge, and then a gradual descent a certain way downwards, as if a sloping slice had been cut off it, after which it descends again in a more rugged and precipitous form into the sea. On the other side, it falls at once from the sharp upper edge already mentioned, straight down into the ocean, with a variety of rents and rocky ledges, which do not interfere with its general character of abruptness.

The lofty peaks of Stack an Armin, one-third of a mile NNE from Borrera, form a very striking feature in the group, which presents an endless variety of most magnificent marine views. For two or three hours after we steamed away from Borrera in the direction of the Sound of Harris, the bold outlines of St Kilda and its satellites continued more or less in sight; and the last glimpse of the wonderful group was eagerly regarded by every member of our enchanted party.

With regard to the noble cliffs on the northern side of St Kilda, it is hard to believe that their height is so great as has been indicated; but it is generally admitted that mere ocular measurements of such objects are very apt to be under the mark, and in other localities my experience has been the same as at St Kilda – viz., a difficulty of persuading oneself that such cliffs actually reach their ascertained altitude. In coasting along the well-known cliffs of Hoy, in Orkney, about a fortnight after my visit to St Kilda, I had the same sceptical feeling; and on a previous occasion, the stupendous precipices of the Romsdal Fiord, in Norway, failed to impress me with an unhesitating belief in their enormous height. Macaulay seems to have been gifted with a much more imaginative mind, inspired, perhaps, by his classical recollections of Pelion and Ossa! 'A view of Conagher from the sea', he says, 'fills a man with astonishment, and a look over it from above strikes him with horror.' I fully concur in the latter part of the minister's statement; but grand as was the appearance of the cliff from the sea, my sensations partook more of admiration than of astonishment.

In more than one instance, the actual appearance and general features of St Kilda seem to have greatly differed from the preconceived notions of its casual visitants. Mr Morgan says that 'the whole character of this solitary isle was less like what I had pictured to myself than any other place I ever beheld. There was a strange, indescribable look about all we saw, as though we had sailed into another planet, or made a voyage to one of the little asteroids.' In like manner, in the case of Mr Wilson, the group of islands far transcended his previous expectations; in alluding to which he states that 'the whole combined form a really magnificent mountain-range, as seen from the sea, and assume a vast variety of shape and aspect in relation to each other, as the vessel from which they are beheld turns round the various points, and passes through the intermediate narrow seas by which they are surrounded.' Dr Angus Smith appears to have first seen St Kilda under a cloudy aspect, the dusky precipices jutting out on every side from the mist, and appearing like huge pillars beneath an impending roof 'Had it been an island of demons,' he says, 'it could not have appeared more dreadful, and had we not heard of it before, we should have said that, if inhabited, it must be by monsters.' Speaking of the sublimity of the atmospheric effects produced by the isolated position of St Kilda, Macculloch says—

Fertile as are the other islands of this sea in all the accidents of colour and light that arise from these changes, they fall far short

of this one, where the variations of the atmosphere are inces-
sant, where they are accompanied by effects, equally various
and changeable, of light and shadow, of rain and mist, and
storm, and of clouds in a thousand new and romantic forms,
and colours such as neither poet nor painter ever imagined; the
whole producing the most splendid and unexpected combination with the land, and with an ever restless and changing sea
. . . If the uniform tints and outlines of grey precipices or
brown mountains require splendid contrasts to give them
interest, so the wider sweep of hill and dale must be rendered
effective by shadows, not by shade, which it seldom displays
with advantage. It is to the pencil of a Turner alone that St
Kilda will furnish employment. A dizzy height from which the
eye looks down over jutting crags, retiring till they are lost in
air; a boiling sea below, without a boundary; dark cliffs beaten
by a foaming surge, and lost in the gloom of involving clouds;
the mixed contest of rocks, ocean, and sky – these are the
subjects which it offers to him who, seeing with the poet's eye,
knows how to speak the language of poetry with his pencil.

Glen Mòr, or the Amazon's Glen, is situated at the west end of St
Kilda, affording extensive pasturage for sheep and cattle. The cliffs
at the extremity of the glen are comparatively low; and at that
point a landing can sometimes be effected, when the weather is
too boisterous on the eastern side. The bay on which the village
stands is divided from Glen Mòr by a lofty ridge, and presents the
appearance of a crescent or half-moon, of which the southern
horn is the Dune already referred to; while on the northern horn
is the mountain of St Kilda proper, with its steep but not altogether precipitous aspect. The intermediate semicircular shore
slopes gently upwards to the village, which stretches in a line
nearly parallel to the curve of the bay, from the margin of which
it is separated by an interval of two or 300 yards of ground, all
under cultivation. About thirty-nine years ago, the Rev. Drs
Dickson and Macleod paid an ecclesiastical visit to St Kilda,

besides making many active exertions in behalf of the inhabitants, by whom the eastern or village entrance has since been sometimes called 'Dickson's Bay', while the western bay has been named after Dr Macleod. Mr Wilson justly regards these designations as 'a fine illustration of the good spirit which pervades the people. They knew nothing,' he continues, 'of Lords of the Admiralty, or of great circumnavigators, or other "men of renown"; but they knew that two kindhearted, pious individuals had come to their almost forgotten shores with "glad tidings", seeking to diffuse the blessings of the Gospel, at their own personal inconvenience and discomfort; and they seek to mark their sense of that holy kindness by the names in question, which are at least as appropriate as Melbourne Mount, or Russell's Reach, or Point Palmerston.'[8]

Many of the published descriptions of the island give a far too unfavourable account of the means of landing. This circumstance is referred to by both Macculloch and Wilson, the former of whom furnishes the following encouraging information to future visitors respecting the argonautics of St Kilda.

The whole shore of St Kilda is so clean that vessels of any draught may range it within gunshot; and the stream of tide is so inconsiderable that there is no danger from calms, if a moderate offing is secured. The bay opens to the south-east, and is perfectly sheltered on three quarters of the compass. Hence it is exposed to few winds, and those not the predominant ones; while, from its depth and semicircular form, the westerly swell cannot often raise such a sea on the shore as to prevent a boat from landing. In this operation, indeed, the natives are uncommonly alert and dexterous; and, with a tolerable steersman, there cannot often be a sea in which a boat might not land, unless that were from the westward. There is good clean holding-ground in depths ranging from four to

8 Mr Maclean connects the name of 'Dickson's Bay' with a somewhat amusing incident – viz, the accidental immersion of the worthy divine.

seven fathoms, where a vessel of any size may lie for a tide or more, with fully as great security as in most ordinary harbours; nor is there any difficulty in weighing and running to sea on either tack, should the wind shift so as to blow in shore.

The only landing-place is under the manse, a little to the north-ward of the store.[9] Captain Otter informs us that the head of the bay is sandy and deepens gradually from the shore. He considers that the best place to anchor is in the middle of the bay, 'with the narrow sound of the Dune open in ten or eleven fathoms, with a sandy bottom and good holding-ground. Great care must be taken to keep the anchor clear, as, except in southerly winds, terrible squalls veer all round the compass, and frequently, in northerly winds, a vessel will be lying with her head out. It is scarcely necessary', he adds, 'to warn the careful seaman to leave this exposed position the moment the wind comes to the south.' Macculloch states that it is high water at St Kilda when the moon is south-east, and that the course of the flood is northerly. According to Captain Otter, 'it is high water, full and change, at 5h. 30m. The ebb sets SW by W, and the flood in the opposite direction; near the islands, and especially at point of Dune, it runs at the rate of three miles an hour.' With certain southerly or east-erly winds, it is difficult, and sometimes impossible, to land; and consequently, in the case of sailing vessels at least, it is not desir-able to have a fair wind for the voyage. On the other hand, if the wind happens to be favourable, vessels of the same description find it very difficult to get out of the bay, owing to its being open to the south-east – a circumstance which also makes it a danger-ous anchorage when the wind blows strongly from that quarter. Accordingly, as Mr Sands informs us, the few adventurous yachts that find their way into the bay usually adopt the precaution of remaining not more than a few hours. In his description of the bay, Martin says that—

9 *Sailing Directions for the West of Scotland*, part i, p. 14.

the only place for landing here is on the north side, upon a
rock with a little declination, which is slippery, being clothed
with several sorts of seaweeds; these, together with a raging
sea, render the place more inaccessible, it being seldom without a raging sea, except under favour of a neap-tide, a north-
east or west wind, or with a perfect calm; when these circumstances concur, the *birlin*, or boat, is brought to the side of the
rock, upon which all the inhabitants of both sexes are ready to
join their united force to hail her through this rock, having for
this end a rope fastened to the fore part; a competent number
of them are also employed on each side; both these are determined by a crier, who is employed on purpose to warn them
all at the same minute, and he ceases when he finds it convenient to give them a breathing.

On the occasion of my recent visit to the island, both wind and
weather were sufficiently favourable to render our landing a
matter of easy accomplishment. On reembarking, however, most
of our party took their places in the large boats belonging to the
islanders, which were drawn up on the shore, and supported on
each side by two or three of the natives, who ran the craft down
into the sea, on entering which the rowers immediately dipped
their oars into the surf. Leaving Obb, in the Sound of Harris,
about 3 a.m., we soon emerged from the Hebridean archipelago
into the wide Atlantic; and between four and five, the islet of
Borrera and its adjacent stacks began to disclose their picturesque
outlines. Masses of white clouds were resting on the summits of
St Kilda as we approached its rocky shores from the north-east
side. We dropped anchor at half-past eight, in smooth water,
within a gunshot of the shore, and the impression produced by
the surrounding scenery was heightened by the stillness that
prevailed. After breakfasting on board the *Dunara*, the passengers
began to land in detachments about half-past nine. Heavy rain fell
during breakfast; but the weather speedily improved, and the sun
shone forth most auspiciously. Some of the party landed in one of

the boats of the islanders which came out to the steamer, while others went in the gig belonging to the *Dunara*. We received a warm and hearty welcome from the inhabitants, who had all assembled on the beach when the steamer entered the bay.

Judging from the effect of the surging waves of the Atlantic upon the rocky shores of St Kilda in a comparatively calm day, a storm must be a very magnificent spectacle. On 28 January, 1877, Mr Sands witnessed a violent gale, when the wind blew from the north-east, accompanied by heavy showers of sleet. 'The huge waves came rolling into the bay against the wind, which caught them as they fell on the shore, and carried them off in spindrift.' The author of *Sketches of St Kilda* gives the following description of the war of the elements against the bulwarks of the lonely isle:

If one would see Nature in her giant gambols, let him go to St Kilda. When the liquid foe, which knew no opposition from the time he left the North Pole – except perhaps an unfortunate ship, which he swallowed – sees St Kilda determined upon breaking his line, he retires a little, swelling as he retires in sullen wrath, and hurling with him stones, or rather fragments of rock, some of them twenty-four tons in weight; then with these rude bullets in his grasp, hurling them against the rocks, he makes one desperate charge, as if in hope to push the island from its seat! The war is vain; but the noise would drown a thousand thunders. The purpose of the assailant is answered, however, in so far that, having mounted a rampart 1,500 (?) feet high, he gets sheer over the island in white spray; dropping salt tears of disappointment upon the natives as he passes. His old grudge may also be satisfied so far that these fragments of rock, thus battered, have literally perforated the island through and through at its foundation.

Both Morgan and Wilson appear to have been struck by the bright, fresh colour of the vegetation. The former was greatly surprised by the rich green hue of the crops in a place where he expected to find a 'howling wilderness'; while the prevailing verdure, the gradual uprising of the land, the absence of trees, and even a certain smoothness and uniformity of aspect and outline in the hills which formed the intermediate background, rather reminded the latter of the pastoral uplands of Peeblesshire and the far-inland shores of 'still Mary's Loch', than of a remote and rocky sea-girt isle. Forewarned of the verdant appearance of the island, I was not, of course, surprised by the brilliancy of its emerald hue, which the rains of the preceding weeks had probably rendered even brighter than usual.

Martin gives a detailed account of the 'excellent fountains or springs' – called by old Isaac Walton the 'eldest daughters of Creation' – with which the island abounds. One of these, named 'St Kilda's Well', is near the little village, between the manse and the factor's house; while another, of which the Gaelic name signifies the 'Well of Qualities or Virtues', in consequence of the supposed efficacy of its water, is situated in Glen Mòr, beside the house of the 'Amazon' or 'Female Warrior', to be afterwards referred to. 'The taste of the water of these wells,' says Martin, 'was so pleasant, that, for several weeks after, the best fountains in the adjacent isles did not relish with me.' Macaulay speaks in equally strong terms, besides alluding to the 'inexhaustible quantities' of water in every corner of the island. 'The whole island', Martin elsewhere states, 'is one hard rock, formed into four high mountains (already enumerated), three of which are in the middle, all thinly covered with black or brown earth, not above a foot, some places half a foot deep, except the top of the hills, where it is above three feet deep, and affords them good turf; the grass is very short but kindly, producing plenty of milk.'

According to Macculloch, who briefly describes the geology of St Kilda in his earlier work, the rocks are all of modern volcanic origin, consisting principally of a dark trap, with a small proportion of syenite, of which the latter occasionally presents cavities containing crystals of both quartz and felspar. As the state of the weather prevented him from approaching Borrera, he only conjectures, from its form and colour, that it consists entirely of the first-mentioned rock. His observations, however, were probably not sufficiently exact to satisfy the accurate research of modern geologists, none of whom, so far as I am aware, have as yet paid a professional visit to the island. Macculloch seems to be quite at fault when he asserts that no stratified rocks can be discovered. Mr Sands states that

> for several hundred feet, the hills are composed of sandstone; the stratification very distinct, and of different colours. Cliffs of igneous rock, trap or granite, arise on the top of the sandstone, marked with vertical furrows, ploughed apparently by the weather. The ridges are brought into bolder relief by the rock-plants which grow in the flutings. To an unscientific eye, it would seem as if the island of St Kilda had been much larger at some time, and that the land had sunk into the sea all around it. It looks as if it had been chopped into its present form by the axe of an earthquake – chopped indifferently through hill and glen.

Professor Geikie informs me that all the specimens of St Kilda rocks submitted to him by Mr Sands were of igneous formation. Along with Mr Dudgeon of Cargen, he contemplated a geological expedition to the island in the course of last summer; and it is to be hoped that, at no very distant date, he will be able to carry his intentions into execution.

Physical Characteristics of the Inhabitants – Their Dress, Food, and Houses

Most of the writers on St Kilda give a favourable account of the physical characteristics of the inhabitants. 'Both sexes,' says Martin, 'are naturally very grave, and of a fair complexion; such as are not fair are natives only for an age or two, but their offspring proves fairer than themselves. There are several of them would be reckoned among beauties of the first rank, were they upon a level with others in their dress.' The minister of Ardnamurchan (Macaulay) expresses the same opinion in even stronger terms. 'The women', he says, 'are most handsome; their complexions fresh and lively, as their features are regular and fine; some of them, if properly dressed and genteelly educated, would be reckoned extraordinary beauties in the gay world.' According to the author of *Travels in the Western Hebrides*, 'The women are more handsome, as well as modest, than those of Harris: they marry young, and address strangers with profound respect.' He elsewhere states that, owing to the oily nature of their sea-fowl food the St Kildans 'emit a disagreeable odour'; but I am not aware that this unpleasant characteristic has been referred to by any recent visitor. Mr Morgan also alludes to the beauties of St Kilda, and gives a graphic description of the 'belle of the island'; but my correspondent, Mr Grigor, pronounces the women to be 'stout and squat'; and although he admits that many of them have a

blond complexion, he considers them to be generally characterised by 'an uncouth comeliness, which is not very taking'. While
Dr Macculloch acknowledges the good physique of the males, his
estimate of the women is not very favourable.

> The men [he says] were well-looking, and appeared, as they
> indeed are, well fed; exceeding in this, as in their dress, their
> neighbours of the Long Island, and bearing the marks of easy
> circumstances, or rather of wealth. But the women, like the
> generality of that little-favoured sex in this country, appeared
> harsh in feature, and were evidently impressed, even in early
> life, by those marks so dreaded by Queen Elizabeth, and
> recorded in the well-known epigram of Plato. This must be
> the consequence of exposure to the weather; as there is no
> want of food here as a cause, and as the children of both sexes
> might even be considered handsome.

The youthful Henry Brougham does not seem to have been
favourably impressed by the appearance of the islanders. 'A total
want of curiosity,' he says, 'a stupid gaze of wonder, an excessive
eagerness for spirits and tobacco, a laziness only to be conquered
by the hope of the above-mentioned cordials, and a beastly degree
of filth – the natural consequence of this – render the St Kildan
character truly savage!'

Mr Macdiarmid appears to have been struck by the fresh-look-
ing, rosy complexions of the population generally; the women,
however, appearing to him, as they did to Mr Grigor, to be 'more
than ordinarily stout'. In the case of both sexes I observed a good
many examples of something more than plumpness; and I am
very much inclined to agree with Captain Thomas in his opinion
that among both men and women there is more than the average
amount of good looks. Traces of a Scandinavian origin seemed to
me as apparent among the natives of St Kilda as in many other
parts of the Western Isles. I believe I came in contact with every
inhabitant of the island; and although I did not make an actual

reckoning, I feel satisfied that a majority exhibit the fair, or Scandinavian, aspect; while the rest are characterised by the olive complexion, accompanied by dark hair and eyes, which usually indicates the Celtic type of countenance. The remarkably healthy look of the children in arms was the subject of universal comment.

In general appearance, the natives of St Kilda bear a strong resemblance to the inhabitants of the Long Island – the men being somewhat less in height, but decidedly fatter. In respect to weight, they are probably above the national average, and they are said to lose flesh when placed upon the comparatively low diet of the inhabitants of the Long Island. Martin refers to the fact of the generation of his day (1697) having come short of their immediate predecessors in point of strength and longevity; but notwithstanding this circumstance, he informs us that

> anyone inhabiting St Kilda is always reputed stronger than *two* of the inhabitants belonging to Harris or the adjacent isles. Those of St Kilda [he continues] have generally but very thin beards, and those, too, do not appear till they arrive at the age of thirty, and in some not till after thirty-five. They have all but a few hairs upon the upper lip and point of the chin.

He elsewhere tells us that their sight is 'extraordinary good', and that they can discern objects at a great distance. Again, in the words of Mr Wilson, 'although most of the men were what we Southrons would call undersized, many of them were stout and active, and several of them handsome-featured, with bright eyes, and an expression of great intelligence.' He particularly refers to one of 'even noble countenance – a sort of John Kemble *rasé*' – who presented a picture of activity and strength combined.

Besides alluding to the strength and healthiness of both sexes, as well as to their capacity for long-continued exertion, Mr Sands makes special mention of the brightness of their eyes and the whiteness of their teeth. The average height of twenty-one male adults whom he measured was about five feet six inches – the tallest being five feet nine inches, and the shortest four feet ten and a half inches. In addition to a woman who is subject to fits, and an aged male of weak intellect, but quiet and peaceable when not contradicted, and who lives by himself in one of the old thatched hovels, there is an elderly man who lost his sight about six years ago. The poor imbecile contrives to cultivate a small patch of ground, and to accompany his neighbours to the fishing; while his blind brother-islesman sits cheerfully at his cottage door, and is still able to sew and make gins. With these three exceptions, all the other members of the little community are at present sound in both body and mind. In allusion to her recent visit to the island, the 'Bartimeus' of St Kilda said to Miss Macleod that 'as Solomon did not go to see the Queen of Sheba, the Queen of Sheba kindly came to see Solomon!'

Mr Wilson describes the prevailing dress of the males as very similar to that of the fishermen of the Long Island – 'small flat blue bonnets, coarse yellowish-white woollen jerkins, and trousers, also of coarse woollen stuff, of a mixed colour, similar to that of heather stalks.' Mr Muir informs us that he found both males and females very decently and comfortably clothed, and, in that respect at least, presenting a very favourable contrast to their equivalents in the Western Islands generally.

> The dress of the females [he says] has some peculiarities, the which it would be difficult for any but a man-milliner, or one of their own sex, to describe. A suit, consisting of a round coat, waistcoat and trousers, made of the coarse kelt manufactured from the short wiry wool of their native sheep, and fashioned very much as such things are in the Lowlands, is the dress universally worn by the men. Even among the children we did not see a single kilt.

According to Martin, the ancient habit of the St Kildans was of sheepskin, which, he says has been worn by several of the inhabitants now living. The men at this day (1697) wear a short doublet reaching to their waist, about that a double plait of plad, both ends joined together with the bone of a fulmar. This plad reaches no further than the knees, and is above the haunches girt about with a belt of leather [apparently an approach to the modern kilt]. They wear short caps of the same colour and shape as the Capuchins, but shorter; and on Sundays they wear bonnets. Some, of late, have got breeches, which are wide and open at the knees. They wear cloth stockings, and go without shoes in the summer time. Their leather is dressed with the roots of tormentil. The women wear upon their heads a linen dress, straight before, and drawing to a small point behind, below the shoulders, a foot and a half in length; and a lock of about sixty hairs hanging down each cheek, reaching to their breasts, the lower end tied with a knot. Their plad, which is the upper garment, is fastened upon their breasts with a large round buckle of brass, in form of a circle . . . They wear no shoes or stockings in summer; the only and ordinary shoes they wear are made of the necks of solan geese, which they cut above the eyes; the crown of the head serves for the heel, the whole skin being cut close at the breast, which end being sewed, the foot enters into it, as into a piece of narrow stocking. This shoe doth not wear above five days, and, if the down side be next the ground, then not above three or four days . . . Both sexes wear coarse flannel shirts, which they put off when they go to bed.

Lane Buchanan informs us that the St Kildans 'are possessed of an equal share of pride and ambition of appearing gay on Sundays and holidays with other people'; while Macculloch refers to the remarkable fact of a community so remote having entirely conformed to the Lowland garb. 'Not a trace of tartan, kilt or bonnet was to be seen; so much has convenience gained the victory over ancient usage. The colours of the *breachan* might

indeed have still been retained: but all was dingy brown and blue.'
Speaking of the rapidity with which 'fashion' travels, he elsewhere mentions that a peculiar kind of shoe-string, which had
been invented in London during spring, had reached the distant
shores of St Kilda by the following summer. Bonnets have for
some time been considered essential for full dress by the female
islanders; and the graceful handkerchief fastened under the chin is
said to be looked upon as vulgar! When the Rev. Neil Mackenzie
went to the island in 1830, his servant-maid, a native, asked
permission to take the hearth-rug to church, by way of a shawl.
Regarding her proposal as a joke, he innocently assented; and to
his infinite astonishment he beheld the girl in his own pew,
enveloped in the many-coloured carpet, the envied of an admir-
ing congregation! All the women in the island were eager candi-
dates for the 'shawl' on the following morning, some of them
offering to give 'ten birds' for its use.

Mr Macdiarmid supplies the following account of the Sunday
dress[1] of the St Kildans:

The men wore jackets and vests of their own making, mostly
of blue colour, woollen shirts, a few had linen collars, and the
remainder cravats on their necks; the prevailing headdress was
a broad blue bonnet. The women's dresses were mostly home-
made, of finely spun wool, dyed a kind of blue and brown
mixture, and not unlike common wincey. Every female wore
a tartan plaid or large shawl over her head and shoulders; and
upwards of twenty of these plaids were of Rob Roy tartan, all
from the mainland. They were fastened in front by an anti-
quated-looking brooch. Several of the women wore the

1 The church is everything to the Western Islanders – 'their play and rout, their ball
and masque and revel' – and only there can their finery be displayed. Our French
neighbours have a special term – *endimanché* – for dressed in Sunday attire, In the
course of his reflections on the Sabbath, Addison pronounces it to be a desirable institution, from the circumstance of its causing poor people to wash and dress themselves
at least once a week!

common white muslin cap or *mutch*; and I noticed one solitary bonnet, of romantic shape, adorning the head of by no means the fairest-looking female present. All the men, and a few of the women, wore shoes; the rest of the women had stockings, or went barefooted.

Mr Sands informs us that

the men all wear trousers and vests of coarse blue cloth, with blanket shirts. On Sundays, they wear jackets in addition. Their clothes are made at home from wool plucked (not shorn) from their own sheep, which is spun by the women with the ancient spindle or more modern wheel. The women also dye the thread, and the men weave it into cloth, and make it into garments for both sexes. The dress of the women consists of a cotton handkerchief on the head, which is tied under the chin, a gown of coarse blue cloth, or blue with a thin purple stripe, fastened at the breast with an iron skewer. [He elsewhere says, 'with a large pin made from a fish-hook'.] The skirt is tied round the waist, and is girded tightly above the haunches with a worsted sash of divers dim colours,[2] and is worn very short – their muscular limbs being visible from near the knee. They wear neither shoes nor stockings in summer. They go barefoot even to church; and on that occasion don a plaid, which is worn square, and fastened in front with a copper brooch, like a small quoit, made by the men from an old penny beat out thin. All the women's dresses are made by the men, who also make their brogues or shoes; for every female owns a pair, although she prefers going without them in summer . . . The brogues are sewed with thongs of raw sheepskin, and look like clumsy shoes. The ancient Highland brogue, which was open at the sides to let out the water, was in use until a few years ago.

---

2 In this garb, the women are said to be *creas*, or 'girdled'.

The same writer refers to the entire absence of ornament in all their works, thereby differing from the ordinary Highlander.

The only exception [he says] to this, is in some of their woollen fabrics, where there is a feeble attempt at colour. And yet they seem fond of bright colours. But everything else appears designed solely for utility. The women's brooches are perfectly plain, and the large pins that fasten their gowns mere skewers. There are no Celtic traceries or 'uncouth sculptures' on their tombstones, or on any building, or any attempt at wood-carving in boat or in house. The aesthetic faculty, if it exists, seems never to have been developed.

In Martin's time, the ordinary food of the inhabitants of St Kilda appears to have been barley and 'oat-bread baked with water', fresh beef and mutton, and the various kinds of sea-fowl, which were merely dried in the small stone houses or 'pyramids' erected for the purpose, without any salt or spice to preserve them. With their fish and other food, they still use an oleaginous accompaniment prepared from the fat of their fowls, termed *giben*, also in a fresh state. It is melted down and stored in the stomachs of the old gannets, like hog's-lard in bladders. 'They are undone', says Martin, 'for want of salt, of which as yet they are but little sensible. They use no set times for their meals, but are determined purely by their appetites.' In one of his letters to the *Scotsman*, Mr Sands states that the islanders usually dine as late as five or six o'clock. That hour appears to be found the most suitable, in consequence of their continuous absence – on fowling expeditions and other avocations – during the greater part of the day. Martin made particular inquiry respecting the number of solan geese consumed by the inhabitants during the preceding year, and ascertained that it amounted to 22,600, which he was informed was under the average. At that time, the common drink was water or whey. According to the same writer they brew ale but rarely, using the juice of nettleroots, which they put in a dish with a little barley-meal dough. These sowens [i.e. flummery] being blended together, produce good yeast, which puts their wort into a ferment and makes good ale, so that when they drink plentifully of it, it disposes them to dance merrily.

Mr Wilson states that the St Kildans are frequently very ill off during stormy weather, and at those periods of the year when the rocks are deserted by their feathered occupants.

Their slight supply of oats and barley [he says] would scarcely suffice for the sustenance of life; and such is the injurious effect of the spray in winter, even on their hardiest vegetation, that savoys and German greens, which with us are improved by the winter's cold, almost invariably perish soon after the close of autumn . . . The flesh of the fulmar is a favourite food with the St Kildans, who like it all the better on account of its oily nature. With it and other sea-fowl, they boil and also eat raw a quantity of *sourocks*, or large-leaved sorrel – a sad and watery substitute for the mealy potatoes of more genial climes. But happy it is for those who, like many a poor St Kildan, know and remember that 'man does not live by bread alone.'[3]

3 The flesh of puffins is not only extensively used as food by the Icelanders, but it is also considered to be the best of bait for cod-fish. Puffins are in great repute for their feathers in Norway, and also for their flesh in some country parts. Yet if the natives could read what Wecker (quoted in the *Anatomy of Melancholy*) says of such food, they would avoid these 'melancholic meats'. All finny fowl [he says] are forbidden; ducks, geese, and coots, and all those teals, curs, sheldrakes and freckled fowls that come in winter from Scandia, Greenland, etc., which half the year are covered up with snow. Though these be fair in feathers, pleasant in taste, and of a good outside, like hypocrites, white in plumes and soft, yet their flesh is hard, black, unwholesome, dangerous, melancholy meat . . . Puffinpie sounds like an abomination, but it is not bad if properly cooked. *Experto crede*. The back-bone must be removed, and the bird soaked in water for some hours before cooking it, or it will taste of fish. Many sea-birds are excellent eating, if this precaution is observed. For instance, a cormorant roasted and eaten with cayenne and lemon, is nearly as good as a wild duck, and better than a curlew. A fisherman of my acquaintance has often told me that 'a fat gull is as good as a goose any day' – Elton's *Norway*, pp. 92–94.

In his extracts from Mr Mackenzie's Journal, we find the following statement relative to the privations of the islanders during the month of July 1841:

The people are suffering very much from want of food. During spring, ere the birds came, they literally cleared the shore not only of shell-fish, but even of a species of sea-weed that grows abundantly on the rocks within the sea-mark. For a time then they were better off, particularly as long as fresh eggs could be got. Now the weather is coarse, birds cannot be found, at least in such abundance as their needs require. Sorrel boiled in water is the principal part of the food of some, and even that grass is getting scarce. All that was near is exhausted, and they go to the rocks for it, where formerly they used to go for birds only.

Mr Wilson refers to Macaulay's important inquiry as to 'whether St Kilda be a place proper for a fishery?' and reasonably concludes, from the enormous number of sea-fowl, that the surrounding waters must be well stocked with fish. According to Martin, the coasts of St Kilda and the lesser isles are plentifully furnished with 'a variety of cod, ling, mackerel, congars, braziers, turbot, greylords, and sythes . . . also laiths, podloes, herrings, and many more. Most of these are fished by the inhabitants upon the rock, but they have neither nets nor longlines. Their common bait is the lympets or *patellae*, being parboiled; they use likewise the fowl called by them *bouger* (puffin), its flesh raw, which the fish near the lesser isles catch greedily. Sometimes they use the bouger's flesh and the lympets at the same time upon one hook, and this proves successful also.' Mr Wilson estimates the number of solan geese alone in the colony of St Kilda at 200,000, their favourite food being herring and mackerel; and, on the assumption that each of them is a feeding creature for seven months in the year, he computes the summer sustenance of this single species at no less than 214 millions of fish![4] 'Think of this,' he remarks, 'ye men of Wick, ye curers in Caithness, ye fair females of the salting-tub. It is also a subject of very grave consideration by all who take an interest in the forlorn St Kildans. A second boat[5] [he adds] would probably be of great advantage, and also a good supply of hooks and lines.'

Mr Grigor considers the St Kildans to be much better off, according to their habits of life, than is generally supposed; and Mr Kennedy, the catechist, assured him that every one of them had some money laid past. Captain Thomas informs me that, in the year 1860, they were able to pay a half-year's rent in advance. According to Mr Grigor, 'their food is principally the flesh of marine birds – the gannet, fulmar and puffin – of which the two first are stored for the winter. They do not care for farinaceous food or fish. They also eat mutton and beef in emergencies, and milk and eggs always. There is plenty of good ling and cod to be got about the islands, and the people have begun to cure.' For that purpose an abundant supply of salt appears to be a great desideratum. In 1860, Captain Otter of the *Porcupine* – engaged on the Admiralty Survey – brought off sixteen cwt. of excellent fish, which were sold for £16, and the proceeds given to the inhabitants. About twelve years ago, some of the younger men having resolved to fish, procured a suitable boat and lines; and at that time it was considered that, if no disaster should occur, they ought to catch from three to four tons of fish, which would be worth upwards of £50.

According to Lane Buchanan, the guillemot supplies the wants of the St Kildans when their fresh mutton is exhausted.

---

4 According to the *Fishing Gazette*, this is equal to 305,714 barrels, or much more than the total average of herrings landed at all the north-east stations. To the number indicated must be added what the cod and dogfish and other fowls and fishes devour. The fruitfulness of the herring to balance this enormous destruction by man, fish and fowl is correspondingly great, as the roe generally contains between 60,000 and 70,000 eggs.

5 In 1841, the St Kildans possessed only one boat.

'Then the solan goose is in season; after that the puffins, with a variety of eggs; and when their appetites are cloyed with this food, the salubrious fulmar, with their favourite young solan goose (called *goug*), crowns their humble tables, and holds out all the autumn. In winter they have a greater stock of bread, mutton, potatoes and salad, or *reisted* [salted] fowls, than they can consume.' While the sea-birds are eaten in a fresh state during summer, they are salted for consumption in winter. I have somewhere seen the number so salted stated at 12,000, which is equal to about 150 birds for every man, woman and child. Mrs McVean mentions that every family has about three or four barrels of fulmars salted for winter use, the flavour of which she considers similar to that of salted pork. Their principal food in summer is roasted puffin. 'For breakfast', she observes, 'they have some thin porridge or gruel, with a puffin boiled in it to give it a flavour. Dinner consists of puffin again, this time roasted, with a large quantity of hard-boiled eggs, which they eat just as the peasantry eat potatoes.[6] They use no vegetables, except a few soft potatoes, not unlike yams. They consume very little meal, as their crops are not good, and are liable to being swept off by the fierce equinoctial gales. Bread is considered a great luxury, and is only used at christenings weddings and the New Year. The latter is quite a time of feasting, as each family kills a sheep, and bakes oatmeal cakes. The principal drink is whey. No vegetables can be raised (as in Martin's time), owing to the showers of spray that dash over the island. Even kail plants are with difficulty reared.'

Mr Sands also states that

the St Kildans subsist chiefly on sea-fowl, the flesh of the fulmar being preferred. This they eat both in a fresh and in a pickled condition. The men when out in their boats dine on oat-cakes and ewe-milk cheese, washed down with milk or

6 In a subsequent chapter, reference is made to the large consumption of eggs by the islanders.

whey. The women when herding use the same viands. The sea-fowl must be nutritious, judging from the lusty looks, strength and endurance of the people. They have a prejudice against fish, and use it sparingly, alleging that it causes an eruption on the skin. They care little for tea, but are fond of sugar, and the women are crazy for sweets. The men are equally fond of tobacco,[7] although they consume it little, probably because it is too costly.

Mr Macdiarmid specifies the following as the ordinary diet of a St Kildan:

Breakfast – porridge and milk.

Dinner – potatoes, and the flesh of the fulmar, or mutton and occasionally fish.

Supper – porridge, when they have plenty of meal.

He also mentions that they take tea once or twice a week, and appear to be rather fond of it. 'They seemed surprised', he adds, 'at the small quantity of tea sent to them in proportion to the amount of sugar.' While he confirms Mr Sands's statement regarding the fondness of the men for tobacco, he says that he 'saw no signs whatever of the partiality for sugar and sweets which has been attributed to them.' I believe, however, that, in common with the other islanders of Scotland, and especially the Shetlanders, the inhabitants of St Kilda have a very decided weakness for sweets. On the occasion of my recent visit, in addition to a number of showy picture-books for the children, I took a supply of sweets, for both adults and juveniles, in the shape of peppermint drops and 'gundy' – a species of strongly-flavoured 'rock' – having previously ascertained, on the best authority, that these two confections would be especially acceptable; and judging from the demonstrations which accompanied the distribution, the common opinion regarding the penchant in question seemed to be fully corroborated. The large quantity of salt food consumed

---

7 Martin alludes to the same predilection.

by the St Kildans during winter has been suggested as the possible cause of their addiction to sweets. Teetotalism does not appear to have reached St Kilda. Mr Grigor partook of both wine and whisky at the house of the catechist, and he was informed that some spirits were to be found in every household – being only used, however, 'on great occasions, or medicinally'.

In Martin's time, the St Kilda houses were of a low form, rounded at the ends, and with all the doors to the north-east, to secure them from the tempestuous shocks of the south-west winds. The walls were rudely built of stone, and the roofs – of wood, covered with straw – secured by ropes of twisted heather, to prevent the thatch from being carried away by the gales. They were built in two rows, with a causeway between called 'The Street'. Mr Wilson believes that the houses which existed up to the beginning of the reign of George IV were the same as those in which the inhabitants had lived during the entire period of their authentic history. He describes these primitive dwellings as consisting of

> a low narrow entrance through the thick stone wall, leading to a first apartment, in which, at least during the winter season, were kept the cattle; and then to a second, in which the natives dwelt.[8] These inner rooms, though small, were free from the incumbrance of beds, for the latter were placed in, or rather formed by deep recesses of the walls, like low and horizontal open presses, into which they crept at night, their scanty bedding being placed upon stones, in imitation of the puffins.[9]

The same author attributes the improved system of house-building to an accomplished and liberal Englishman, Sir Thomas Dyke Acland, who visited the island in his yacht upwards of forty years

---

8 This primitive practice is referred to by both Herodotus and Juvenal.
9 According to Macaulay, these recesses, or croops, were large enough to accommodate three persons.

ago, and left a premium of twenty guineas with the minister (the Rev. Neil McKenzie) for the first person who should demolish his old house and erect a new one on an improved principle. A tenacious adherence to uniformity had long formed a characteristic feature in the social polity of the inhabitants, and it was some time before anyone was bold enough to take a step in advance. At length a comparatively energetic individual commenced the double work of demolition and reconstruction, which resulted in a general movement; and under the judicious superintendence of the worthy minister, 'the ancient city of St Kilda was razed to its foundations, and one of modern structure erected in its place.' When Mr Wilson visited the island in 1841, only a single roofless hut of the olden time remained to illustrate the peculiar construction of these rude dwellings.

There are at present eighteen inhabited houses on the island – viz., sixteen cottages with zinc roofs, and two thatched huts, arranged in the form of a crescent, from fifteen to twenty yards apart, and numbered from right to left.[10] The occupants of each of the cottages range from two to seven, while the two huts are respectively tenanted by a bachelor and a spinster. The cottages were built about fifteen years ago by Sir John Macpherson Macleod, the late proprietor of St Kilda. Most of the other old huts still stand, alternating with the cottages, and are used by the inhabitants as byres and cellars.[11] They are constructed of rough stones, without mortar. The walls are of great thickness, varying from five to eight feet, and about five feet high on the outside; or, rather, they really consist of two strong dykes within a foot or two of each other, the intermediate space being tightly packed with earth, so as to fill up all the interstices. The doorway is very low

10 At the census of 1851, the number of houses in St Kilda was thirty-two. Ten years later they amounted to twenty-five, containing twenty-three rooms with one or more windows, and classified as follows: inhabited, twenty; uninhabited, one; building, four. In 1871, the number of inhabited houses was nineteen, with forty-two windowed rooms.
11 For the benefit of English readers, not 'buyers' and 'sellers'.

– somewhere about three feet in height – and in consequence of the great thickness of the double walls, the entrance may be almost termed a passage, resembling, in miniature, that of the celebrated Maeshowe in Orkney. The shape of the huts is oval, and internally they are divided into two apartments by a removable partition of loose stones. Most of them can boast of a small four-paned window, which, however, admits a very limited amount of light, in consequence of the great thickness of the walls. The door is secured by a wooden lock, worked with a key of the same material, and of ingenious construction.[12]

> One feature [says Mr Muir] belonging to the houses rather amused us. On our return from the day's excursion, the people being assembled in the church, we found the doors in most instances secured by a large wooden lock, so ingeniously contrived that we were utterly unable so much as to conjecture by what means it could be opened. The thing, made up of a square of several sturdy bars immovably jammed, ends and sides together, and without catch or keyhole, was certainly a puzzle that would have honoured a Chubb or a Chinaman. Yet more puzzling than the lock seemed the necessity for its existence.

The roofs, which are of thatch, are circular or somewhat rounded, and are secured by ropes of straw with heavy stones attached to their extremities, as in many other parts of the Hebrides, for the purpose indicated by Martin. Instead of the thatch projecting beyond the walls, in accordance with the ordinary practice, its edge springs from the inner side of the thick wall, and thus counteracts the effects of the wind. In the case of a few of these old houses, the walls contain boot-shaped vaults or recesses, similar to those described by Martin, which were formerly used as beds, and which are accessible through small apertures, about two feet from

---

12 The same kind of locks has been introduced into the modern cottages.

the floor, resembling the mouth of a baker's oven. One of these, which I inspected with the aid of a light, was certainly not very inviting. The fireplace used to occupy the middle of the room, being a circular cavity in the floor, round which the natives sat before smouldering ashes of dry turf, cut or scraped together from the hills. Most of the smoke made its exit through the doorway; but, owing to the scarcity of fuel, the smoke was not very troublesome. The absence of chimneys, however, was to some extent compensated for by the accumulation of soot on the under side of the thatch.[13] Once a year, usually in May – as is still the practice in Lewis and other parts of the Hebrides – the huts were unroofed, in order to remove the lower portion of the sooty straw for the purpose of manure, and in October a fresh coating of thatch was laid upon the part that remained. The want of peat in St Kilda makes a glowing fire a rare spectacle. Occasionally a log or other fragment of wood is cast upon the island; but owing to the limited extent of shore, such godsends are not very frequent. The memoranda furnished to Mr Wilson by the Rev. Neil McKenzie contain several allusions to the scarcity of fuel. Sometimes when the islanders run short of turf, they are compelled to burn grass (*phiteach*) as a substitute. In referring to the important subject of fuel, Mr Macdiarmid very naturally speculates on the probable result of the present disastrous but apparently unavoidable system of stripping the turf from the pasture as a substitute for peat. Many hundreds of acres have already been thus bared; and only where a little soil is left on the surface of the rock is there anything like an approach to the original sward. In other parts of the Western Isles, such as Iona, Tiree and Canna, the deficiency of fuel is a very serious circumstance. The author of *Agriculture of the Hebrides* says

---

13 Among the illustrations which accompany Captain Thomas' communication on 'Primitive Dwellings' to the Society of Scottish Antiquaries will be found accurate ground-plans of one of the older cottages, with a *crub* or wall-bed, and of one of the houses erected about forty years ago, and occupied by the unfortunate Betty Scott. The position of the furniture and other internal arrangements are shown in both of the engravings. – *Proceedings of the Society*, vol. vii, plates xxx and xxviii.

that 'the man who opens a colliery in the Hebrides, or opposite the mainland of the west of Scotland north of Cantyre, will confer a greater favour on those sequestered regions than the whole dictionary of praise can express. He will literally kindle the flame of gratitude, and "cheer the shivering native's dull abode."

Mr McKenzie gives the following account of the domestic usages of the St Kildans, as they continued up to a comparatively recent date (1863), when they took possession of their present abodes:

The apartment next the door (as in Martin's time) is occupied by the cattle in winter, and the other by themselves. Into their own apartment they begin early in summer to gather peatdust, which they use with their ashes, and moisten by all the foul water used in making their food, etc. By these means the floor rises gradually higher and higher, till it is, in spring, as high as the side-wall, and in some houses higher. By the beginning of summer a person cannot stand upright in any of their houses, but must creep on all fours round the fire.[14]

The modern cottages, which, as already stated, were erected by the late proprietor of the island in 1861–62, present a favourable contrast to these squalid abodes, and in respect of house accommodation, the St Kildans may now be regarded as far ahead of the inhabitants of the Long Island. Mr Macdiarmid furnishes the following detailed account of their construction:

The walls are well built, with hewn stones in the corners, and about seven or eight feet high; chimney on each gable; roof covered with zinc; outside of walls well pointed over with cement, and apparently none the worse as yet of the many wild wintry blasts they have withstood. Every house has two windows, nine panes of glass in each, one window on each side

14 A more detailed description of the process will be found in Macaulay's work, p. 41.

of door; good, well-fitting door, with lock. The interior of
each house is divided into two apartments by a wooden partition, and in some a bed-closet is opposite the entrance-door.
Every house I entered contained a fair assortment of domestic
utensils and furniture – kitchen-dresser, with plates,[15] bowls,
pots, kettles, pans, etc., wooden beds, chairs, seats, tables, tin
lamps, etc. There is a fireplace and vent in each end of the
house, which is certainly an improvement on the majority of
Highland cottars' dwellings, where the fire is often on the
middle of the floor, and the smoke finds egress by the door or
apertures in the wall, or it may be a hole in the roof.

The zinc plates are nailed down over wooden planks. The minister told Dr Angus Smith that he considered the roofs to be a
failure, 'since it rained inside whenever it rained outside', the
plates not being made to overlap sufficiently to produce perfect
security. When the inhabitants first took possession of these new
houses, they found them colder as well as airier than their former
abodes; but this is the ordinary experience among the humbler
classes, when they are persuaded to occupy improved dwellings.
At the time of Mr Wilson's visit to St Kilda in 1841, the furniture
was very scanty, each house then having 'one or more bedsteads,
with a small supply of blankets, a little dresser, a seat or two with
wooden legs and a few kitchen articles'. About twelve years later,
an assortment of crockery was furnished to the islanders by the
Rev. Dr McLauchlan and a small party of friends, on the occasion
of an expedition to St Kilda; and before they left the island, they
were not a little amused to find certain utensils, to which I cannot
more particularly allude, freely used as porridge-dishes!

On 3 October, 1860, a dreadful storm swept across St Kilda,
and the roofs of some of the houses were carried away by the gale.
A large sum was collected in Glasgow to provide for the

15 According to Mrs McVean, spoons were unnecessary when she resided on the
island, as the natives *drank* their porridge!

destitution which it was believed to have occasioned, and it was proposed to devote a portion of the fund to the erection of new houses. It appears, however, that this was opposed and prohibited by the proprietor, who himself sent masons and carpenters from Skye the year following, for the purpose of building four houses, each containing two rooms and two closets.

Besides the cottages of the islanders, the little township of St Kilda embraces four other fabrics of a more pretentious kind – to wit, the manse, church,[16] store, and factor's house. Situated on the north-east side of the bay, about a hundred yards from the beach, and twice that distance from the village, the manse is a one-storeyed, slated building, with a porch, and contains four apartments. It is protected on one side by a high wall by way of shelter, and in front is an enclosed patch of tilled ground, where a rain-gauge is placed. On looking into the rooms, I was struck by their unfurnished and comfortless aspect – the absence of a help-mate being painfully apparent. The manse must have presented a better appearance at the time of Mr Wilson's visit. He describes the apartment in which he was received by the minister as 'a neat enough room, carpeted, and with chairs and tables, but with some appearance of damp upon the walls, which, on tapping with our knuckles, we found had not been lathed'. At the same period, the minister – or rather the *prime minister* – of St Kilda was the Rev. Neil Mackenzie, now pastor of Kilchrenan, Argyllshire, who also acted in the capacity of teacher, and who appears to have done everything in his power to improve both the spiritual and physical condition of the inhabitants. Some interesting extracts from his manuscript memoranda relative to the weather, the condition of the people, and the arrival of the various sea-fowl, to which I have already referred, are printed in Mr Wilson's work.

---

16 Martin speaks of three chapels in St Kilda at the close of the seventeenth century, to which reference will afterwards be made. They all appear to have been in existence when Macaulay wrote, upwards of sixty years later, but not a vestige of any of them now remains.

The church, built at a cost of about £600, is situated immediately behind the manse – a plain, substantial structure, with a door and four windows. Like the manse, it has a slated roof, but only an earthen floor – the pews consisting of rude deal benches. On each side of the pulpit, which is accompanied by the ordinary precentor's desk, is an enclosed pew, of which one is for the use of the elders, and the other for visitors. Two wooden chandeliers, recently presented by Sir Patrick Keith-Murray, are suspended from the ceiling, each charged with three excellent candles made from the tallow of the sheep; and the islanders are summoned to worship by a small bell which was recovered from a wreck.

The little burial-place, elliptical in form, and surrounded by a wall, is situated behind the village, and, like most Highland churchyards, is overgrown by nettles, and otherwise in a very neglected condition. A better state of matters appears to have prevailed at the close of the seventeenth century. Martin says 'They take care to keep the churchyard perfectly clean, void of any kind of nastiness, and their cattle have no access to it.' With the solitary exception of a slab, erected by a former minister, none of the tombstones bear any inscriptions. The ruins of one of the ancient chapels – removed a few years ago – occupied the centre of the burial-ground. One of the stones bearing an incised cross, which I unfortunately neglected to look for, is built into the wall of a cottage. Gray's well-known lines seem peculiarly applicable to the 'God's acre' of St Kilda:

> Perhaps in this neglected spot is laid
> Some heart once pregnant with celestial fire;
> Hands that the rod of empire might have swayed,
> Or waked to ecstasy the living lyre:
>
> But Knowledge to their eyes her ample page
> Rich with the spoils of time did ne'er unroll;
> Chill penury repressed their noble rage,
> And froze the genial current of the soul.

> Full many a gem of purest ray serene
> The dark unfathomed caves of ocean bear:
> Full many a flower is born to blush unseen,
> And waste its sweetness on the desert air.

Close to the landing-place is the store, built of stone and lime, and with a slated roof, in which feathers and oil – the staple exports of the island – are deposited; and in its immediate neighbourhood is another very tolerable house, resembling the manse in form, in which the factor resides during his periodical sojourns. On the occasion of my visit, we found that it had been occupied, for upwards of a fortnight, by Miss Macleod of Macleod, the sister of the proprietor of St Kilda, who returned with us in the *Dunara*. As already mentioned, she had accompanied Lord and Lady Macdonald in their yacht on the 15 June, and had spent sixteen days on the island, with the view of making herself acquainted with the condition of the inhabitants. The scene at her departure was not a little touching. While she was affectionately kissed by the women, the men 'lifted up' their voices. I was, however, fully prepared for this display of attachment, having heard so much of the benevolent lady's acts of kindness at Dunvegan, where a woman, to whom I happened to speak of Miss Macleod's absence from Skye being a cause of regret in that quarter, warmly informed me that she was 'an angel in human form'!

Climate, Crops and Livestock

I have already referred to the tempestuous gales – chiefly from the south-west – which occasionally sweep across the island. Speaking generally, however, the climate of St Kilda is by no means rigorous – in consequence, no doubt, of the beneficial influences of the Gulf Stream, in the midst of which the island is situated. Martin describes the air as 'sharp and wholesome'.

> The hills [he says] are often covered with ambient white mists, which in winter are forerunners of snow, if they continue on the tops of the hills; and in summer, if only on the tops, they prognosticate rain, and when they descend to the valleys, excessive heat. The night here, about the time of the summer solstice, exceeds not an hour in length, especially if the season is fair; then the sun disappears but for a short space, the reflex from the sea being all the time visible. The harvest and winter are liable to great winds and rain, the south-west wind annoying them more than any other; it is commonly observed to blow from the west, for the most part of, if not all July.

He elsewhere gives an elaborate account of wind and weather prognostics, connected with the appearance of the sky and the character of the waves; and mentions that the sea between St Kilda and the Long Island is most boisterous during the prevalence of a north wind. A terrific gale took place at St Kilda in January 1866; and Dr Macdonald refers to a hurricane that occurred on 8 July, 1827, during his last visit to the island, when 'the billows rose mountains high, and dashed with fury against the lofty rocks'. He also states that when the sun happens to be obscured, the natives determine the time of day by the ebb and flow of the sea – 'their knowledge of the tides depending upon the changes of the moon, which they likewise observe, and are very nice in it'. Mr Wilson pronounces the climate of St Kilda to be 'extremely mild', adding that the ice which is formed during the coldest winter night is scarcely thicker than a penny, and usually melts away, under the influence of the sun, in the course of the following day. Mr Macdiarmid, however, was told that snow sometimes falls so heavily as to bury the sheep, and that frost is occasionally severe.

The soil, according to Martin, is 'very grateful to the labourer', producing from sixteen to twenty-fold.

> Their grain [he says] is only bere and some oats; the barley is the largest produced in all the Western Isles. They use no plough, but a kind of crooked spade; their harrows are of wood, as are the teeth in front also, and all the rest supplied only with long tangles of sea-ware tied to the harrow by the small ends ... The chief ingredient in their composts is ashes of turf mixed with straw and urine ... They join also the bones, wings and entrails of the sea-fowl to their straw. They sow very thick,[1] and have a proportionable growth. They pluck all their bere by the roots in handfuls, both for the sake of their houses, which they thatch with it, and their cows, which they take in during the winter.

It appears from Macaulay's account of the island that about eighty acres were under cultivation in 1758, in the immediate neigh-bourhood of the village. He refers to the fact of the soil being well

---

1 Thick sowing is still considered absolutely necessary, as a thin crop would not be able to withstand the gales to which the island is subject.

manured and carefully pulverised, in accordance with the advice of Virgil, whose opinions he frequently quotes. He describes the quality of barley as excellent, and mentions that the harvest is usually over by the beginning of September. At the time of Mr Wilson's visit, the arable land, fronting the village and within a large enclosure, was chiefly laid out in small rigs of barley, subdivided into about twenty portions, and belonging to a corresponding number of families. Besides these, there were eight smaller families not so portioned. In ordinary years, they were then believed to raise sufficient grain for their own consumption. The hill pastures were common – seven shillings being paid for each cow's grazing, and one shilling for each sheep, above ten, annually. The *caschron*, or spade-plough (referred to by Martin), was in ordinary use on Mr Mackenzie's arrival in 1830,[2] but he contrived to render the use of the English spade almost universal; and the introduction of drains nearly doubled the produce of the arable land. Mr Wilson further informs us that a few cabbages and potatoes grew in smaller enclosures, by courtesy called gardens, and that the minister had tried both carrots and onions with some success. 'Turnips', he says, 'seem to thrive well for a time, but are speedily cut off by some kind of destructive insect; and peas and beans blossom, but produce no pods.'

In proportion to the number of inhabitants, the present quantity of arable land seems to be considerably less than at the middle of last century. Probably the total extent enclosed and under cultivation does not amount to forty acres – about an acre and a half for each family – but it could easily be doubled. The devotion of the islanders to the more profitable pursuit of fowling induces them to neglect farming operations. Mr Sands, however, makes special mention of the industry of the islanders in the matter of agriculture. 'Every little spot of earth', he says, 'on the stony hills that will yield a crop is enclosed with a stone fence, and

2 An engraving of the *caschron* will be found in Macdonald's *Agriculture of the Hebrides* (1811).

cultivated. And even where the soil is too thin to be productive in itself, it is artificially deepened, by shovelling on it the thin soil adjacent. They preserve [he adds] the ashes of their turf fires for manure, mixing it with the entrails and carcases of fowls . . . but they have not yet learned the value of fish-offal.' The crops which Mr Grigor saw in July 1861 consisted of bere, oats and potatoes, and looked exceedingly well, having been much improved by the application of guano, which had been supplied to the inhabitants after the ravages of the storm of 3 October, 1860, already referred to. A few drills of turnips came up well in the plot occupied by the catechist and registrar; and in other plots there were a few cabbages. A proper supply of vegetables would be a desirable addition to the diet of the inhabitants. The land under cultivation is enclosed by a stone fence, and occupies a gentle slope between the village and the foot of the hills. The rest of the island produces good green pasture, there being little or no heather or moss. The implements of husbandry are few and simple – spades, hoes and picks being now in use; but there does not seem to be any desire on the part of the inhabitants to extend cultivation. In one of his recent letters in the *Scotsman*, Mr Sands asserted, on the authority of some of the older inhabitants, that there had been no change of seed-corn for at least sixty years, and that the crops had greatly deteriorated. This, however, was distinctly contradicted, at a subsequent meeting relative to St Kilda, by one of the speakers, who mentioned that he had been the means of sending a fresh supply of seed about fifteen years ago; and further, that he was aware of potatoes having been supplied last year.

The plants enumerated by Martin as growing on the island are the following: dock, scurvy-grass, milfoil, shepherd's purse, silverweed or argentine, plantain, sage, chick-weed, sorrel, all-hail or siderites (starwort?), sea-pink, and tormentil or 'scurf upon the stones', which (he says) 'has a drying and healing quality, and is likewise used for dyeing'. He adds that the St Kildans are 'ignorant of the virtues of these herbs', being thus unconscious of the truth announced by the Franciscan friar in *Romeo and Juliet*—

> O, mickle is the powerful grace that lies
> In herbs, plants, stones, and their true qualities!

As in many other parts of the Western Islands, large tracts of ground are carpeted with the delicately coloured sea-pink. Martin elsewhere states that 'no sort of trees, no, not the least shrub, grows here, nor is ever a bee seen at any time.' Mr Mackenzie induced the inhabitants to plant two willow-trees in the church-yard; but if they still exist, I have no recollection of seeing them.

Mr Macdiarmid gives the following circumstantial account of the tillage and pastoral operations:

The soil is a fine black loam, resting on granite, and, by contin-ued careful manuring and cleaning, looks quite like a garden. Yet with all this fine fertile appearance, the return it gives is miserable; and this can only be accounted for from the land never being allowed any rest under grass. The only crops grown are potatoes and oats, with a little bere. Within the remembrance of some of the older men, the returns were double, or nearly treble, of what they now are . . . From a barrel of potatoes [about 2 cwt], scarcely three barrels will be lifted. They require to sow the oats very thick – at the rate of from ten to twelve bushels to the acre – and the return is never above three times the quantity of seed sown; formerly it used to be six or seven times. I was shown some of the oats, but they were very small and thin, and thick in the husk. If possible, they avoid sowing home-grown seed, as it never gives a good return. Flails are the instruments used for separating the grain from the straw. The ground is all turned over with the spade, of which they have a number in very good order . . . The land is harrowed with a sort of strong, roughly-made wooden hand-rake. They have iron 'grapes' for spreading their manure. The dung-pits are situated generally a few yards in front of the house, at the end of the patch of land, sunk a few feet in the ground – rather convenient for being conveyed to the land,

which is done by wooden creels or baskets. Saw no wheelbar-
rows; but there are one or two hand-barrows. They have sufficient manure for their land. Sometimes they gather a little seaware for manure; but there being no beach, it is not to be got
in any great quantity . . . Noticed one or two small enclosures
planted with cabbages – not this year's plants. Turnips were
once grown rather successfully, but of late years they have not
thriven . . . The pasture-land is excellent, and forms as fine a
sheep-run of its size as can be seen anywhere . . . I should say
the grazing extent would be about one and a half times the size
of Arthur's Seat and the Queen's Park, Edinburgh . . . Nothing
is to be seen growing naturally on the island but grass, which I
believe to be very nutritive. In some parts, last year's grass was
lying quite thick where it had not been eaten.

Every visitor to St Kilda must have been struck by the large
number of little dome-shaped stone buildings, resembling ovens,
scattered all over the island and the adjacent islets, eight or ten feet
in diameter, and from four to five feet in height, with a small
doorway capable of admitting an ordinary person on all-fours.
Their form is round when they occupy a level position on the
summit of a hill, and oval when placed on a hillside. They are
ingeniously constructed by gradually diminishing the courses of
dry stone; affording a free current to the air at the sides, the top
being closed by heavy stones, and protected from wet by a covering of turf. These are the 'pyramids', or *cleits*, referred to by Martin
as being 500 in number,[3] and used for preserving various kinds of
produce – sea-fowl, eggs, turf, hay and corn. No attempt is made
by the St Kildans to dry their grass or grain outside. Immediately
after being cut, both are thrown loosely into these receptacles,

3 Their present number is probably much larger. In 1838, one of the natives told the
author of *Sketches of St Kilda* that they amounted to about 5,000. A plan and section of
a cleit accompanies Captain Thomas's paper on 'Primitive Dwellings', already referred
to, of which the internal dimensions are 8 × 21/2 × 5 feet. Some of them are considerably larger – See *Proceedings of Society of Scottish Antiquaries*, vol. vii, pl. xxxviii.

and thus secured against all risk of injury from the weather – an example which might be prudently followed by many other Highland farmers.

It appears from Martin's account that, at the end of the seventeenth century, the number of sheep in St Kilda and the adjacent islands amounted to about 2,000. 'Generally,' he says, 'they are speckled, some white, some philamort (dun?), and of an ordinary size. They do not resemble goats in anything, as Buchanan was informed, except in their horns, which are extraordinarily large, particularly those in the lesser isles.' About one-fourth of the sheep were then fed on the island of Soa, 'each of them having generally two or three lambs at a birth, and every lamb being so fruitful that it brings forth a lamb before itself is a year old'; thus reminding us of the flock referred to in the Song of Solomon, 'whereof every one bears twins, and none is barren among them'. These sheep, Martin further informs us, are never milked, 'which disposes them to be the more prolific'. At the same period, the island of Borrera fed about 400 sheep, and 'would feed more, did not the solan geese pluck a large share of the grass for their nests'. Macaulay also refers to the remarkable fecundity of the St Kilda sheep. He was informed that, in the course of thirteen months, a single sheep had been the means of adding nine to the flock. 'She had brought three lambs in the month of March, three more in the same month the year after, and each of the first three had a young one before they had been thirteen months old.' Dean Monro describes the sheep of Hirta as 'fairer and greater and larger-tailled than in any uther ile about'; while the Lord Register (Sir George McKenzie) says that they are 'far different from all others, having long legs, long horns, and, instead of wool, a blewish hair upon them; for the figure and description they seem to approach in resemblance to the *Ovis Chilensis*'.

According to Macculloch:

the breed of sheep is exclusively the Norwegian (now nearly extirpated elsewhere), distinguished by the extreme shortness of their tails; and the wool is both thin and coarse. They are occasionally of a dun colour; and are subject here, as well as in Iceland, to produce an additional number of horns. The mutton is peculiarly delicate, and highly flavoured. The cattle are small, and both the ewes and the cows are milked. The cheese, which is made of a mixture of these milks, is much esteemed, forming one of the prevailing articles of export to the Long Island, the mart in which all their little commerce centres.

In Martin's time, the number of horses did not exceed eighteen, 'all of a red colour, very low and smooth-skinned, being only employed in carrying their turf and corn, and at the anniversary cavalcade. The cows, which are about ninety head, small and great, all of them having their foreheads white and black, are of a low stature, but fat and sweet beef. The dogs, cats and all the sea-fowl of this isle are speckled.' When Mr Wilson visited St Kilda in 1841, two or three small horses – originally imported to carry turf – still existed in St Kilda, but practically they were found to be of little use. The number of cows was then about fifty, of small size, but 'yielding a delicious milk, which in the making of cheese is mingled with that of ewes'. The sheep, including those on Soa and Borrera, were about the same number as in Martin's time, the Soa sheep being 'chiefly of the Danish breed, with brown and black wool, and one or two more horns than the usual complement'. About twenty-five years ago, some specimens of sheep resembling those of St Kilda were to be seen at the home-farm of Abercairney, near Crieff. The Abercairney breed, which the proprietor procured in 1822, has generally been known by the name of 'Barbary sheep'; and if not identical with those of St Kilda, they bore a striking resemblance to them.

In 1861, there were forty-three head of cattle and 1500 sheep in the group of islands, of which all the cattle and nearly half of the sheep were in St Kilda. About 500 sheep found pasture in Borrera, and 300 in Soa. The latter of these islands was grazed by the families who emigrated to Australia in 1856; and when they left St Kilda, the stock was purchased by the proprietor, and was held in 'steel-bow' by the other tenants – that is, they had to return their equivalent in quantity and quality at the end of the lease.

Mr Macdiarmid was unable to ascertain the number of sheep on the island at the time of his visit in May last, and estimates it at not less than 400. Mr Mackenzie, the factor for the proprietor, recently informed me at Dunvegan that the islanders are entitled to keep 1,200 sheep and fifty head of cattle, and that, at present, they actually possess between 1000 and 1200, but only admit having about the half of that number. The same tendency to conceal the actual number appears to have prevailed in the middle of last century. 'The St Kildans,' says Macaulay, 'have their own mysteries of state. In proportion to the number of sheep he possesses, every man must pay a certain heavy tax to the steward . . . and, according to the laws of their land, every Hirta householder must pay to the person he calls his master every second he-lamb, every seventh fleece, and every seventh she-lamb.' The proprietor's charge for a sheep's grass on St Kilda is ninepence per head, and sixpence on the adjacent islands; and for a cow's grass, seven shillings – the rates at Dunvegan being five shillings and three pounds respectively. The breed of sheep has already been improved by crossing; and Mr Mackenzie considers that, with good management, a much greater improvement might take place. Most of the sheep on St Kilda are white; the dun or native breed, which run wild, and are only caught at plucking time, being chiefly on the smaller islands. In appearance, the latter are something between sheep and fallow deer, with light-brown wool, long necks and legs, and short tails. It would appear that the sheep receive very little attention, and many of them are blown over the cliffs in seeking shelter from the storms. A system of mutual insurance, however, has long existed on the island, the owners of the lost sheep being indemnified by their neighbours in proportion to the number which the latter themselves possess. The smallest number owned by one man is eleven, and the largest 150. Mr Macdiarmid strongly condemns the present system of sheep-farming, under which every man has his own, and no two tenants the same number, instead of the flock being held in common, and the wool and carcases equally divided. He states that

the yeld sheep are plucked about the beginning of June, and the ewes about the middle of summer. They sell neither sheep nor wool. From two to five sheep are killed by each family for the winter's supply, and the wool is made into blanketing and tweed, which they sell. They keep about twelve tups ... The breed of sheep may be called a cross between the old St Kilda breed and the blackfaced ... Nothing is applied to the sheep by way of smearing; and, so far as could be ascertained, they are quite free from scab and other skin diseases common to the class. The St Kildan should be initiated in the art of clipping his sheep; for plucking must be a sort of cruelty to the animals.

He considers that, by proper management, the number might be doubled; and that, instead of levying a payment on each head, the proprietor ought to receive a fixed rent for pasturage. The sheep are said to be very fat in autumn when killed, in consequence of the fine quality of the pasture; and the mutton that was presented to Mr Macdiarmid and his friends for dinner 'would favourably compare, in flavour and quality, with the best-fed blackfaced'. The islanders consume a great deal of mutton at certain periods, as no sheep are exported.

The total number of cows and other cattle – including a brindled bull – at present on the island is about fifty, of the West Highland breed, chiefly black, or red and black in colour, and all in very good condition. Mr Macdiarmid estimates the average value of the young cattle, on the mainland, at £3 15s per head – and about £3 per head – the rate paid by the factor in 1875 – if purchased on the island. There are now no horses within its bounds. The older inhabitants, however, remember when some of the crofters had as many as four or five ponies. It is reported that a lessee of the island, about thirty years ago, shipped them all away, on the pretext of their being destructive to the grass! There are numerous dogs – a mongrel breed of collie – used for fowling purposes, as well as by the shepherds. A cat is to be seen in almost every cottage, the mouse being the only wild animal on the island, and rats are still unknown. According to Mr Macdiarmid, there are only two hens in St Kilda.[4] It has been suggested that a few goats might be appropriately introduced; and perhaps the rabbit also might form a useful addition to the fare of the St Kildan. The experience of the inhabitants of Barra, however, is not very encouraging – the destruction of the crops having been the result of the importation of rabbits into that island.[5]

At the date of Dr Macculloch's visit (1815), the rental of St Kilda appears to have amounted to only forty pounds. In 1841, Mr Wilson was told that it was about sixty pounds; and twenty years later, the three islands were entered in the Valuation Roll of Inverness-shire at £100. From £90 to £100 is stated to be the annual revenue derived by the present proprietor; but, in some quarters, an impression appears to prevail that he receives a considerably larger return. The rents are paid in kind, consisting chiefly of feathers, oil, cloth, cattle, cheese and barley. The oil is extracted from the stomach of the fulmar, and is eagerly purchased by the farmers of Skye for smearing purposes. When Mr Wilson visited St Kilda, each family was bound to furnish about twenty-three pecks of barley annually; which failing, an additional supply of feathers. The quantity of the latter which the entire nation required to supply was 240 stones (of 24lb each?) – the rugged cliffs, in the language of the poet, thus 'turning to beds of down'.

4 Such scarcity of poultry will doubtless remind some of my readers of the Cockney schoolmaster reproving his pupil when he smiled on being found fault with for misspelling 'Venice'. 'Don't you know, sir,' he said, 'that there is only one hen ['n'] in Venice?' 'In that case,' rejoined the pupil, 'eggs must be uncommonly scarce there!'
5 Otter's *Sailing Directions for the West of Scotland*, part i, p. 4.

Sixteen families, constituting the present 'crofters', pay rent, while the rest of the inhabitants are only 'cottars', each possessing a few sheep. The annual charge for each croft and cottage is two pounds. The present rents were fixed by Mr Norman McRaild, the factor for the late proprietor, each tenant being credited with a certain number of sheep; and they have not been altered since the change in the ownership. Accordingly, in some cases tenants may be paying for too many, and in others for too few sheep. Mr Macdiarmid states that

> It is impossible to arrive at the actual value given to the proprietor. None of the men keep an account of the quantity of produce they give to the factor, and the amount of goods they take in return. They have great confidence in Mr Mackenzie, who, they say, is just and generous, and easy to deal with . . . They are never pressed for arrears; and, so far as could be made out, they are contented with their lot, and consider that they are very fairly dealt with. They are very much attached to their island home; and there is no inclination to emigrate. They speak of their landlord, Macleod, in the very best terms, and consider themselves very fortunate in being under his guardianship; and I must say that I did not hear one single word or expression implying want of confidence or distrust in his dealings with them.

Mr Macdiarmid refers to the unsuccessful attempt made by a recent visitor – I presume Mr Sands – to induce the islanders to carry their produce to the Long Island or the mainland, and to discontinue the system of barter which has so long prevailed. It appears that the minister (Mr McKay) strongly objected to the proposed change, reminding his flock that, in dispensing with Macleod's assistance, they might expose themselves to risk and danger. A document was sent to the island by the proprietor calling upon all who wished to adhere to the existing system to give in their names; and ultimately, the minister succeeded in getting a clause inserted in a formal agreement between the owner and his tenants, granting them permission, if they thought proper, to go to the mainland, with the view of selling their produce and buying such commodities as they might wish. This fair and reasonable arrangement appears to have given perfect satisfaction to all the islanders.

As already indicated, the principal exports are feathers, oil, cloth, cattle, cheese and barley. The price paid by the present factor for feathers is, per stone of 24lb, five shillings for grey, and six shillings for black feathers, which it appears can be sold in Edinburgh or Glasgow at from seven to eight shillings per stone. For fulmar oil the islanders receive one shilling per Scotch pint, or about two shillings per imperial gallon.[6] On a recent occasion, the factor brought away fourteen barrels of oil, each containing about thirty gallons. The quantity of cloth – tweeds and blanketing – sold by each family ranges between 12 and 80 yards. For the former, they receive two shillings and sixpence; and for the latter, about two shillings and threepence per Scotch ell or 'big yard' = 4 feet 1 inch. The tweed, which is of a natural, drab colour, is sold by the factor at four shillings per English yard, which certainly appears to constitute a liberal profit. The price paid for cattle has already been indicated. The islanders are able annually to dispose of not more than four stones (24 lb each) of cheese, of a fair quality, chiefly made from sheep's milk, for which they receive six shillings and sixpence per stone. As they have no churns, butter is very rarely made by them. In Mr Mackenzie's time, they sometimes attempted the process by placing the milk in a wooden dish, or 'noggin', and shaking the vessel up and down until butter was produced. Another plan is to pour the milk into a pail, and put it in motion by the use of the hands. I have no information as to the price paid to them for barley. Tallow and salted ling are among their other occasional exports – the former bringing from seven to eight shillings per stone, and the

6 According to Mr Sands, the price paid for the oil is one shilling per 'St Kilda pint' = about five English pints; and he states that upwards of 900 St Kilda pints were exported in 1875.

latter sevenpence each, the proprietor supplying the salt free. In 1875, the factor paid the islanders upwards of forty pounds for fish, last year about six pounds, and in the current year nothing at all, which he regards as an indication of their now being comparatively independent, and unwilling to undergo the labour and hardship which fishing involves.

Mr Macdiarmid gives the following list of imports, with the respective prices charged during the last few years:

Meal	25s per boll
Oats	25s "
Potatoes	5s per barrel
Salt	3s 6d per cwt
Sugar	6d and 7d per lb for the coarsest
Tea	5s per lb (in 1876, 4s)
Whisky	4s per bottle
Tobacco	5s per lb
Leather	⌈2s per lb for sole ⌊2s 3d per lb for upper
Indigo	6d per ounce
Bonnets for the men	4s each
Caps	3s "
Cravats	3s "
Coloured cotton handkerchiefs	1s "
Sweeties	1s 6d per lb

The following have been the highest and lowest prices of some of the above-mentioned articles, in the Edinburgh market, during the last two years:

Meal	25s	21s 6d per boll
Oats (good)	24s 6d	20s "
Salt	3s 6d	3s per cwt
Sugar (coarse)	3¾d	3d per lb
Tea (good)	3s 6d	2s "
Whisky	3s 6d	2s 4d per bottle
Tobacco (ordinary twist)	4s per lb	
Leather	⌈3s	2s 3d per lb for sole
	⌊5s 6d	3s per lb for upper
Sweeties (peppermint drops)	1s per lb and 1d per ounce	

During each of the past three years, the proprietor's smack, the *Robert Hadden*, a craft of sixty-two tons, has made from one to three trips to the island. She went thrice in 1875; only once in 1876, in consequence of unfavourable weather; and at the time of my visit in the beginning of July, she had been twice since the spring, with a third trip in prospect. Mr Mackenzie, the factor, resides at Dunvegan, in Skye, and generally goes only once a year to St Kilda. This year he accompanied the smack on her second voyage, and remained for about a week on the island. One of the inhabitants acts as his local representative in the capacity of sub-factor, his designation in Gaelic being maor, or ground-officer. The present functionary is Neil Ferguson, who, by the way, has a handsome profile and otherwise a good physique. The factor for the late proprietor, Sir John Macpherson Macleod, who also resided in Skye, paid a yearly visit to St Kilda, in May or June, and remained for a good many weeks, receiving the feathers and other articles already specified. He usually took with him meal, tea, sugar, salt, clothing, etc., for the use of the inhabitants, in fulfilment of commissions given the preceding year. In 1853, he was obliged to spend several months on the island, in consequence of the vessel which was sent for him not having been able to accomplish the voyage; and it was only in April of the following year that he succeeded in reaching Skye. Seven years later (1860), the expected craft was lost, with its entire cargo, in the east bay; and Mr McRaild would have been again detained on the island but for the arrival of HMS *Porcupine*, which conveyed him to his home.

It appears from Dean Monro's brief notice of Hirta that a similar visitation took place towards the end of the sixteenth century. He states that

the inhabitants thereof ar simple poor people, scarce learnit in aney religion; bot McCloyd of Herray, his stewart, sailes anes in the zeir ther at midsummer, with some chaplaine to baptize bairnes ther, and if they want a chaplaine, they baptize ther bairnes themselfes. The said stewart, as he himself tauld me, uses to take ane maske of malt ther with a masking fatt, and makes his malt, and ere the fatt be ready, the commons of the town, baith men, weemen, and bairns, puts their hands in the fatt, and findis it sweeit, and eets the greyns after the sweeitness thereof, quhilk they leave nather wirt or draff unsuppit out ther, quharwith baith men, weemen, and bairns were deid drunken, sua that they could not stand upon their feet. The said stewart receives their dewties in miell and reisted [salted] mutton, wyld foullis reisted, and selchis [seals].

At the time of Martin's visit, the factor or 'steward' was one Alexander Macleod. 'Upon his arrival,' says our author, 'he and his retinue – consisting of about fifty persons – have all the milk of the isle bestowed upon them in a treat' – a second such treat, in which Martin himself participated, taking place on St Columba's Day, 15 June. After stating that 'the steward lives upon the charge of the inhabitants until the time that the solan geese are ready to fly, which the inhabitants think long enough', Martin gives some detailed information relative to the daily allowance made by the inhabitants in proportion to their respective holdings, and also regarding their rigid adherence to ancient laws and measures. At that period, in the absence of the steward, the St Kildans were governed by a *meijre*, or officer, nominated by the former, of whose duties and jurisdiction Martin furnishes a curious account. Besides some acres of land in return for his services, the steward gave the officer 'the bonnet worn by himself on his going out of the island'; while the steward's wife left with the officer's wife her *kerch*, or head-dress, and also an ounce of indigo. On the other hand, the officer was bound to present to the steward, at every meal, a large cake of barley, 'sufficient to satisfy three men at a time', and also to furnish him with mutton or beef for dinner 'every Sunday during his residence in the island'.

When Macaulay visited St Kilda in 1758, the proprietor had

given a lease of the island to a cadet of his own family, at a yearly rent of about eleven pounds; and the predecessors of that lessee had enjoyed the same privilege for three generations. This steward, he states, required to be 'at the annual expense of fitting out a large Highland boat to bring his grain, feathers, or any commodities he bought from the people to Harris, where he generally resided. It must be confessed that the voyages made by him thither were attended with some danger. In former times,' he adds, 'the principal persons of this little commonwealth came yearly in their own boat to Dunvegan, the proprietor's chief seat, and brought the small taxes they had to pay.'

From Lord Brougham's *Autobiography* it appears that, forty years later, the steward, or tacksman, paid two visits yearly to the island, 'to plunder, under the name of "Macleod's factor". He pays only twenty pounds sterling to Macleod, and makes above twice as much himself. For this purpose, all the milk of cows is brought into his dairy from May Day to Michaelmas, and all the ewes' milk together for the whole year. Every second lamb-ram and every seventh ewe go to the same quarter – and this sanctified to his use under the name of a tenth. The rest of the rent is made up in feathers, at the rate of three shillings per stone, and the tacksman sells them in the Long Island for ten shillings. He is quite absolute in dispensing justice; punishes crimes by fines, and makes statutes of his own account, which are implicitly obeyed . . . There is no money current here – nothing like barter – and the rate of assessing the rent to Macleod is the only criterion of the prices of articles. According to this, we found that a fat sheep is valued at 3s 6d, a cow at 30s, a horse at 20s, barley at 16s per boll and potatoes at 3s per barrel, which may contain about eight pecks.' In referring to the purchase of St Kilda by Colonel Macleod from the heir of the ancient owners, a few years after Lord Brougham's visit, Macdonald, in his *Agriculture of the Hebrides*. indirectly alludes to the same system of pillage, describing the transference as 'a blessing to the inhabitants, who are no longer fleeced to the skin, but encouraged to industry'. In a subsequent chapter I shall venture to make a few remarks on the relative position of the islanders and their present lord.

Population of St Kilda –
Surnames, Occupations, etc.

St Kilda was, for the first time, officially enumerated in 1851. The report of the census of that year refers to a tradition that the population of the island had been nearly stationary for 200 years, sometimes falling below, and sometimes exceeding, 100 persons. Martin, however, informs us that at the time of his visit in 1697, the inhabitants amounted to about 180; but twenty-seven years afterwards, as already stated, a contagious distemper, believed to have been smallpox, swept away the greater part of the population. Since that date – that is, for a period of rather more than 150 years – the number of the islanders has not very materially fluctuated, ranging from a maximum of 110 to a minimum of seventy-one. During the first half of the eighteenth century, the diminution of the population was very marked, falling, as it did, to eighty-eight – thirty-eight males and fifty females – at the time of Macaulay's visit in 1758. Thirty-seven years later (1795), the number of the inhabitants was almost precisely the same; but from that date it gradually rose till it reached 110 – forty-eight males and sixty-two females – at the census of 1851; while, during the last twenty-six years, the movement has been in the opposite direction. For upwards of a 100 years, the average population of the island has been, as nearly as possible, ninety-three souls. The number of inhabitants at the several dates already referred to, and also at various other periods since the middle of last century, is set forth in the following table, males and females being separately stated, wherever it was possible to distinguish them.

Date	Authority	No. of families	M	F	Total
1697	Martin's *Voyage to St Kilda*	27	...	...	*c.* 180
1758	Macaulay's *History of St Kilda*	...	38	50	88
1764	Walker's *History of the Hebrides*	...	...	...	92
1773	Buchan's *Description of St Kilda* (2nd ed.)	30	...	...	...
1795	Macdonald's *Agriculture of the Hebrides*	...	...	...	87
1799	Lord Brougham's *Life and Times*	...	...	...	100
c. 1803	Sir George S. Mackenzie of Coul, Bart	...	...	...	97
1815	John Macculloch, MD	20	...	...	103
1822	Rev. John Macdonald, of Urquhart	...	...	...	108
1841	Wilson's *Voyage round the Coasts of Scotland*	*c.* 26	...	...	105
1851	Government Census	32	48	62	110
1861	"	20	33	45	78
1871	"	19	27	44	71
1877	2 July Author and party in the *Dunara Castle*	19	31	45	76[1]

It appears from a statement in the *Gazetteer of Scotland*, that the first epidemic of cholera (1832–33) was fatal in this remote region; but I have been unable to find any definite information on the subject. Any consequent diminution of population that may have occurred appears to have been very nearly made up a few years afterwards. It ought to be borne in mind that thirty-six of the inhabitants of St Kilda emigrated to Australia in the year 1856; and accordingly, but for that circumstance, the natural increase of the population in 1861 would have been four (that is, 114 instead of seventy-eight), on the assumption that all the emigrants survived to that date. It appears, however, that several of them died on the passage, and others after their arrival in the colony. About fifteen years ago, only thirteen of the thirty-six survived,

1 From a return from the registrar of St Kilda, posted at Dunvegan and received at the General Registry Office, 4 September, 1877, it appears that one birth and one death – both females – have occurred on the island since 2 July; and accordingly the number of the inhabitants, up to the first-mentioned date, was unaltered.

and appeared to be doing well, as they sent occasional remittances to their relatives in St Kilda. The same decrease in the population between the censuses of 1861 and 1871 is fully accounted for by the eight deaths by drowning which occurred in the spring of 1863. Had all the deceased survived till the summer of 1871 – and the oldest of the party was only forty-six – the population at that date would have been almost exactly the same as ten years previously. Notwithstanding their precarious mode of life and the hardships which they are called upon to endure, it must not be supposed that the inhabitants of St Kilda are not strongly attached to their island home. 'The very reverse of this,' says Mr Wilson, 'may be inferred from the few examples of their migrating to foreign countries, or even settling in other Scottish islands, or on the mainland' – the devotion of the St Kildans to their native shores thus forming a confirmation of the sentiment implied in the sarcastic lines of one of the most distinguished travellers in the Western Islands:

> For who could leave, unbribed, Hibernia's land,
> Or change the rocks of Scotland for the Strand?[2]

With regard to the supposed capacity of the island in respect to population, Macaulay ventures to affirm that, 'if under proper regulations, it might easily support 300 souls'; while an embryo Lord Chancellor, some forty years later, indicated as his opinion that 'with crops, cattle, and the vast resources of sea-fowl, eggs and fish, St Kilda is capable of supporting a population of 1,500 souls with ease'.[3] If even the former of these calculations may be regarded as approximately correct, the prospects of the present

2 Johnson's *London*.
3 Brougham's *Life and Times*, i, 107.
In another part of his *Voyage*, Macaulay surpasses Brougham's estimate. After alluding to the extraordinary abundance of sea-fowl and eggs during the summer, he says that 'the place could easily afford enough of these different articles to support two thousand persons more during that season!'

inhabitants cannot be regarded as particularly gloomy. There are two other Scottish islands which, in respect to magnitude, geographical position, and general characteristics, bear a very considerable resemblance to St Kilda – namely, Fair Isle and Foula, both in the county of Shetland. The population of the former fell from 380 to 226 in the ten years ending 1871, in consequence of the removal of a large number of the inhabitants under the auspices of the Board of Supervision for the Relief of the Poor; while that of Foula increased from 233 to 257 during the same period. The present population of Fair Isle is 187, and that of Foula about 240.[4]

The annexed table exhibits a comparative statement of the surnames of the inhabitants of St Kilda in 1841, and at the three subsequent decennial periods, under the two-fold classification of families and persons. The particulars pertaining to 1841 are derived from Mr Wilson's work:

Surnames	1841		1851		1861		1871	
	Families	Persons	Families	Persons	Families	Persons	Families	Persons
Gillies	5	25	...	33	7	33	7	27
McDonald	7	26	...	23	5	18	4	16
Ferguson	4	11	...	13	2	9	3	10
McKinnon	3	9	...	9	2	10	2	8
McQueen	4	15	...	20	1	4	2	8
McCrimmon	2	4	...	9	2	3	0	0
McLeod	2	3	...	1	0	0	0	0
Morison	1	2	...	2	0	0	0	0

4 Although smaller than any of the three Scottish islands mentioned in the text, Pitcairn Island, in the Pacific, at the south-eastern corner of the great Polynesian archipelago, resembles them in a good many particulars. First discovered by Carteret in 1767, its colonisation by the mutineers of the *Bounty* in 1790 is too well known to require repetition. It may, however be stated that, in 1831, the number of its inhabitants (eighty-seven) having become too great for the island, they were transported by the British Government to Tahiti, from which they shortly afterwards returned to Pitcairn, in consequence of the immorality of the Tahitians. Again finding their numbers too great (*c.* 219), they were removed in 1856 to the more productive shores of Norfolk Island, from which seventeen of them returned to Pitcairn three years afterwards.

Surnames	1841		1851		1861		1871	
	Families	Persons	Families	Persons	Families	Persons	Families	Persons
McKenzie (minister)	1	9	0	0	0	0	0	0
Kennedy (catechist and registrar)	0	0	0	0	1	1	0	0
McKay (minister and registrar)	0	0	0	0	0	0	1	2
Total	29	105	32	110	20	78	19	71

It will be observed that, in 1871, only five surnames prevailed among the native population – viz, Gillies, McDonald, Ferguson, McKinnon, and McQueen – McLeod and Morison having disappeared before 1861 and M'Crimmon before the last official census. The M'Crimmons were the hereditary pipers of the McLeods, and, according to Lane Buchanan, held their lands in Skye from Macleod of Macleod 'for attending the chief's person and family'. Among the last of the race in St Kilda was Euphemia McCrimmon, some of whose stories (*sgeulachdan*) will be afterwards referred to. In 1871, the prevailing Christian names among the males were John, Neil, Donald and Finlay; and among the females, Catherine, Rachel, Anne, and Mary. In many cases, for the sake of distinction, a characteristic epithet is added to the Christian name, after the manner of the 'tee-names' of the fishermen of Banff and Moray – e.g. Donull Og, or 'Young Donald'; Callum Beag, or 'Little Malcolm'.

Mr Wilson says that 'in addition to whatever slight knowledge a few of them may possess of certain handicrafts, the whole of the male sex who have attained to and have not passed the prime of life, are what we may call "practical ornithologists", or cragsmen'. At the census of 1851, while eight of the softer sex were described as 'weaveresses in wool', all the men were designed 'farmers and bird-catchers', each farmer then occupying about three acres of land. In 1861, a few of the females were described as 'cottars' or 'servants', the males being designed as follows:

Cottars and cragsmen	15
Cragsmen and fishermen	6
Fowlers	6
Cragsmen	2
Scholars	3
Catechist and registrar	1
Total	33

Accordingly, at that date, it would appear that twenty-nine of the thirty-three male inhabitants either partially or exclusively followed the avocation of fowling.

In 1871, the occupations were thus specified—

I – MALES

Joint cottars	12
Joint cottars and cragsmen	10
Scholar	1
FC minister and registrar	1
Undesigned (ages 3–9)	3
Total	27

II – Females

Scholars	4
Servants	2
Undesigned	38
Total	44

Martin states that 'the women have their assemblies in the village, where they discourse of their affairs, but in the meantime employing their distaff and spinning, in order to make their blankets'. The wool of the St Kilda sheep is very fine, and excellent stockings are knitted by the females – soft and somewhat similar to those made in Shetland. The women, however, who spin the yarn, have no idea of fine work. Some of the men are good weavers; and the cloth which they produce resembles that which is manufactured in Harris, now so well known on the mainland through the philanthropic efforts of Mrs Thomas. Each of the adult males acts as his own tailor and shoemaker; and in every house there is a loom, also a spinning-wheel and a large pot in which the yarn is dyed. 'Mr Mantilini' is a familiar character in St Kilda – the dresses of the women, as already mentioned, being made by the men. Macaulay refers to the successful tanning of leather with the root of tormentil, which, as already stated, is also employed for dyeing purposes. 'The St Kildans', he says, 'lay the leather, when sufficiently prepared, in the warm infusion of this bark for two nights, and afterwards keep it in the hollow of a rock, which is under water at every full sea, with some of this root pounded about it, until it is sufficiently tanned.' Forty years ago, it would appear that the St Kildans manufactured earthen pots, of clay brought from the Long Island, which they used for boiling milk.[5]

Both men and women are extremely industrious, and the assertions that have been made in some quarters relative to their lazy habits appear to be utterly untrue. Mr Sands alludes to the activity which prevailed during his last sojourn in the island, towards the end of the year, in the way of spinning and weaving – both sexes working from dawn of day till an hour or two after midnight. Their assiduity quite astonished him.

The men vary their sedentary occupation [he says] by going to fish when the weather permits. In spring they scale the crags, and visit the adjacent islands for eggs and birds, and cultivate their plots of ground . . . In summer they fish for ling, which they cure and sell to the factor. About the end of July they require to be on the alert to catch the young fulmars, before they are quite ready to take wing; and after their perilous labours during the day, they are often obliged to sit up all night to pluck the feathers. Then comes the season to knock the young solan geese on the head – and so on.

---

5 The art of the potter is still practised, in a somewhat rude form, in the parish of Barvas in Lewis. In the course of last summer I there purchased, from an elderly woman bearing the romantic name of 'Flora Macdonald', a small cup and saucer, which she was good enough to fabricate for my special benefit.

His account of the industry and activity of the women, which is fully confirmed by Mrs McVean, is even more striking – the manner in which they carry heavy loads of turf from every corner of the island; the powerful aid which they render in dragging boats on their arrival over the rocks; their milking, cheesemaking and herding in all states of the weather; their washing, spinning and occasionally dyeing of wool; their alertness in knitting stockings while tending the flocks or when engaged in conversation; their snaring of puffins and plucking the feathers; their help in tilling the land; and their grinding the corn in hand-mills, after it has been thrashed with a flail, and scorched in a pot or basket containing hot stones.

Notwithstanding the prohibitory statute of Alexander III in 1284, the quern or bra, though much disused since the erection of country mills, is still pretty common in some parts of Lewis and Harris, as well as in St Kilda, where it is to be found in every cottage. It consists of two circular stones of granite, from fifteen to eighteen inches in diameter, and about four inches thick, laid flat upon each other. In the centre of the lower stone, which has a hollow of some five inches in depth, there is an iron pivot on which the upper stone, which is flat, is turned by means of a wooden handle. The grain is dropped into a round hole in the centre of the upper stone, finds its way between the two stones as the upper one is kept revolving, and is supposed to be sufficiently ground when it comes out at the edge between the stones. Mrs McVean mentions that in her infancy the practice in St Kilda was to place the quern on a sheep-skin, in the centre of the floor, while two women, in accordance with the language of Scripture, sat cross-legged on each side – one feeding the mill with grain, while the other turned the handle with great rapidity. In referring to the same process, Mr Sands describes the present female islanders as working 'like furies'! When Pennant wrote (1772), the quern was made on the mainland, and cost about fourteen shillings. In alluding to the tediousness of the process, he states that it occupied two pairs of hands four hours to grind a single bushel of corn. He gives a pictorial illustration of hand-mill grinding, and also of the process of cloth-waulking, at both of which the usual custom was for the women to sing 'slow and melancholy' tunes.[6]

Mr Macdiarmid refers to the well-built walls which surround the patches of cultivated ground, as an indication of the masonic skill of the males. They possess axes and hammers, and in one house he saw a large box of joiner's tools. 'They are rather scarce of nails,' he adds, 'which are always of use to them in the case of accidents to their boats.'

Incidental reference has already been made to the capabilities of St Kilda as a fishing station, and several writers have noticed the disregard, on the part of the islanders, of that important source of food and emolument.

> The neglect of fishing [says Macculloch] proceeds from the wealth of the inhabitants. They possess already as much food as they can consume, and are under no temptation to augment it by another perilous and laborious employment added to that to which they seem to have a hereditary attachment; while their distance from a market, and the absence of commercial habits, prevent them from undertaking a fishery for the purpose of foreign sale. Yet the coast abounds in cod and ling, and may perhaps hereafter prove a source of increased population; if not of a greater disposable produce, and consequent increase of rent to the proprietor.

At the time of the doctor's visit, the islanders possessed only two boats, one of which was not serviceable, in consequence of its having been allowed to go to decay for want of some trifling repairs. A few years later, Dr Macdonald refers in one of his journals to the abundance of fish in the immediate neighbourhood of St Kilda, and to the disinclination of the inhabitants to secure the

6 *Tour in Scotland*, ii, 323, 329.

treasures of the deep. Martin gives a curious account of the solitary boat, 16 cubits in length, which the islanders possessed at the end of the seventeenth century. It was divided into apartments proportioned to their lands and rocks; 'every individual having his space distinguished to an hair's-breadth, which his neighbour cannot encroach so much as to lay an egg upon it'. Mr Maclean describes the sail of the *Lair-dhonn* (or brown mare), the designation of the St Kilda boat at the time of his visit in 1838. 'It is made up', he says, 'of twenty-one patches of varied sizes and shades, like what you would have fancied Joseph's coat to have been, and of coarse plaiding, the contribution of twenty-one partners, in proportion to their share of land and rocks severally. The reefs are as varied as the sail, made of old garters or woollen ropes.'

An anonymous visitor to St Kilda in August 1875, in a relative contribution to the *Scotsman* newspaper, stated that there were then no fewer than eight boats upon the island, but that the fishing seemed to be carried on 'in a kind of scrambling way'. Mr Sands, on the other hand, states that two boats, with crews of eight and nine men respectively, went to sea almost every night during the time he resided on the island, to fish for ling with long lines. 'Each boat would return in the morning, with perhaps, on an average, about thirty-five ling and a few cod, besides other fish', such as lithe, halibut, black-mouths, skate and conger-eels. He also mentions that, in the July evenings, a number of elderly men were in the habit of angling for mullet from the top of the crags near the village. Mr Macdiarmid found four boats on the island in May 1877, two of which had been recently presented to the islanders by casual visitors. Although very good of their kind, he does not consider them sufficiently strong to withstand the rough usage of being hauled over the rocks at landing. He states that, on the recommendation of Captain Digby of the *Jackal*, Government intends to send another boat forthwith, and suggests that the most judicious course would have been for the authorities to have ordered a boat to be specially built at Stornoway, on the model of the ordinary herring-boats of that seaport. He also refers to the important question of a suitable landing-place, in which Captain Otter took a deep interest, the continued want of which is the source of so much inconvenience and danger. In his *Sailing Directions for the Hebrides*, Captain Otter states that a very fair landing-place was actually constructed at the north edge of the nearly vertical rock below the manse. The large boulders when blasted were cleared away to some distance, and a small breast-work erected; but, in the course of two years, the drawback of the winter swells rolled back the stones and destroyed it. It appears that the captain intended to have cleared away the rock, and then to have made a cutting of about forty or fifty yards into the bank to the right of the minister's house, with the view of letting the sea run in at high water. Mr Macdiarmid considers that some such project might be carried out at a comparatively small cost, and judiciously suggests that any public fund which may hereafter be raised on behalf of the St Kildans could not be better applied than to the construction of a proper landing-place, The islanders are known to be very expert in the management of rowing-boats, but inexperienced in the use of sails, as is believed to have been indicated at the loss of the *Dargavel* in 1863. Judging, however, from their unequalled daring as cragsmen, to which reference will be made in the following chapter, it may fairly be conjectured that, with proper training, they would prove themselves to be intrepid and skilful sailors.

With regard to the civil, or conjugal condition of the St Kildans, it appears from the report on the census of 1861, that, at that date, the island contained thirteen married couples, one widower, and four widows; while there were eight bachelors and nine spinsters between the ages of twenty and forty-six. In 1871, however, the proportions of the latter were materially altered – the spinsters between twenty and forty-six then amounting to no fewer than fourteen, and the bachelors of the same age to only three. The condition and ages of the entire population at the last census (1871) are exhibited in the two following tables, from the first of which it will be observed that the number of unmarried and widowed females was then twenty-nine, while the males in the same conditions amounted to only twelve.

I – CONDITION

	Married	Unmarried	Widowed	Total
Males	15	10	2	27
Females	15	25	4	44
Total	30	35	6	71

II – Ages

	Years				
	0–5	5–20	20–60	above 60	Total
Males	1	4	17	5	27
Females	2	9	29	4	44
Total	3	13	46	9	71

All the inhabitants of St Kilda enumerated at the census of 1861 were natives of the island except two – viz, Mr Kennedy, the catechist and registrar, who was born at Ardchattan, Argyllshire; and poor Betty Scott – who perished with the *Dargavel* in 1863 – wife of one of the McDonalds, and mother of the belle of the island, already referred to, whose birthplace was Lochinver, in the county of Sutherland. Mr Morgan describes her as 'the Mrs Poyser of the village – smart, energetic, talkative and shrewd' – and appears to have been equally impressed with her pretty, fair-haired daughter, and her 'firmly-knit, frank-looking son' – a lad of seventeen or eighteen summers – whose elastic step and cool, daring expression of eye, induced that gentleman to single him out as one of the boldest cragsmen in St Kilda. Such was the Duke of Athole's admiration of these two young islanders, that he seriously proposed to transplant them, along with their vigorous mother, to his Perthshire estate.

In 1871, all the inhabitants were natives of the island except Mr McKay, the minister, and his sister (since deceased) – who were respectively born in the town of Inverness, and at Jeantown in Ross-shire – and Isabella Munro, daughter of a surveyor in Glasgow and wife of Neil McDonald, afterwards referred to.

Sea-birds and Cragsmen

If the human population of St Kilda is somewhat sparse, during eight or nine months of the year every island and stack in the group is tenanted by myriads of feathered inhabitants, which impart no small amount of life and bustle to what would otherwise be a desolate and lonely scene. It is, of course, impossible to indicate an approximation to the number of the various kinds of sea-fowl which annually occupy the beetling cliffs; and even with the king of birds as registrar-general, and a select staff of sharp-eyed falcons as enumerators, an ornithological census of these islands would probably prove a very arduous task!

Macculloch refers to Swift's description of a land of feathers in his *Tale of a Tub*, but as I have failed to find the passage, I must content myself with his own account of one of the special characteristics of St Kilda.

The air [he says] is full of feathered animals, the sea is covered with them, the houses are ornamented by them, the ground is speckled with them like a flowery meadow in May. The town is paved with feathers, the very dunghills are made of feathers, the ploughed land seems as if it had been sown with feathers, and the inhabitants look as if they had been all tarred and feathered, for their hair is full of feathers, and their clothes are covered with feathers. The women look like feathered Mercuries, for their shoes are made of a gannet's skin; everything smells of feathers, and the smell pursued us all over the islands – for the captain had concealed a sack-full in the cabin.

The same writer, in his notice of the Flannan islands, makes some interesting observations on the *harmony* of the sea-birds, for the introduction of part of which I think it unnecessary to offer any apology.

I have often been entertained [he says] with the extraordinary concerts of the sea-fowl in Ailsa, the Shiant islands and elsewhere; but I never heard any orchestra so numerous, so various, and so perfect as this one, which seemed to consist of almost all the birds that frequent the seas and rocks of these wild coasts. I should perhaps do injustice to the performers, did I attempt to assign the parts which each seemed to take in this concert: but it was easy to distinguish the short, shrill treble of the puffins and auks, the melodious and varied notes of the different gulls, the tenors of the divers and guillemots and the croaking basses of the cormorants. But the variety of tones was far beyond my power of analysis, as I believe Pennant had found it before me. It may appear ludicrous to call this music melodious, or to speak of the harmony formed by such ingredients: yet it is a combination of sounds to which a musician will listen with interest and delight, although the separate cries of the different individuals are seldom thought agreeable. Few of the notes in this concert could perhaps have been referred to the scale, if separately examined; yet the harmony was often as full and perfect as if it had been the produce of well-tuned instruments, and the effect was infinitely superior to that which is often heard in a spring morning among the singing birds of the forest, while it was so entirely different as not to admit of any comparison.

After alluding to the special characteristics in the notes of the cuckoo, nightingale, thrush, and other songsters of the grove, he goes on to say that:

in the sea-birds there are few tones and few notes, but they are decided and steady. The body of sound is also far greater; and, however inferior in variety or sweetness the notes of the individuals may be, there is much more variety in the harmonious combinations, and in that which musicians would call the contrivance and design. Very often they remind me of some of the ancient religious compositions, which consist of a perpetual succession of fugue and imitation on a few simple notes; and sometimes it appeared as if different orchestras were taking up the same phrases ... I will not say that the gulls, the auks, the gannets and the cormorants will compete for the palm of music with Haydn's 'Chaos', or with the solemn and wild strain of extraordinary and superhuman harmonies with which the ghost first addresses Don Giovanni: but the educated musician who shall choose to attend to these marine symphonies will find that modern inventions have unwittingly been only following nature, and may thence borrow valuable hints for his own art.

In the course of my insular rambles, I have more than once been struck by the wild and curious music of the feathered orchestras – particularly at the little island of Handa, off the west coast of Sutherlandshire, and at the wonderful 'Noss' of Bressay, in Shetland. During a visit to the former, about eight years ago, I ascertained that its cliffs were tenanted by not fewer than twelve different kinds of sea-fowl, including the razor-bill, kittiwake, puffin, sea-swallow and oyster-catcher, besides several species of gulls, guillemots, and cormorants. All these, I believe, with the fulmar and solan in addition – and probably three or four other species – are to be found in the St Kilda group. Captain Macdonald of the *Vigilant* cutter informed me, on our return voyage, that he thinks the sea-birds are not quite so numerous as when he first visited St Kilda several years ago; but this does not appear to be the impression of the islanders themselves. It is difficult to convey the very faintest idea of their countless number. When coasting along the rugged shores in the *Dunara*, besides the occasional discharge of two fowling-pieces, a small gun was fired in the immediate proximity of one of the most densely animated cliffs; and without going the length of asserting that the sky was actually darkened by the myriads of wings set in motion by the report as it echoed from rock to rock, I can honestly declare that the cobalt of the heavens was at least partially concealed by a canopy of feathery clouds. In disputing the accuracy of the popular assertion relative to the interception of light by an infinite multitude of sea-birds, Mr Wilson poetically compares them to 'the spray of sparkling waters, or the mild effulgence of the milky way ... shining with a pearly lustre, pure as "the bolted snow".'

Apropos to the harmony of the sea-fowl, Martin mentions that two distinct cries – 'grog, grog', and 'bir, bir' – are uttered by the sentinel of the solan geese under different circumstances. Mr Wilson being curious, as an ornithologist, to ascertain the truth of this statement, paid particular attention to the matter during his visit to St Kilda; and he solemnly asserts that he distinctly heard a voice giving utterance to the words 'grog, grog', 'but whether it came from the solan geese or the sailors, still remains to be proved. The other monosyllable "bir, bir" (pronounced "beer, beer"), was also heard frequently, but almost always in the earlier portion of the day, especially during the prevalence of warm weather!' From the dictation of one of the islanders, Mr Sands wrote down the following cries of four of the principal birds, that of the puffin being of a peculiarly mournful and melancholy tone:

Solan goose – 'Gorrok! beero! hurro boo!'
Scraber – 'Kickogoo, hoo! kickogoo, hoo!'
Puffin – 'Oh! oh! oh! oh!' (*ad infinitum*)
Fulmar – 'Ok! ok! ok! ok!' (*allegro*)[1]

Independently of the friendship that existed between Thomson and Mallet, the tragedy of 'Alfred' was their joint production; and

---

1 Professor Macgillivray compared the torrent of crackling sounds uttered by the solan goose to the words 'Varroch, varroch, kirra, kirra, cree, cree, krak, krak', for which a loud call for 'grog' is ultimately substituted!

When an unfortunate kittiwake is mercilessly shot dead upon its nest, the neighbours immediately flit about, calling in pitiable tones, 'Kittawee, kittawee! ah! get away, get away!' But probably the most curious cry is that of the long-tailed duck (*Fuligula glacialis*), which does not appear in my list of St Kilda birds. Mr Gray states that, a few years ago, in the neighbourhood of Dunbar, he carefully noted the cry of a group of these beautiful birds as bearing a remarkable resemblance to the words 'Coal an' can'le licht' (in a good Scotch accent) – the whimsical name by which the bird is known in many parts of Scotland.

it is somewhat curious that both poets, in their individual compositions, devote several graphic lines to the transmigration and other habits of the sea-birds of the Western Islands. The following passage occurs towards the middle of Thomson's 'Autumn', after a reference to the annual departure of the swallow and the stork:

> Or where the northern ocean, in vast whirls,
> Boils round the naked melancholy isles
> Of farthest Thule, and the Atlantic surge
> Pours in among the stormy Hebrides;
> Who can recount what transmigrations there
> Are annual made? what nations come and go?
> And how the living clouds on clouds arise?
>
> Infinite wings! till all the plume-dark air,
> And rude resounding shore are one wild cry.
> Here the plain harmless native his small flock,
> And herd diminutive of many hues,
> Tends on the little island's verdant swell,
> The shepherd's sea-girt reign; or, to the rocks
> Dire-clinging, gathers his ovarious food;
> Or sweeps the fishy shore; or treasures up
> The plumage, rising full, to form the bed
> Of Luxury.

In like manner, the author of 'Amyntor and Theodora' thus discourses of the feathered tribes in his first canto:

> But high above the season full exerts
> Its vernant force in yonder peopled rocks,
> To whose wild solitude, from worlds unknown,
> The birds of passage transmigrating come,
> Unnumbered colonies of foreign wing,
> At Nature's summons their aerial state
> Annual to found, and in bold voyage steer

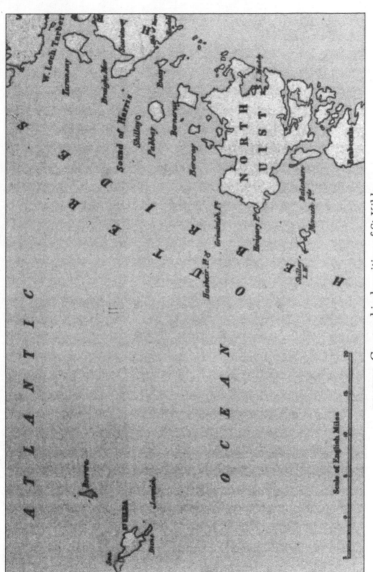

PLATE I. Geographical position of St Kilda.

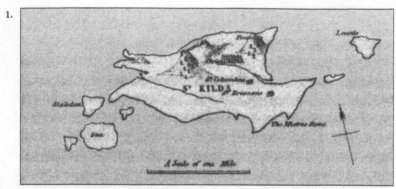

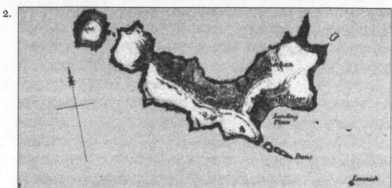

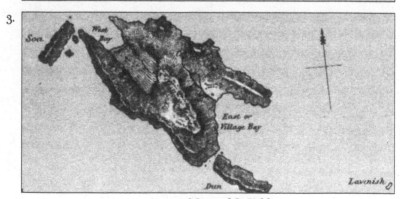

PLATE II. Maps of St Kilda.
1. Martin. 2. Macculloch. 3. Wilson.

PLATE III.

Levenish   St Kilda   Soa   Borrera

PLATE IV. East Bay with Conagher.

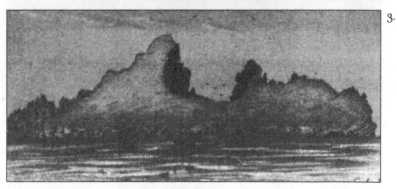

PLATE V.
1. Levenish. 2. Borrera. 3. The Dune.

PLATE VI. St Kilda Man.

PLATE VII. St Kilda Women.

PLATE VIII. St Kilda Children.

PLATE IX. St Kilda Cottages.

PLATE X. Great Auk.

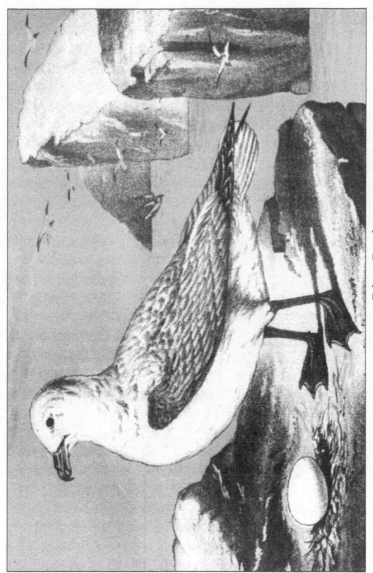

PLATE XI. Fulmar Petrel.

PLATE XII. St Kilda Cragsman.

O'er this wide ocean, through yon pathless sky,
One certain flight to one appointed shore,
By heaven's directive spirit here to raise
Their temporary realm, and form secure,
Where food awaits them copious from the wave,
And shelter from the rock, their nuptial leagues;
Each tribe apart, and all on tasks of love,
To hatch the pregnant egg, to rear and guard
Their helpless infants, piously intent.

Again, towards the end of the poem, he alludes to the movements and music of the birds during the glory of an Atlantic sunset:

Above, around, in cloudy circles wheeled,
Or sailing level on the polar gale
That cool with evening rose, a thousand wings,
The summer nations of these pregnant cliffs,
Played sportive round, and to the sun outspread
Their various plumage, or in wild notes hailed
His parent-beam that animates and cheers
All living kinds: he, glorious from amidst
A pomp of golden clouds, the Atlantic flood
Beheld oblique, and o'er its azure breast
Waved one unbounded blush; a scene to strike
Both ear and eye with wonder and delight!

The St Kilda land birds enumerated by Martin are the hawk, eagle, plover, crow, wren, stone-chaker (stonechat or wheat-ear), craker (corncrake) and cuckoo, the last being very rarely seen, and that only on extraordinary occasions, 'such as the death of the proprietor MackLeod, the steward's death, or the arrival of some notable stranger!' When our author expressed his incredulity respecting this belief on the part of the natives, they were astounded by his want of faith, and on appealing to the steward, he at once confirmed the truth of the allegation. Two sons of a distinguished living ornithologist accompanied the party in the *Dunara Castle*; but I am not aware that either of them was able to detect the sound of the 'magic' note! In his larger work, Martin describes the hawks of St Kilda as the finest in the Western Isles, adding that 'they go many leagues for their prey, there being no landfowl in St Kilda proper for them to eat, except pigeons and plovers'. Both the peregrine falcon and the kestrel are to be found on its shores. He also speaks of a couple of large eagles having a nest at the north end of the island, respecting which the inhabitants informed him that 'they commonly make their purchase [depredation] in the adjacent isles and continent, and never take so much as a lamb or hen from the place of their abode, where they propagate their kind.' Besides several of the birds specified by Martin, Macaulay mentions the raven ('of the largest sort'), heron, curlew, magpie (very rare in other parts of the Hebrides), pigeon, starling, lark and sparrow. Next to the sea-fowl, the starling is probably the most common bird in St Kilda. Whether such small birds as wrens and sparrows reach the island by their own efforts or with the aid of boats, he leaves 'undetermined'; and with regard to the herons – 'the most watchful fowls in the world' – he says that their capture by the St Kildans, 'by dint of stalking', may perhaps be hardly credited, 'though the fact seems to be very well attested'. He partially confirms Martin's statement relative to the eagles being perfectly harmless on the island, and conjectures that this may arise from their necessities being more than supplied, at least in summer, by the inexhaustible stores of eggs which fall in their way. In winter, he presumes that they must make frequent excursions to the neighbouring isles. At present, the eagle is not to be found at St Kilda. Mr Wilson saw no sparrows; but, in addition to the birds mentioned by Martin and Macaulay, he enumerates the hooded crow, thrush, blackbird (an occasional visitant), corn-bunting, twite and two species of titlark. There are no grouse or other game birds; but the minister informed Mr Wilson that, on a winter day, he once saw a single ptarmigan on the hillside, after the prevalence of strong easterly winds. The snipe remains all the year round. Towards the close of the year, wild geese, mireducks and a few straggling swans sometimes make their appearance on the island; and occasionally birds with foreign plumage find their way to its lonely shores.

Eight years ago (24 June, 1869), an Act for the Preservation of Sea-Birds was passed, which is known in statutory language as 32 & 33 Vic., cap 17. Section 1 enumerates thirty-two different species as included under the term 'sea-birds' – viz, auk, bonxie, Cornish chough, coulterneb, diver, eider duck, fulmar, gannet, grebe, guillemot, gull, kittiwake, loon, marrot, merganser, murre, oystercatcher, petrel, puffin, razor-bill, scout, sea-mew, sea-parrot, sea-swallow, shearwater, shelldrake, skua, smew, solan goose, tarrock, tern-tystey and willock. Of these, however, the coulterneb and sea-parrot, the gannet and solan goose, the guillemot and marrot, the gull and sea-mew, and the murre and razor-bill, are respectively one and the same species. Section 2 defines the period – four months – within which these sea-birds are not to be slaughtered – viz, from 1 April to 1 August; and imposes a penalty of one pound on every contravener of the enactment. The eighth clause declares that the operation of the Act 'shall not extend to the island of St Kilda', the cause of the exemption being indicated in the 9th and concluding section – to wit, 'the necessities of the inhabitants'. As stated in a previous chapter, many a long day is likely to elapse before the inhabitants of the remote island will enjoy the ordinary legal protection of her Majesty's lieges; and, on the other hand, if the exemption in question had not been made, it would not have been a very easy matter to have convicted a St Kildan of a breach of the statute.

Nearly all the sea-fowl of St Kilda belong to three of the five families of the order of *Palmipedes*, or web-footed birds[2] – viz, Alcadoe, or auks; *Pelicanidae* or pelicans; and *Laridae*, or gulls. I have been unable to compile a complete list, but have reason to believe that the following are to be found on the group of islands:

Common or foolish guillemot – *Uria troile*
Black guillemot – *Uria grylle*

2 The *Natatores*, or swimmers, of Illiger and other ornithologists.

Alcadoe[3]	[Puffin – *Fratercula arctica*
	Razor-bill – *Alca torda*

	Common cormorant – *Phalacrocorax carbo*
Pelicaridoe	[Shag, or green cormorant – *Phalacrocoraxgraculus*
	Gannet, or solan goose – *Sula alla* (or *bassana*)

	Black-headed gull – *Larus ridibundus*
	Kittiwake gull – *Larus tridaclylus* (or *rissa*)
	Common gull – *Larus canus*
	Lesser black-backed gull – *Larus fuscus*
Laridoe	[Herring gull – *Larus argerfatus*
	Great black-backed gull – *Larus marinus*[4]
	Fulmar-petrel – *Procellaria glacialis*
	Manx shearwater – *Puffinus Anglorum*
	Fork-tailed petrel – *Thalassidroma Leachii*[5]
	Stormpetrel – *Thalassidroma pelagica*

In addition to these seventeen birds, at least two others occur – viz, the eider-duck (*Somateria mollissima*), belonging to another family (*Anatidae*) of the same order,[6] and the oystercatcher (*Hoematopus ostralegus*), pertaining to the order *Grallatores*, or waders. 'Every fowl', says Martin, 'lays a single egg three different times (except the gairfowl and fulmar, which lay but once); if the first or second egg be taken away, every fowl lays but one other egg that year, except the

3 Brunnich's guillemot (*Uria Brunnichlii*) has also been said to be a native of St Kilda; but Gray, in his *Birds of the West of Scotland*, says that none of his correspondents who have visited the island appear to have recognised it. The great auk (*Alca impennis*) – to be afterwards referred to – was formerly an occasional visitor.

4 This appears to be the large gull which, according to Macaulay, is cordially detested by every St Kildan, on account of the destruction which it effects among the eggs and young fowls of other species.

5 At one time St Kilda was supposed to be the only breeding-place in the United Kingdom of the fork-tailed petrel; but it has now been ascertained that there are several other stations.

6 On the occasion of my visit to St Kilda, a specimen of the eiderduck was shot by Major Colquhoun. Although abundant on the island of Colonsay and elsewhere, it is only occasionally seen at St Kilda. It is said to breed on the Flannan islands, 37 miles NW of St Kilda.

seamalls, and they ordinarily lay the third egg, whether the first and second eggs be taken away or no.' In alluding to the instinct and sagacity of the various sea-birds, he elsewhere observes: 'So powerful is their στοργή, or natural affection for their offspring, that they choose rather to die upon the egg or fowl than escape with their own lives (which they could do in a minute), and leave either of these to be destroyed.' Of the trilichan, or sea-pie, he says that it is cloven-footed, and 'consequently swims not. If it comes in the beginning of May, it is a sign of a good summer; if later, the contrary is observed.'

The following is a list of the sea-birds specified by Martin as occurring on the St Kilda group, with the dates of their arrival and departure:

Local Name	Synonym	Arrival	Departure
Gairfowl	Great Auk	May 1	c. June 15
Solan Goose	Gannet	c. March 15	
Fulmar	Fulmar-petrel	November	August
Scraber or Scràbaire	Puffinet, Greenland-dove, or Shearwater	March	August
Lavy or Làmhaidh	Guillem or Guillemot	Feb. 20	*
Falk	Razor-bill, Auk, or Murre	Before May	c. July 15
Bougir	Coulterneb, Sea-parrot, or Puffin	c. March 22	August
Assilag or Aisealag	Stormpetrel	c. March 22	c. Nov. 25
Sea-malls (3 kinds)	Gulls		
1[– Tuliac, size of a goose	Great black-backed Gull (?)	?	?
2 – considerably smaller.	Lesser black-backed Gull (?)	?	?
3 White – Ruideag, less than a tame duck	Kittiwake	April 15	August
Trilichan	Tirma, Sea-pie, or Oyster-catcher(?)	May	August

* In the case of the solan and lavy, the time of departure is said to depend on the inhabitants 'taking or leaving the first, second, or third egg'.

The memoranda of the Rev. Neil McKenzie embrace numerous references to the habits of the various seafowl. 'All the birds,' he says, 'are so regular in the time of leaving and coming, laying and hatching, that a kind of calendar might be constructed from their migrations', in forcible illustration of the language of Scripture, 'Yea, the stork in the heaven knoweth her appointed times; and the turtle and the crane and the swallow observe the time of their coming.' He also informs us that all the different kinds of seafowl are to be found on the islands by the month of April, and that the following month (May) – during which almost all the birds lay their eggs – is by far the most important season in the year to the fowler. Macaulay states that, on the arrival of the principal birds, 'the most considerable persons in this small state assemble together to congratulate one another on the great occasion'. Most of the feathered inhabitants leave the cliffs during August and September. By November, the rocks are almost entirely deserted; and for about three months the islands present a lonely and desolate appearance.

Some special remarks seem to be called for respecting a few of the principal birds of St Kilda; and my title warrants the assignment of the place of honour to a 'thing of the past', the extinct Garefowl or Great Auk, which Martin pronounces to be 'the stateliest as well as the largest of all the fowls in the island' and which appears to have recently excited great interest among naturalists. In his valuable work on the *Birds of the West of Scotland*, Mr Gray recapitulates all that appears to have been written regarding the garefowl. With respect to the etymology of the name – garefowl or gairfowl – Jamieson defines both *gare* and *gair* as 'keen or rapacious', which may perhaps have been characteristic of its nature. Various writers, however, seem to regard it as identical with the *geirfug* or *geyr-fugl*,[8] formerly common in Iceland and other high latitudes, from which it may have found its way to St Kilda. Influenced, no doubt, by a recollection of the proverb

8 The *gorfuglir* of Faroe.

'*Rara avis in ferris*', Macaulay suggests that the men of Hirta may perhaps have conferred the appellation of garefowl on the great auk as a corruption of rarefawl, 'a name,' he adds, 'probably given to it by some one of those foreigners, whom either choice or necessity drew into the secure region'! The author of the *Agriculture of the Hebrides*, in his brief notice of St Kilda, refers to this remarkable bird under the unpronounceable Gaelic name of *bunnabhuachäille*.

Martin describes the garefowl as—

> above the size of a solan goose, of a black colour, red about the eyes, a large white spot under each eye, a long broad bill; stands stately, his whole body erected; his wings short. He flyeth not at all;[9] lays his egg upon the bare rock, which, if taken away, he lays no more for that year. He is palmipes, or whole-footed, and has the hatching-spot upon his breast – i.e. a bare spot from which the feathers have fallen off with the heat in hatching. His egg is twice as big as that of a solan goose, and is variously spotted black, green and dark.[10]

Whether Martin actually saw the garefowl does not positively appear, but his detailed description seems to indicate that his information was at least derived from the personal observation of others. Macaulay admits that he 'had not an opportunity of knowing the very curious fowl, sometimes seen on the coast of St Kilda', but his notice of the bird seems to be worthy of transcription.

> It is [he says] above four feet in length, from the bill to the extremities of its feet; its wings are, in proportion to its size, very short, so that they can hardly poise or support the weight

---

9 Hence called by naturalists '*Alca impennis*'.
10 The Lord Register, Sir George McKenzie, says that the eggs of the garefowl are 'as big almost as those of the ostrich'. Two specimens are to be seen in the Edinburgh Museum of Science and Art.

of its very large body. Its legs, neck and bill, are extremely long. It lays the egg (which, according to the account given me, exceeds that of a goose, no less than the latter exceeds the egg of a hen), close by the sea-mark, being incapable, on account of its bulk, to soar up to the cliffs. It makes its appearance in the month of July. The St Kildans do not receive an annual visit from this strange bird as from all the rest in the list, and from many more. It keeps at a distance from them, they know not where, for a course of years. From what land or ocean it makes its uncertain voyages to their isle is perhaps a mystery.

The wings of the great auk appear to have been so short as to bear the character of *paddles*, thus resembling the penguin, of which it was the northern representative. It laid its solitary egg – about 5 inches long and 3 inches at the greatest breadth – on the bare rock, without any nest.

Little more than fifty years ago the great auk appears to have regularly visited the island of Papa Westray, in Orkney, where, about the year 1812, Mr Bullock had the gratification of chasing a widowed male bird for several hours in a six-oared boat, the speed of which was entirely eclipsed by that of the auk. According to Wilson, 'its powers of swimming and diving probably exceeded those of any other species of the feathered race'. Shortly after Mr Bullock's departure, the object of his pursuit was secured by the native boatmen, and is now preserved, in excellent condition, at the British Museum. Another live specimen, captured off St Kilda by the tacksman of the island of Scalpa, in Harris, was seen there by Dr Fleming in the year 1821. While being indulged with a swim in the sea, restrained by a cord fastened to one leg, it contrived to escape from a subsequent owner. A former tacksman of St Kilda (McNeill) informed Professor Macgillivray that the bird occurred in that island 'at irregular intervals of two or three years',[11] but no recent visitor appears to have obtained any trust-

11 *Edinburgh Journal of Natural and Geographical Science*, 1830.

worthy particulars regarding its existence in that quarter. Mr Elwes, who was at St Kilda in 1868, made particular inquiries there and elsewhere respecting the great auk, without eliciting any information.[12] A detailed description of the bird will be found in Dr Fleming's History of British Animals, and accurate representations of it are given in the works of Audubon, Wilson, Jardine and other ornithologists. In 1871, Mr Gray estimated the value of a specimen at not less than £100, but it is now probably very much greater; and at an auction in London, in 1865, four eggs of the great auk were sold at prices ranging from twenty-nine pounds to thirty-three pounds. Their present value is said to be not less than from fifty to sixty pounds. Admirably manufactured forgeries of the eggs have been offered for sale within the last few years. It has been ascertained that there are thirty-four specimens of the auk and forty-two eggs in different parts of the world. The eggs vary in size, colour and markings, some being of a silvery-white, and others of a yellowish-white ground – the spots and streaks also differing in form and colour. One of the four eggs in the possession of Mr Champley is five inches one line long, three inches wide, and thirty-eight scruples fifteen grains in weight. Martin's description of the colour of the auk is only correct so far as it goes. The upper surface of the body is black, except a patch of pure white, round and in front of the eye, and the ends of the secondaries, which are also white. All the under surface is white, and in winter the chin and throat assumed the same colour.

Several valuable contributions relative to the great auk have recently been made to the *Ibis* by Professor Newton of Cambridge, who fondly cherishes the belief that the interesting bird may not, after all, be actually extinct; and cannot, accordingly, persuade himself to address it in the tender words of Milton, some of which, at least, are sufficiently applicable:

12 Unsuccessful inquiries appear to have been also made in Greenland and Iceland respecting the auk by Sir L. McClintock, Dr Rae and other scientific travellers.

Aye me! whilst thee the shores and sounding seas
Wash far away, where'er thy bones are hurled,
Whether beyond the stormy Hebrides,
Where thou, perhaps, under the whelming tide,
Visit'st the bottom of the monstrous world;
Or whether thou, to our moist vows denied,
Sleep'st by the fable of Bellerus old,
Where the great vision of the guarded mount
Looks towards Namancos, and Bayona's hold.

The general impression of ornithologists, however, as already indicated, is that the garefowl, like the dodo, has entirely passed away, and that his abode knows him no more, while the winds and the waves chant his requiem.

The only existing sea-birds of St Kilda to which I intend specially to refer are the solan goose or gannet, the fulmar, and the puffin.

The solan goose, spectacle goose, or gannet, frequents the islets and stacks adjacent to St Kilda,[13] but not the island itself, thus exhibiting the opposite characteristic of the rook and some other birds, which seem to prefer the proximity of human habitations. Its favourite haunt is Stack Ly or Leath – already referred to – in the immediate vicinity of Borrera, which, as a breeding-place for the solan goose, Mr Wilson pronounces 'one of the wonders of the world'. Not only the top of the stack, but every crack and crevice all around is tenanted by sea-fowl, chiefly gannets. The minister informed him that 'although he himself could not perceive the slightest diminution of their amount, it consisted with his knowledge that fifteen thousand had been captured and carried off within the last few weeks'. Like most of the other

13 The only other breeding stations of the solan goose in Scotland are the Bass Rock; Ailsa Craig; the small island of Suleskeir, or North Barra, ten miles west of Rona; and Stack of Suleskerry, about forty miles west of Stromness, in Orkney. The bird appears to have been recently driven away from certain parts of the Bass by the intrusion of visitors.

sea-fowl, the gannets are accompanied on their arrival by a considerable number of barren birds, which have no nests, and sit upon the bare rock, at a distance from their mated kinsfolk, with whom they do not interfere. It has been suggested that these separatists might be young birds; but Mr Wilson states that in the case of the solan geese this was proved not to be so, the plumage being that of the adult bird. Accordingly, the same author observes that they were probably 'bachelors and old maids!' Martin states that the solan goose—

equals a tame goose in bigness. It is by measure, from the tip of the bill to the extremity of the foot, thirty-four inches long, and to the end of the tail thirty-nine; the wings extended very long, there being seventy-two inches of distance betwixt the extreme tips. Its bill is long, straight, of a dark colour, a little crooked at the point; behind the eyes, the skin of the side of the head is bare of feathers; the ears of a mean size; the eyes hazel-coloured. It hath four toes; the feet and legs black as far as they are bare: the plumage is like that of a goose. The colour of the old ones is white all over, excepting the extreme tips of the wings, which are black, and the top of the head, which is yellow, as some think the effect of age.[14] The young ones are of a dark-brown colour, turning white after they are a year old. Its egg, somewhat less than that of a land goose, small at each end, casts a thick scurf, and has little or no yolk . . . The solan geese hatch by turns.

The name Solan is said by some to be a corruption of *Solent*, an old designation of the English Channel; while, according to others, the bird derives its name from the Gaelic word *sùler* (from *sùl*, an eye), which indicates sharpness of sight – *qui oculis irretorfis*

14 Gannets with black tails have been observed at St Kilda, but Mr Gray suggests that they may have been birds with the last of their immature plumage uneffaced. The solan does not assume its adult plumage till the third or fourth year.

e longinquo respicit praedam. He soars in midair, flying slowly up the wind, and balancing himself upon expanded wings till he sees his prey, on which he darts down with unerring precision and incredible force. The herring-fishers sometimes amuse themselves by fixing a fish upon a board sufficiently loaded to float a little below the surface of the sea. On observing the herring, the solan pounces down upon it with so much energy that he perforates the board with his bill, and falls an easy prey to the fishermen. The principal food of the solan goose consists of whiting, haddock, pilchard, mackerel, and herring.[15] Martin says that 'when it returns from its fishing, it carries along with it five or six herrings in its gorget, all entire and undigested, upon whose arrival at the nest, the hatching fowl puts its head in the fisher's throat, and pulls out the fish with its bill as with a pincer, and that with very great noise; which I had occasion frequently to observe.' The nest, which is strong and deep, is made of various materials – grass, turf, sorrel, branches, sea-weed, rags, shavings, etc. – whatever the old birds come across by land or by sea; and it is asserted that they never gather grass but on a windy day, which is the solan's 'vacation from fishing.' Martin states, on the authority of the steward of St Kilda, that a red coat had been found in one nest, and a brass sun-dial, an arrow, and some Molucca beans in another! Failing a supply of suitable materials, the solan does not hesitate, if he gets a chance, to steal from the nest of a neighbour; and the same author gives a graphic account of a 'bloody battle' between two gannets, consequent upon a transgression of the eighth commandment. According to Mr Gray, the flight of the St Kilda gannets cannot be much short of 200 miles in one day, without reckoning the

15 Lane Buchanan mentions that on the occasion of a voyage to St Kilda, the barge of the tacksman, sailing rapidly before the wind, passed over a fish so quickly that a gannet which had marked it for his prey rushed with such violence through the air that he sent his bill through the plank of the boat, instead of capturing the fish, and in that position was carried back to Harris. The same author refers to an Act of Parliament directed against the cruel practice in question, with 'a severe penalty against transgressors'; but I have hunted the statute-book in vain for the alleged enactment.

distance traversed while they are engaged in fishing; and he inclines to think that fatigue sometimes compels them to discontinue their journeys. They seldom fly over land, generally making a circuit when they meet with a promontory or island. As in the case of the garefowl, the place whence they come in spring, and whither they go in autumn, is not well known. They direct their course southwards, and are occasionally met with at the mouths of the Tagus and Guadiana.[16] The young solan, or *goug*, is fit for use in September, if the first egg is left untouched – otherwise, about a month later. As at the Bass, it is slaughtered by blows on the head with a stick. The flesh has a somewhat fishy flavour, but when baked makes a tolerably palatable dish.[17] Before the bird is able to fly it is larger than its mother, and excessively fat – a most precocious baby – the fat on the breast being sometimes as much as three inches deep. 'The inhabitants of Hirta', says Macaulay, 'have a method of preserving their grease in a kind of bag, made of the stomach of the old solan goose, caught in March. In their language it is called *gibain*; and this oily kind of thick substance, manufactured in their way, they use by way of sauce, or instead of butter, among their porridge and flummery.'[18]

The old solan geese are captured in the dark during the latter part of March. Macaulay gives the following account of the mode of procedure.

While the creeping fowlers hear them cry *grog, grog*, they continue to approach without any fear of alarming them; but as soon as they hear *bir, bir*, they halt.[19] If the fowls who were alarmed of the approaching danger are not able to discover the enemy, they give the signal of security, *grog, grog*; the fowlers then advance, and lay, with great caution, the first solan goose

16 See Gray p. 132.
17 '*Anseres Solanae quae mixto ex carne et pisce sapore, gulae mire adblandiuntur.*' – Sibbald's *Scotia Illustrata*, p. 46.
18 Oatmeal steeped in water till it turns sour.
19 Mr Sands makes the calls 'gorrok' and 'beero' respectively.

which they kill among his old companions: and the St Kildans [he adds] have given me repeated assurances that the living begin to mourn immediately over their departed friend, with a lamentable tone of voice, examining his body very narrowly with their bills, and are so deeply affected that the fowlers improve their sorrow and confusion much to their own advantage.

After giving the purport of this passage, Mr Sands states that it sometimes happens that the entire flock flies away with a 'Beero! hurro! boo!' when the fowlers have the mortification of crawling back without any victims.

Probably the most interesting of the existing sea-birds of St Kilda is the fulmar or fulmar-petrel,[20] which may almost be regarded as peculiar to that island and the adjacent rocks. According to Mr Gray, it formerly bred in the south isles of Barra, and perhaps also in Mull; and one of his correspondents recently informed him that its eggs are still to be obtained on a stack off the far-famed Talisker in Skye. It is seen pretty frequently in Orkney and Shetland, where, however, it is said never to breed. There can be no doubt that its headquarters have long been St Kilda, with which it is, in more than one respect, intimately associated. One of its favourite haunts in the group is the precipitous stack of Briorach, already referred to, lying between St Kilda and Soa. On the main island it generally selects a lofty position on the cliffs, and builds its nest on the grassy ledges. The fulmar is about as large as a middle-sized gull – or, as Martin expresses it, 'a mall of the second rate', – which it greatly resembles, except in the

---

20 According to some authorities, from *Fýl-már* (Norse) = 'the vomiting man' and 'foul man'. *Fýla* = *foetor, res rejectanea* (Haldorsen). See, however, page 26, note 2, *supra*. It has been called 'the skunk of birds'.

  The name petrel is said to have been given by certain devotees in allusion to the attempt of the Apostle Peter to walk upon the sea. 'Mother Carey's chicken' is the term usually applied by sailors to the storm petrel. Jamieson gives 'malduck' as a synonym of fulmar.

formation of the bill. From a stuffed specimen of a full-grown bird now before me, which I saw noosed on one of the cliffs, I may give the following description: the head, neck, breast and tail are of a dingy white colour; the back and wings (which are long) being slate-grey, and the latter tipped with black; head round, neck short and thick; bill large, strong, and sub-cylindrical, about an inch and a half in length, and of a pale-yellow colour; the upper mandible hooked at the point like that of the eagle, and the tip of the lower one curved upwards – the tips of both mandibles appearing as separate pieces firmly joined to the straight part of the bill, which is marked by longitudinal grooves; the nostrils enclosed in a tube open at the extremity, and extending along the ridge of the upper mandible; legs dark brown, and about three inches long; feet pretty broad, and of a paler colour than the legs, with sharp claws and a small hind toe.[21] Martin's engraving of the bird is about as like the original as the secretary-falcon, or serpent-eater, of South Africa. The egg, which is white, is rather larger than that of the solan goose, sharpish at one end and somewhat blunt at the other; shell thin and tender, being liable to break in a rainy season.

> When his egg is once taken away [says Martin] he lays no more for that year, as other fowls do both a second and third time. The young fowl is brought forth in the middle of June, and is ready to take wing before 20 July. He comes in November, a sure messenger of evil tidings, being always accompanied with boisterous west winds, great snow, rain, or hail, and is the only sea-fowl that stays here all the year round, except the month of September and part of October. The inhabitants prefer this, whether young or old, to all others. The old is of a delicate

---

21 Audubon's magnificent work on the *Birds of America* (vol. iv, plate 264) embraces an adult male fulmar in summer plumage. The head is represented as sunk down upon the neck, indicative of a recumbent position. The colour of the bill is bright yellow, and that of the legs and feet pale orange.

taste, being a mixture of fat and lean – the flesh white; no blood is to be found but only in his head and neck. The young is all fat, excepting the bones, having no blood but what is in his head.

The male and female hatch by turns for six weeks, and take the same period to nourish their progeny. The weight of the fulmar is from two to three pounds. Every family has from three to four barrels, each containing about 200 birds, salted for winter use. Martin further informs us that 'if the fulmar comes to land, there is no west wind to be expected for some time; but if he keeps at sea, or goes to sea from the land, whether the wind blow from the south, north, or east, or whether it is a perfect calm, his keeping the sea is always a certain presage of an approaching west wind'.

> Screaming from his nest
> The fulmar soared, and shot a westward flight
> From shore to sea.[22]

According to Macaulay, 'so exquisitely nice are his feelings, and so strong his resentment, that he conceives an unconquerable aversion for his nest if one breathes over it, and will never pay it any more visits: for this reason, to plunder his nest, or to offer indignity to it, is in Hirta a high crime and misdemeanour.'

With its long wings extended, its flight is easy and elegant – gliding as it does in graceful curves, and seldom moving a pinion – the Camilla of the ocean, like whom

> She sweeps the seas, and as she skims along,
> Her flying feet unbathed on billows hung.

On our return from St Kilda on 2 July, two or three fulmars followed the *Dunara* at least as far as the Sound of Harris, and I

---

22 'Amyntor and Theodora', i, 186.

thus had a good opportunity of watching their movements. The fulmar is extremely voracious, its principal food being fish; but it constantly attends upon whale-ships, in order to pick up any offal that is thrown overboard; and it follows, in flocks, the track of a wounded whale, alighting on the carcass for the purpose of devouring the blubber. Sailor boys often amuse themselves by catching attendant fulmars, by means of lines and hooks baited with fat.

Besides being highly esteemed by the islanders as food, the feathers and oil of the fulmar form, as already stated, two important articles of export. Beds made of the feathers are supposed never to harbour insects; but it is alleged that they are difficult to keep dry. Mr Gray gives a detailed statement relative to the oil, furnished to him by Mr Edward C. C. Stanford, FCS, from which it appears that

> when genuine, it is of a clear, dark, slightly reddish cherry colour, and has a powerful and peculiar odour – an odour of which the whole island and all the inhabitants smell. It is certainly a fish oil, and possesses nearly all the properties of cod-liver oil. Its specific gravity is midway between cod-liver and sperm—
>
> | | Specific gravity |
> | --- | --- |
> | Fulmar oil | .902 |
> | Cod-liver, light | .924 |
> | ” brown | .926 |
> | Sperm oil | .875 |

After indicating other chemical characteristics, Mr Stanford says: 'I shall be glad if this short notice of fulmar oil will induce any one to experiment with it for medicinal purposes. I have no doubt a good deal might be obtained, and a good market would be a boon to that isolated people.'

Fulmar-fowling begins on 12 August – an ominous day on the mainland to another noble bird – and lasts between two and three weeks. The fowlers are usually accompanied by a few of the younger women, some of whom can carry about 200 weight of birds. The oil is extracted from the stomachs of both the old and the young birds, and enclosed in long distended bags, formed of the stomachs of old solan geese. The receptacle is held open by one man, while another, squeezing the body of the fulmar, forces the oil through its gaping bill. It proves of great service to the islanders during the long-continued darkness of the winter nights. In order to obtain the oil, the fowler requires to seize and strangle the bird in a rapid manner, otherwise it is immediately squirted in his eyes, as a defensive movement; not, as is commonly supposed, through the tubular nostrils in the surface of the upper mandible, but through the throat and open mouth. Each fulmar contains about half a pint of oil.

The estimation in which the fulmar is held by the islanders may be gathered from the following words of a St Kildan, which are recorded in the pages of Macaulay: 'Can the world exhibit a more valuable commodity? The fulmar furnishes oil for the lamp, down for the bed, the most salubrious food, and the most efficacious ointments for healing wounds. Deprive us of the fulmar, and St Kilda is no more.' But we must also look at the other side of the picture. What says the worthy Sysselmand, the king's sheriff in Faroe, and deeply learned in fowl-lore? 'Thirty years ago, the fulmar knew his place: our fishers saw him out at sea 100 miles away, and only a stray bird now and then was driven hither by a heavy gale; but now he has set his ugly foot on my Holm of Myggenaes, and on the Goblin's Head of Sando, and every year he spreads further and further, and breeds in more places. Nasty, stinking beast! why, even his egg keeps its stench for years; his flesh no man can eat; and if you sleep on a bed on which even a handful of his feathers have been put by mistake, you will leave it long before morning: and yet this fellow thrusts his nose in among my gannets, and is slowly but surely driving them away . . . just as the Germans are overrunning Schleswig'!

The last as well as the least of the St Kilda sea-fowl to which I intend specially to refer, is the Puffin, Tammie Norrie, or Sea-parrot, a fat and consequential little bird, so well described by a writer in the *North British Review* (May 1864), as looking 'like a respectable butler at his master's door, in a black coat and white waistcoat, with a Roman nose red at the tip with many a bottle of port!' Probably greater numbers of this bird are annually captured by the islanders than of all the others put together. Mr Gray inclines to think that the puffin is the most abundant species of sea-fowl on the west of Scotland, from Cape Wrath to the Mull of Galloway, Ailsa Craig and St Kilda being two of its favourite haunts. In 1826, nearly 1,000 puffins were killed, for a wager, in a single day, by the powerful tacksman of Ailsa; and a few years ago, the number annually captured in Faroe was estimated at 235,000 – an experienced fowler slaughtering about 900 in one day. Mr Sands calculates that upwards of 89,000 puffins must have been killed by the St Kildans in 1876. 'The bougir of Hirta', says Macaulay, 'is by some called the coulterneb, and by others the puffin. This is a very fine sprightly bird, in size much like a pigeon: it seems to be conscious of its own beauty, cocking its head very smartly, and assuming great airs of majesty. Its colour is black on the outer parts, and about the breast red and white; the legs and feet are red (or rather orange), and the beak fashioned like a coulter, edged above, and most charmingly painted with red and yellow below.' The form of the bill is very peculiar, being of a triangular shape, short, broad, and very much compressed, the depth at the base about the same as its length – an approach, indeed, to an equilateral triangle – the ridge of the upper mandible as high as the top of the head, both mandibles being arched, and transversely grooved. Like its wings and tail, the puffin's legs are short and placed far back, in consequence of which arrangement the bird sits very erect, like the auk and penguin, resting on the tarsus as well as on the foot. Its flight is rapid, straight, and strong, though not long sustained; and its swimming and diving powers are very remarkable. It breeds in burrows of its own making, among stones and splintered rocks, somewhat similar to rabbit-holes, from which it is dislodged by dogs trained for the work. The shaggy coat of a Skye terrier is extremely serviceable for the purpose. The birds seize it with their powerful beaks, as the dog traverses the long passages; and an accomplished terrier has been seen to emerge from a burrow with half-a-dozen puffins dangling from different parts of his body! Like the solan and fulmar, the male and female puffins hatch by turns. The single egg which is laid is usually deposited, by way of protection, at the farthest extremity of the subterranean passage. Originally pure white, and mottled with ashy spots, it ultimately becomes very much soiled, and before the young bird is hatched, the shell assumes a dark-brown colour. The infant puffins are chiefly fed with sand-eels, which the old birds carry in their beaks in large numbers, and from great distances, hanging down on each side like a beard. The Faroe fowlers allege that an old puffin can carry as many as fifty sand-eels in his beak at once!

Had my space permitted, I should have liked to say a few words about some of the other sea-fowl of St Kilda – the guillemot,[23] the razor-bill, the cormorant, the shearwater, the stormpetrel and the kittiwake and other gulls; but 'the line has to be drawn somewhere', and the puffin must close my catalogue of feathered portraits, which an impatient reader may perhaps consider already too long. A history of St Kilda, however, without a notice of the birds, would have been the play without Hamlet. The mode in which they are captured by the hardy islanders will form the conclusion of the present chapter.

*   *   *

23 The term 'foolish' is applied to one species of guillemot, from the circumstance of its suffering itself to be taken by the hand rather than leave its breeding-place. According to Mr Morgan, it is usually captured at St Kilda in the following manner: 'A man with a white cloth about his neck is let down from the summit of the crags at night, and hangs, like the weight of a clock, immediately before the nests. The birds, attracted by the bright colour, mistake the intruder for a projecting portion of rock, and settle upon him in great numbers, a freedom which the cragsman resents by quietly dislocating their necks. In this manner, three or four hundred are sometimes taken by a single fowler in the course of a night.'

Fowling, as we have already seen, is the principal avocation of the St Kildans; and the great ambition of every male on the island is to excel as a cragsman. In the words of the Lord Register Mackenzie, 'the exercise they affect most is climbing of steep rocks. He is the prettiest[24] man who ventures upon the most inaccessible, though all they gain is the eggs of the fowls, and the honour to dye, as many of their ancestors, by breaking of their necks.' According to the 'Apostle of the North', 'the impulsive Celt likes the excitement of an occasional risk, rather than the monotony of safe and continuous employment.' Nearly all the published accounts of St Kilda refer to the feats of the fowlers, and the various modes in which they prosecute their hazardous calling. Probably the earliest notice of the cragsmen is embraced in the paper communicated by Sir Robert Moray to the Royal Society exactly 200 years ago, in which he describes the dangers connected with the capture of sea-fowl by the 'men of Hirta' on the apparently inaccessible Stacca Donna.

> After they have landed [he says] with much difficulty, a man having room but for one of his feet, he must climb up twelve or sixteen fathoms high. Then he comes to a place where, having but room for his left foot and left hand, he must leap from thence to such another place before him, which, if he hit right, the rest of the ascent is easie; and with a small cord, which he carries with him, he hales [hauls] up a rope, whereby all the rest come up. But if he misseth that footstep (as oftentimes they do), he falls into the sea, and the company takes him in by the small cord, and he sits still until he be a little refreshed, and then he tries it again; for every one there is not able for that sport.

Both Martin and Macaulay furnish curious details respecting the ropes formerly used by the cragsmen. In Martin's time, there appear to have been only three ropes in the whole island – the

---

24 That is, bravest or most intrepid – so applied in *Rob Roy*.

property of 'the commonwealth' – each being twenty-four fathoms in length; and these were either tied together or used separately, according to circumstances.

> The chief thing upon which the strength of these ropes depends is cows' hides, salted and cut out in one long piece; this they twist round the ordinary rope of hemp, which secures it from being cut by the rocks. They join sometimes at the lower end two ropes, one of which they tie round the middle of one climber, and another about the middle of another, that these may assist one another in case of a fall; but the misfortune is that sometimes the one happens to pull down the other, and so both fall into the sea; but if they escape (as they do commonly of late), they get an incredible number of eggs and fowls . . . They catch their fowls with gins made of horse-hair; these are tied to the end of their fishing-rods, with which the fowlers creep through the rocks indiscernibly, putting the noose over their heads about their necks, and so draw them instantly. They use likewise hair-gins, which they set upon plain rocks, both the ends fastened by a stone.

He then proceeds to describe the wonderful dexterity of the fowlers, which he himself witnessed, and refers to the early initiation of the young men of St Kilda in the dangers of the cliffs. 'The young boys', he says, 'of three years old begin to climb the walls of their houses; their frequent discourses of climbing, together with the fatal end of several in the exercise of it, is the same to them as that of fighting and killing is with soldiers, and so is become as familiar and less formidable to them than otherwise certainly it would be.' Macaulay's description of the ropes is more minute than that of Martin. He states that each party of fowlers, which usually consists of four skilful and agile men, possesses at least one rope, about thirty fathoms long, 'made of a strong, raw cow-hide, salted for that very purpose, and cut circularly into three thongs, all of equal length. These thongs being closely twisted together, form a threefold cord, able to sustain a great weight, and durable enough to last for about two generations.' To prevent injury from friction on the rocks, the cord was lined with sheepskin. 'In the testament of a father, it constitutes the very first article in favour of his eldest son; should it happen to fall to a daughter's share, in default of male heirs, it is reckoned equal in value to the two best cows in the isle.' He elsewhere mentions a less costly rope made of horse-hair, nine or ten fathoms in length, which they use in more accessible places. 'Linked together in couples, each having either end of the cord fastened about his waist, they go frequently through the most dreadful precipices. When one of the two descends, his colleague plants himself on a strong shelf, and takes care to have such sure footing there, that if his fellow-adventurer makes a false step and tumbles over, he may be able to save him.' Like Martin, Macaulay describes, what he saw with his own eyes, the performance of two noted cragsmen.

> One of them fixed himself on a craggy shelf; his companion went down sixty fathoms below him, and after having darted himself away from the face of a most alarming precipice, hanging over the ocean, he began to play his gambols. He sung merrily and laughed very heartily . . . The fowler, after having performed several antic tricks, and given us all the entertainment his art could afford, returned in triumph and full of his own merit, with a large string of fowls round his neck, and a number of eggs in his bosom.

As in the moral world (where every schoolboy knows something about a certain *facilis descensus*), the ascent of the cliffs, which is occasionally unavoidable, is more difficult than the converse process. This is effected by fastening a rope to two cragsmen, who ascend by turns. In the event of the foremost slipping his foot, he falls only the length of his cable-tow, his fellow usually breaking the fall. Sometimes loose stones are dislodged by the feet of the uppermost fowler, and the rope is apt to be cut or weakened by the sharp edge of the rock, giving way under the weight of the man below. At other times, the strain of the rope is relieved when the lower cragsman happens to reach a grassy resting-place; and if the turf gives way before he has time to warn his comrade, he falls into the yawning abyss, dragging the other along with him.

Mr Wilson gives a very graphic account of the performances of the St Kilda cragsmen as witnessed from a boat. After the minister (Mr McKenzie) had made a preconcerted signal,

> three or four men [he says] from different parts of the cliff, threw themselves into the air, and darted some distance downwards, just as spiders drop from the top of a wall. They then swung and capered along the face of the precipice, bounding off at intervals by striking their feet against it, and springing from side to side with as much fearless ease and agility as if they were so many schoolboys exercising in a swing a few feet over a soft and balmy clover field. Now they were probably not less than seven hundred feet above the sea . . . A great mass of the central portion of the precipice was smoother than the wall of a well-built house . . . so that any one falling from the summit would drop at once sheer into the sea . . . We could perceive that the cragsmen, having each a rope securely looped beneath their arms, rested occasionally upon their toes, or even crawled, with a spider-like motion, along projecting ledges; and ever and anon we could see them waving a small white fluttering object, which we might have taken for a pocket handkerchief, had we not been told it was a feathery fulmar.

He states that the cragsmen usually work in couples, each of whom has, as it were, two ropes between them. 'One man', he adds, 'stands on the verge of the precipice, and the rope which he holds in his hands is fastened round the body and beneath the arms of him who descends, while another rope is pressed by the foot of the upper man, and is held in the hand of the lower . . . It is said that scarcely more than one or two accidents have happened within the memory of the present generation.' Mr Wilson was told that on one occasion two men had descended close together, suspended by the same rope, when suddenly the higher of the two perceived that several strands above his head had given way, and that the rope was rapidly rending from the unaccustomed weight. Believing the death of both to be inevitable if he delayed an instant, and with but small hope even of his own life under existing circumstances, he cut the cord close beneath his own body, and consigning his companion to immediate death, was himself drawn to the crest of the precipice just in time to be seized by the neck as the rope gave way.[25] Speaking of the boldness of the St Kilda fowler, Mr Morgan says:

> Not content with the mere routine discharge of his calling, he swings and careers down the cliff like a plaything jerked by an elastic cord. Sometimes when the portion of the crag to be visited lies within the perpendicular – that is, under that portion of the rock from which his comrade tightly grasps the oft tried cord – he strikes out from the cliff with the steady sweep of a pendulum, the impetus landing him at the wished-for ledge. About the age of twelve or fourteen, they first essay the cliffs, no unimportant day to a St Kilda youth. During the last thirty years, five men have, in the language of the island, 'gone over the rocks'. In these words are registered the deaths of the daring spirits who fall victims to the dangers of their calling. Their bodies are seldom, if ever, recovered, being ruthlessly engulfed by the voracious deep.

On the occasion of my visit to St Kilda in July, one of the principal features in the programme was, of course, a practical display of the prowess of the cragsmen. The minister having made suitable

---

25 A nice question in casuistry, which will probably remind some readers of the dastardly conduct of one of the Zermatt guides while ascending the Matterhorn, with a party of travellers, about ten years ago.

arrangements with some of the most experienced fowlers in the island, we ascended to the summit of the cliff, which commands a magnificent view of Borrera and the adjacent stacks – a pretty stiff pull of fully half an hour – and from the verge of the precipice looked down a sheer descent of some eight hundred feet upon the heaving rollers of the Atlantic. Furnished with the requisite ropes and other appliances, four or five of the cragsmen approached the edge of the cliff. One of the most agile of the party – a vigorous, bright-eyed islander of about thirty years of age – taking one rope[26] in his hand, in order to steady his movements, and having another firmly secured round his waist, was gradually lowered down the perpendicular face of the precipice by two of his comrades. Uttering a shrill Gaelic cry, he descended barefooted,[27] skipping and singing as he went, and occasionally standing out nearly at a right angle from the beetling cliff! Arrived at the narrow rocky ledges where the fulmar and puffin sit in supposed security, a long stick, resembling a fishing-rod, with a noose at the extremity, was let down to him from above, which he cautiously extended, making the noose fall rapidly over the head of the bird, the fluttering victim being immediately captured. Several fulmars and puffins were thus secured for different members of our party, one of the former – of which an accurate representation is given – being now in my possession. It is difficult, by means of verbal narration, to convey anything like an adequate idea of the sensation produced by the wonderful performance which I have endeavoured to describe; but with the aid of Mr Carlyle Bell's clever illustration, some slight notion may perhaps be formed. To

26 The ropes at present in use are of Manilla hemp. Very recently they were formed of tightly-twisted horse-hair, enclosed, as in Martin's time, within cases of salted cows' hide. They were handed down as heirlooms, and sometimes given as a dowry to a favourite daughter.

27 The object of going without shoes or stockings is to secure a better footing on the face of the rock, which the bare sole contrives, in the expressive language of the Leslie motto, 'to grip fast'. The great toes of the cragsmen are widely separated from the others, from the circumstance of their frequently resting their entire weight on that part of the foot in climbing.

any one who has witnessed the daring procedure of the St Kilda cragsman, the most startling feats of a Blondin or a Leotard appear utterly insignificant; and if the most venturesome member of the Alpine Club had been of our party, I feel satisfied that he would have been compelled to 'hide his diminished head'! Some sensitive people are quite unable to contemplate the fowler's miraculous movements; and even in the case of the most callous spectator, the blood inclines to run cold, and for once in his life he discovers that he is possessed of a nervous system.

The exploits of the cragsmen on the cliffs of Borrera and Soa and adjacent stacks are, if possible, even more astonishing than their performances on the main island. Stack Briorach, the pointed rock between Soa and St Kilda, is regarded as the crucial test of a fowler's pluck. Here the rope is of no avail, and the rock can only be climbed after the fashion of the celebrated 'steeple-Jack', lately gone to his rest. The man who fails to accomplish the ascent never gets a wife in St Kilda. Only two of the islanders achieved the feat during the first eight years of Mr McKenzie's incumbency – the inducement being a quid of tobacco presented by an English visitor! The minister, who was present, described the undertaking as 'fearful'. When the fowlers reached the summit of the stack, they committed great havoc among the unsuspecting fulmars, tying them in large bundles, and flinging them into the sea, which was crimsoned with blood, 'as if the second angel had sounded'! Macaulay gives an account of the mode in which the fowlers formerly carried out their expeditions to Briorach and the other stacks. When the weather was favourable, they manned a boat with eight of their most skilful hands – the factor's deputy, who on such occasions acted as captain, under the local designation of *gingach*, being the first to land and the last to quit the rock. His description of the procedure is very similar to that already quoted from Sir Robert Moray's communication to the Royal Society, but somewhat fuller in its details.

The exciting sport of bird-catching is not confined to the male sex. Like the maids of ancient Sparta, the young women of St

Kilda employ themselves in fowling, their hunting expeditions being chiefly directed against the puffins. Mr Sands accompanied a detachment of seven vigorous girls to Borrera, returning to St Kilda with the men of the party, while the women remained on the islet for a period of three weeks. After two or three of the men had landed, as already explained, 'the girls in succession jumped into the arms of the man at the foot of the cliff, who lifted them on the slope, where, by the help of the rope, they attained a level spot.' Laden with their stores, they then fearlessly ascended by a hazardous route to a height of some 500 feet, where they reached a sort of terrace, on which were a number of the *cleits*, or pyramids, already referred to. After a few minutes' rest, the damsels proceeded vigorously to business, and with the aid of their sagacious and well-trained dogs, soon secured a considerable number of birds. They also set snares, by means of which each girl bags several hundreds in a single day. Mr Sands was informed that their place of abode, during their temporary sojourn in the islet, was an old hut 'across the hill', which he conjectures to be the hermitage of Stallir, described by Martin and Macaulay, and to be afterwards referred to.

The eggs of the different sea-fowl constitute an important article in the diet of the St Kildans. Martin mentions that he had the curiosity to make a 'calcule' of the number of eggs bestowed upon his party during a three weeks' residence on the island, and he came to the conclusion that they amounted to 16,000. 'Without all doubt,' he adds, 'the inhabitants, who were triple our number, consumed many more eggs than we could.'[28] He elsewhere states that he has seen the natives bring home, in a single morning, twenty-nine baskets full of eggs, the least of them containing 400 large eggs, and the others 800 and upwards of smaller ones. He refers to the astringent quality of the eggs, and the effect produced upon some members of his party, in the shape

28 From a statement at p. 79 of his entertaining *Voyage*, it would appear that Martin's party embraced as many as seventy persons.

of swollen veins, by a too abundant consumption of them. Dr Macdonald, in one of his *Journals*, also alludes to the large quantity of eggs collected by the islanders. 'The eggs of the solan geese', he says, 'resembling those of our common country geese, eat well; but those of a small black bird called by the natives the *bougir* (puffin), resembling in size and taste our hen eggs, relish most of any I have eaten on the island.'

The following are a few of the many anecdotes that have been preserved in illustration of the dangers connected with fowling. On one occasion, the rope having given way, a young cragsman, the only support of a widowed mother, fell down a depth of several fathoms, lighting upon a grassy shelf, where unfortunately no assistance could be rendered. All that his friends could do was to approach as near as possible with a boat and comfort him by words at a distance. On the evening of the third day, parched with thirst, and starving with hunger, he became deranged, and was heard chanting a simple native song, till death sealed his lips. On another occasion, a father and son happened to descend by a single rope. When they were being drawn up, the son observed that a sharp rock had nearly cut through the rope, but he came to the conclusion that it was still capable of bearing the weight of one of them. On hearing this, the father urged his son to avail himself of it, as *he* was old and of comparatively little use in the world. The son burst into tears, and urged his father to ascend. With great reluctance he yielded, and reached the summit of the cliff in safety. On the son trying the rope after him, it gave way, as was expected, and the anxious father saw his son mangled by the projecting rocks, before he had reached the yawning gulf below.[29] Martin gives an account, on the authority of the natives,

29 According to another version of this anecdote, the party consisted of a father and *two* sons, but the details of the narrative are somewhat confused and unintelligible.

A very graphic account of the manner in which fowling is conducted in the Faroe Islands will be found in the article in the *North British Review* for May 1864, to which I have already referred. The appliances used by the Faroe cragsmen appear to be of a more elaborate and safer character than those of St Kilda. The second volume of

of an 'extraordinary risque' which one of them incurred while engaged in setting his gins. Walking barefoot along the rock where he had fixed a gin, he happened to put his toe in the noose, and fell over the rock, where he hung by the toe for a whole night, twenty fathoms above the ocean, the gin proving strong enough to support him. One of his comrades hearing his cry for assistance, came to the rescue, and drew him up to the summit of the cliff!

Pontoppidan's *Natural History of Norway* contains an interesting chapter relative to birds and fowling, from which it appears that there was a law in that country in former times, that when the body of any one killed on the rocks was found, his nearest relation was required to go the same way. If, however, he could not do so, or declined to venture, the deceased was not allowed a Christian burial, and was treated as a criminal who had been his own executioner; but the law is no longer in force.

Diseases of the Islanders

With the view of obtaining the most authentic information on the subject of the diseases of the St Kildans, I have analysed the causes of death and other relative particulars in the register kept by the Rev. Neil McKenzie during his residence on the island (1830–44), now in the custody of the Registrar General; also the duplicate registers of deaths in St Kilda, pertaining to the fifteen years ending 1870, kept under the provisions of Lord Elcho's important statute, and the returns subsequently transmitted by the registrar to Edinburgh up to the end of 1876 – embracing in all a period of about thirty-four years, if we deduct the interval between the close of Mr McKenzie's record and the commencement of the new system of registration. My attention has been called to an interesting article on the 'Diseases of St Kilda' by Mr John E. Morgan, already referred to, in the *British and Foreign Medico-Chirurgical Review* for January 1862. Mr Morgan, who is a member of the Royal College of Physicians, Manchester, appears to have made a partial analysis somewhat similar to my own; and I shall avail myself of some of the opinions and conjectures which his paper contains.

From a note prefixed to Mr McKenzie's register, it appears that he went to St Kilda on 3 July, 1830, as a missionary from the Society for Propagating Christian Knowledge – and finding that no record was kept of baptisms, marriages and deaths, he determined to supply the omission while he remained on the island. He was translated to Duror, in Appin, in 1844, visited St Kilda in 1845, and again in 1847, and is now minister of the parish of Kilchrenan, in

Argyllshire. The register in question embraces seventy-two baptisms between 4 July, 1830 and 18 July, 1851; twenty-two marriages between 20 August, 1830 and 10 July, 1849; and sixty-eight deaths between 18 July, 1830 and 31 October, 1846. Three of the deaths, as well as a few of the baptisms and marriages, occurred after Mr McKenzie's departure in 1844. The following table exhibits the comparative mortality of the two sexes from the various causes specified by Mr McKenzie.

CAUSES OF DEATH

	Males	Females	Total
'Eight-day sickness',	23	9	32
'So called, because the children which are seized with it are generally so on the 8th or 9th day. They die in a day or two afterwards.'			
Dysentery (M 50 and 60 years – F 30, 35, 45, 50 and 70 years)	2	5	7
Cold (M. 'an infant,' ★9, 22, ★62 years, and ★1 age not stated – F 30 years)	5	1	6
In the cases indicated by an asterisk, 'boat cough' in addition to cold. In the case of the female, 'cold after child-birth'.			
Dropsy (both 65 years)	1	1	2
Liver complaint (M 61 – F 55)	1	1	2
'Green-sickness',[1] (25 and 34 years)	. . .	2	2
Chincough (twins – 6 weeks)	. . .	2	2
Consumption (70 years)	. . .	1	1
Cancer (*c.* 45 years)	1	. . .	1
Inflammation (50 years)	1	. . .	1
Nervous disorder (65 years)	. . .	1	1
Teething (2¼ years)	. . ..	1	1
Child-bed (age not stated)	. . .	1	1

1 This disease, known to the medical faculty as *chlorosis* (from the Greek word signifying green), chiefly affects females, and is characterised, among other symptoms, by a pale lurid complexion. Shakespeare. however, in his Antony and Cleopatra (Act III, sc. 2), assigns it to one of the sterner sex:

Octavia weeps
To part from Rome; Caesar is sad; and Lepidus,
Since Pompey's feast, as Menas says, is troubled
With the green-sickness.

Fall over rocks (2 adults, of whom one 25 years, the age of the other not being stated)	2 ...	2
'Suddenly in the fields' (60 years)	... 1	1
Still-born	2 1	3
Cause not specified (2 M infants and 1 F 75 years)	2 1	3
	<u>39</u> <u>29</u>	<u>68</u>

[Total infantile mortality, including the 2 chincough cases = 37: 26 males and 11 females.]

My next table illustrates the comparative mortality of the two sexes with respect to age in the same sixty-eight cases.

AGES AT DEATH

	Males	Females	Total
'Eight-day sickness' (No. of days not stated)	23	9	32
'An infant'	1	...	1
Six weeks	...	2	2
2¼ years	...	1	1
9 "	1	...	1
22 "	1	...	1
25 "	1	1	2
30 "	...	2	2
34 "	...	1	1
35 "	...	1	1
45 "	...	2	2
50 "	2	1	3
55 "	...	1	1
60 "	1	1	2
61 "	1	...	1
62 "	1	...	1
65 "	1	2	3
70 "	...	2	2
75 "	...	1	1
'Still-born'	2	1	3
Age not stated	<u>4</u>	<u>1</u>	<u>5</u>
	39	29	68

Shortly after the passing of the Scottish Registration Act, the Registrar-General suggested to Mr Macleod – afterwards Sir John Macpherson Macleod, KCSI – the proprietor of St Kilda, the expediency of having a registrar appointed in the island; and both that gentleman and his factor, Mr Norman McRaild, entered very cordially into the proposal. Accordingly, in the year 1856, St Kilda was formally constituted a registration district by the sheriff, on the application of Mr Macleod, as sole heritor; and Mr Duncan Kennedy, then Free Church catechist in the island, was appointed to the post of registrar. He left St Kilda about the middle of the year 1863, and was succeeded in the office by the Rev. A. Cameron, who took up his abode in the island in the month of September following. About two years later (October 1865), the Rev. John McKay supplied the place of Mr Cameron, and now acts as registrar. In one of his letters to the Registrar-General, Mr McRaild mentions that St Kilda is 'not overlooked'[2] by the poor-law authorities of the parish of Harris, to which it belongs – adding, however, that 'meantime the proprietor directs me to make up the want of the inhabitants'.

Owing to the limited population and the rarity of communication with the island, an arrangement was made, in terms of which the duplicate registers of births, deaths and marriages in St Kilda should be transmitted to the central office every ten years, instead of annually, as in the case of other districts.[3] Accordingly, when the census of St Kilda was taken by Mr Grigor, as examiner of the district embracing the Hebrides, in the summers of 1862 and 1871, he collated the registers for the five and ten preceding years respectively, and transmitted the duplicates to the Registrar-General. Since 1871, as already indicated, the registrar has made

2 A somewhat Delphic expression, but intended to signify looked after or supervised. The English language contains more than one example of words with ambiguous meanings. A Frenchman once happened to pop his head out of the cabin window of an English steamer, on hearing a jolly tar shout 'Look out!' from the deck – the consequence being that he received an avalanche of dirty water on his head. 'Keep in!' would have been more intelligible to the unfortunate *voyageur*.

3 The duplicate registers are annually transmitted from all the districts in Scotland – upwards of 1,000 in number – except St Kilda, Fair Isle and Foula. In the case of the two Shetland Islands, they are transmitted every five years.

periodical returns of the births, deaths, and marriages. During the twenty-one years ended 31 December, 1876, the births amounted to fifty-six (thirty-two males and twenty-four females), and the deaths to sixty-four (thirty-seven females and twenty-seven males), being at the rate of rather more than two and a half births and three deaths annually. Of the fifty-six births, three were illegitimate, in the years 1862, 1864 and 1876 respectively, the last being an adulterous case.

The causes of death and the ages of the deceased are stated below. The seven deaths by drowning occurred 3rd April 1863, at the loss of the *Dargavel*, already referred to. The death of one of the males who perished on the occasion does not appear to have been registered. It will be observed that the total infantile mortality amounted to forty-one – twenty-six males and fifteen females.

I – CAUSES

	Males	Fem.	Tot.
1. Lockjaw (all children, except one of the females, 25 years old)	13	2	15
2. Tetanus (34 years)	0	1	1
3. Asthma (44 and 83 years)	0	2	2
4. Colic (the female 6 days old)	1	1	2
5. Quinsy (27 years)	1	0	1
6. Consumption (75 years)	0	1	1
7. Pleurisy (6 days)	0	1	1
8. Influenza (88 years)	0	1	1
9. Swelling in the belly (12 days)	1	0	1
10. Cold (20 days)	1	0	1
11. Old age (84 and 86 years)	0	2	2
12. Dropped down suddenly (54 years)	0	1	1
13. Fall over precipice (18 and 27 years)	2	0	2
14. Drowned (from 21 to 46 years)	6	1	7
15. 'Unknown' (all children, except 3 of the females)	6	12	18
16. Not specified (all children, except 1 of the males)	6	2	8
	37	27	64

Note. – The two females under Nos. 4 and 7, the two males under Nos. 9 and 10, and all the children (22) under Nos. 15 and 16, might probably be tabulated under 'Lockjaw' or 'Eight-day Sickness'.

II – AGES

1. Children				2. Adults			
Days	M	F	Total	Years	M	F	Total
4	0	1	1	18	1	0	1
5	1	1	2	21	1	0	1
6	0	3	3	22	1	0	1
7	5	1	6	24	2	0	2
8	5	4	9	25	0	1	1
9	4	3	7	26	0	1	1
10	2	0	2	27	3	0	3
11	1	0	1	28	1	1	2
12	3	0	3	34	0	1	1
13	1	0	1	44	0	1	1
14	2	0	2	45	0	1	1
16	0	1	1	46	1	0	1
17	0	1	1	54	0	1	1
20	1	0	1	63	1	0	1
22	1	0	1	75	0	1	1
				83	0	1	1
	26	15	41	84	0	1	1
				86	0	1	1
				88	0	1	1
					11	12	23

	M	F	Total
Children	26	15	41
Adults	11	12	23
Total	37	27	64

From these tables it will be seen that in a total mortality of 132, the infantile mortality, during the two periods of sixteen and twenty-one collectively, amounted to seventy-six cases, of which no fewer than fifty-two – or more than double – were males, the remaining twenty-four being females. Of the seventy-six deaths, thirty-five occurred during the sixteen years ended 1846, and forty-one during the twenty-one years ended 1876. Taking the population of the island in 1841 (105) as the basis of comparison for the mortality of the earlier period, and the population of 1871 (71) as that for the later period, it would appear that the infantile mortality was less during the earlier than during the later period, being in the one case at the annual rate of rather more than 2 per cent (2.08), and in the other exactly 2¾ per cent (2.75), or 208 and 275 deaths respectively in a population of 10,000. During the thirty-seven years in question, the number of deaths from eight-day sickness has been remarkably equal – viz, a fraction above two deaths annually, ranging from a minimum of one to a maximum of four.

During the same period, the deaths of four young men are attributed to 'fall over rocks', and three deaths (all males) are assigned, in Mr McKenzie's register, to 'boat cough', to which, as well as to some of the other causes specified in the tables, reference will afterwards be made.

In St Kilda, as elsewhere, it may be reasonably concluded that the health of the inhabitants is more or less affected by the character of their climate, habits, and occupations, and the nature of their food and condition of their dwellings; and, at least in the case of the most prevalent diseases, it certainly appears that one or more of these circumstances exercise no inconsiderable influence. Probably the most remarkable of the St Kilda diseases is the 'eight-day sickness', or infantile lockjaw (*trismus nascentium*), known in some parts of Ireland under the name of '*nine*-day fits'. It receives its English name from the circumstance of its victims being usually attacked on the eighth or ninth day after birth; but, as shown in one of the preceding tables, the fatal issue occurs as early as the fourth day, and as late as the twenty-second day, after birth. This disease is not referred to by Martin, but it is distinctly mentioned by Macaulay, who states that 'the St Kilda infants are peculiarly subject to an extraordinary kind of sickness. On the fourth or fifth day after their birth, many of them give up sucking; on the seventh their gums are so clenched together that it is impossible to get anything down their throats. Soon after this symptom appears, they are seized with convulsive fits, and, after struggling against excessive torments till their strength is exhausted, die generally on the eighth day.' Mr Morgan refers to the evidence of the 'nurse of the isles-women', who herself lost twelve out of fourteen children born alive. In these, and in all the other fatal cases which she had known during a period of thirty years, the children were all 'proper bairns' up to the fifth or sixth day after birth. The same writer describes the various symptoms in detail, directing special attention to the relaxed condition of the jaw. The nurse informed him that when once the jaw falls, all hope is lost – adding, 'I have never seen a child come round when that happened.'

In the fifth volume of the *British and Foreign Medico-Chirurgical Review* we are told, on the authority of a gentleman who visited St Kilda in 1838, that the disease proves fatal to eight out of every ten children born alive. Mr McRaild, the factor for the late proprietor, in a letter addressed to the Registrar-General, gives an even higher proportion – viz, *nine* out of ten. According to Mr Morgan's calculations, on the other hand, the deaths from *trismus* since 1830 have only amounted to five out of nine – the disease proving fatal, in the great majority of cases, between the fifth and tenth day after birth. This mortality, however, is said to be far exceeded in the Westmann Islands, off the coast of Iceland. In the appendix to Sir George Mackenzie's *Travels in Iceland* it is stated, on the authority of Sir Henry Holland, with reference to Heimacy, one of the group, that the population, then amounting to less than 200, was 'almost entirely supported by emigration from the mainland, scarcely a single instance having been known, during the twenty years preceding his visit, of a child surviving the period of infancy'. In a relative table, he shows that out of 185 deaths, seventy-five took place on the seventh day, twenty-two on the sixth, eighteen on the ninth, and sixteen on the fifth and eighth – the second and twenty-first days being the earliest and latest respectively on which the disease terminated fatally. Dr Arthur Mitchell,[4] on the other hand, asserts,

4 'On Consanguineous Marriages', *Edinburgh Medical Journal*, 1865.

that while the Westmann mortality from *trismus*, over a period of twenty years, amounted to 64 per cent, that of St Kilda was more than 3 per cent higher. 'Out of 125 children,' he says, 'the offspring of the fourteen married couples residing on the island in 1860, no less than eighty-four died within the first fourteen days of life, or, in other words, 67.2 per cent . . . The pestilential lanes of our great cities present no picture so dark as this. It is doubtful if it is anywhere surpassed, unless in some of the foundling hospitals of the Continent.' One of the remarkable results of this abnormal infant mortality, referred to by Dr Mitchell, is the increased fecundity of the mothers. 'One woman in St Kilda, at the age of thirty, has given birth to eight children, of whom two live; while two others have borne fourteen each, or twenty-eight in all, of whom twenty-four are in their graves.' The absence of children about the cottages of the remote island has struck many visitors – a circumstance which naturally recalls the old Gaelic saying that 'a house without the cry of bairns is like a farm without kye or sheep'.

Being aware that a disease called '*five*-nights' sickness', somewhat similar to *trismus*, was believed to prevail in the parishes of Barvas and Uig, on the west coast of Lewis – the former being about eighty, and the latter about sixty miles distant from St Kilda – I have prepared the following tabular statement from the registers of deaths pertaining to these two parishes, for the six years ended 1874. Crediting all the juvenile deaths in the table to *trismus*, it appears that out of the 446 deaths which occurred in Barvas during the six years in question, they only amounted to fifty-one, or at the annual rate of 0.171 per cent of the population as at 1871; while in Uig, during the same period, in a total mortality of 169, they amounted to only sixteen, or 0.124 per cent, or seventeen and twelve deaths respectively in a population of 10,000 – in both cases, a very different proportion from that which is exhibited by the registers of St Kilda.

| Year | Total deaths | Between 1 and 28 days, both inclusive, of which 9 one hour and under | | | Registered causes |
		M	F	Tot.	
Barvas					
1869	80	5	1	6	`Unknown', no medical attendant
1870	91	3	4	7	”　　　　”
1871	62	7	8	15	”　　　　”
1872	71	4	2	6	”　　　　”
1873	69	3	7	10	”　　　” (5); croup (4); bronchitis (1) – *certified*
1874	73[a]	4	3	7	”　　　” (6); croup (1)
	446	26	25	51	[Population of Barvas in 1871 = 4950]
Uig					
1869	35	2	1	3	`Lockjaw', – not certified
1870	24	5	1	6	”　　　” (5); influenza (1) – not certified
1871	33	1	2	3	`Lockjaw', croup, and influenza – no medical attendant
1872	31	1	2	3	`Lockjaw' (2), 'unknown' (1) – no medical attendant
1873	20	1	0	1	`Lockjaw' – no medical attendant
1874	26	0	0	0	
	169	10	6	16	[Population of Uig in 1871 = 2159[b]]

a Exclusive of 19 cases of drowning by the wreck of a ship.
b The population here given is that of the registration district of Uig, that of the entire parish (which is partly in two other districts) being 3,143.

For the purpose of further comparison, I annex another table, showing the number of children under three months of age who died from tetanus[5] in Scotland and its five groups of districts during each of the three years ended 1873.[6] It is questionable

5 *Tetanus* (from τειγνω, 'I stretch') involves a contraction of the muscles, and bears a strong resemblance to *trismus* (from τριδω, 'I gnash the teeth').
6 The Registrar-General's detailed report for the year 1873 is the latest that has been published.

whether any useful conclusions can be drawn from the figures, beyond the general fact that the proportion of these deaths was very much larger in the insular districts than in the rest of Scotland. During the three years in question, the total number of infantile deaths from tetanus appears to have been forty-eight, of which eleven occurred in the insular districts, with an estimated population of 131,418. If the mortality had been in the same proportion in the rest of Scotland, with a population of 3,267,807, instead of thirty-seven deaths, as indicated in the table, there would have been no fewer than 273.

Groups of Districts	Population estimated to mid. of 1872	1871			1872			1873		
		M	F	Tot.	M	F	Tot.	M	F	Tot.
Principal towns	1,094,061	4	2	6	3	0	3	2	1	3
Large towns	342,611	0	0	0	3	2	5	2	1	3
Small towns	783,599	2	0	2	0	1	1	1	0	1
Mainland (rural)	1,047,536	3	1	4	1	2	3	3	3	6
Insular (rural)	131,418	2	1	3	2	2	4	4	0	4
Scotland	3,399,225	11	4	15	9	7	16	12	5	17

As to the cause of this remarkable disease in St Kilda, various explanations have been offered. According to some, the excessive mortality arises from the mismanagement of the umbilical cord at birth, while others consider that it is produced by the infants being exposed to sudden alternations of temperature. We have already seen, however, that the climate of St Kilda is remarkably mild and equable; and Mr Morgan informs us that the treatment of new-born children is precisely the same as that which is followed on the west coast generally. But he is very much inclined to think that the chief cause of the mortality is a vitiated atmosphere dependent on deficient ventilation; and he asserts, moreover, that imperfect ventilation is a condition which exists in other places where the disease prevails. Although externally very similar to ordinary huts in all parts of the Scottish Highlands, the former houses of St Kilda were in some respects essentially different. In almost every instance, there was no hole in the roof for the escape of smoke; and the walls, instead of being constructed of unhewn stones loosely piled together, and more or less pervious to the atmosphere, consisted, as already explained, of a double stone dyke, separated by an interval of eighteen or twenty inches, which was completely filled with closely-packed layers of sod, with a view to the indoor manufacture of soot, which they use as a manure. Within these rude fabrics the inmates may be said to have been hermetically sealed, and their unfortunate infants were thus debarred from the invigorating influences of the purest air in this quarter of the globe. The very unsatisfactory condition of the former cottages of St Kilda is referred to in the report on the census of 1851, where it is stated that, through the ignorance of the inhabitants, they are 'dirtier than the dens of wild animals'. In a letter which he contributed to the *Scotsman* in August 1875, Mr Sands erroneously states that the eight-day sickness has only recently appeared in the island, and, instead of pointing to the older houses as the cause of the disease, suggests that the zinc roofs of the modern cottages may have something to do with it. Their comparative deficiency in warmth has also been indicated as having a possible connection with the fatal malady.

Dr Collins's well-known *Treatise on Midwifery* contains some interesting particulars relative to the disease in question. It embraces a record of the 16,654 children born in the Dublin Hospital during the seven years ended 1833, of whom 284 died before the mother left the institution. Of the 284, thirty-seven died from *trismus nascentium*, 'A disease', he says, 'of much interest to the medical practitioner, from its obstinate resistance to all modes of treatment.' He mentions, as the result of the experience of one of his predecessors, Dr Clarke, that at the end of the year 1782, out of 17,650 live births in the hospital, 2944 children died within the first fortnight – i.e., nearly every *sixth* child, or about 17 per cent; and about nineteen out of every twenty died of nine-day fits. As the foul and vitiated state of the air in the wards was supposed to be the principal cause of this alarming mortality, an attempt was made to introduce a counteraction, apertures being formed in the ceiling of each ward (since changed for air-tubes passing to the roof), while small holes were made through the tops of the window-frames and of the doors opening into the galleries. The result of this simple process was a free circulation of air; and out of 8033 subsequent births, 419 children died = about one in nineteen and a half, or from 5 to 6 – instead of 17 – per cent. Dr Collins considers that extreme vigilance as to cleanliness, combined with free ventilation, might banish the frightful disease from lying-in hospitals. The mode in which *trismus* attacks the children is described in Dr Clarke's relative treatise in the third volume of the *Transactions of the Royal Irish Academy*. Dissection appears to have thrown no light on the pathology of the disease. No treatment hitherto adopted, including calomel, opium, tobacco, oil of turpentine, tartar emetic, leeching and warm bath, has produced a shade of relief. Accordingly, prevention is the only alternative where cure seems to be hopeless. The following tables have been prepared from Dr Collins's statements, in order to show the particulars connected with the thirty-seven deaths from *trismus* which occurred during his mastership. The diminution in the mortality exhibited in table No. III is attributed to the removal of impure air. The total number of deaths was, no doubt, in the inconsiderable proportion of 1 in 450; but for the last four years (1830–1833), it was only 1 in 666.

No. I		No. II		No. III	
Day on which attacked	No. of children	When died No. of hours after seizure	No. of children	Year of Dr Collins' mastership	No. of deaths
2nd	1	18	1	1st	14
4th	2	19	1	2nd	7
5th	11	20	1	3rd	3
6th	12	21½	1	4th	3
7th	5	24	12	5th	3

No. I Day on which attacked	No. of children	No. II When died No. of hours after seizure	No. of children	No. III Year of Dr Collins' mastership	No. of deaths
8th	2	26	1	6th	3
9th	1	29	1	7th	4
not noted	3	30	3	37	
	37	33	2		
		36	1		
		38	1		
		40	1		
		48	1		
		70	2		
		72	1		
		not noted	7		
			37		

One of the Edinburgh death-registers for the year 1873 contains an entry relative to a male child who died, at the age of twelve days, from '*tetanus* (*trismus nascentium*)', after four days' illness. The following note of the medical attendant – a well-known and skilful practitioner – occurs immediately below the cause of death, in the sixth column of the register: 'This child was born on board, and remained on board ship till it was taken ill. The ship was loaded with bones and bone-ash – the atmosphere consequently impure. The child had never been in the open air. This is the only case I have seen for many years. As certified by J.S., MD'.

In common with some other writers, Dr Arthur Mitchell considers that the mortality from *trismus* is intimately connected with the peculiar character of the houses; and he seems to have satisfied himself that there was nothing exceptional in the mode of dressing the umbilical cord to account for the results. He also declines to accept, as applicable to St Kilda, the explanation offered by Schleisner with reference to the infantile mortality of Iceland[7] – viz, the use of birds' excrements as fuel, and birds' fat

7 Between 1827 and 1837, it amounted to 30 per cent.

for lighting purposes; discrediting the idea that the consumption of fulmar-oil in the lamps of St Kilda has any connection with the disease in question. As already indicated, Mr Morgan attributes what may be termed the 'slaughter of the innocents', to the insanitary character of the domestic arrangements, and more especially to the indoor manufacture of manure – the former cabins of the inhabitants having been constructed, as already stated, without smoke-holes, with the view of preventing its escape, owing to the scarcity of manure. For twelve long months the soot was deposited in pitchy layers upon the inner surface of the roof, and collected in the manner already indicated. As stated by Mr W. H. Corfield of University College, London, in a letter to the *Times*, towards the end of August 1871, this view of the matter is referred to in the *First Report of the Health of Towns Commissioners*, published in 1844; and after mentioning the filthy habits of the St Kildans, Mr Corfield expresses great surprise that nothing should have been done to improve their sanitary condition, and points to the fact of there being only one child in the island, at the time he wrote, in a population of seventy-one, and that one dying! A reply was sent by the owner of the island, in which he admitted the large infantile mortality. 'What the *cause* of this is,' he says, 'I have never been able to ascertain, but I am certain that it is not what Mr Corfield desires the public to 'rest assured' that it is. The state of things on the island is very different from what he imagines it to be. The inhabitants are well fed, well clothed, and, for a Hebridean peasantry, particularly well housed. I have no doubt that the habits of the people in respect of cleanliness admit of improvement; but the disgusting practice described in Mr Corfield's letter – though something of the kind did prevail in former times – is unknown to the present generation.' A few days afterwards, Rear-Admiral Otter, who frequently visited St Kilda, and to whom I have already more than once referred, wrote another letter to *The Times*, in which, after mentioning the proprietor's other acts of kindness to the inhabitants, he specially alludes to the erection, about ten years previously, of a series of 'neat detached two-roomed cottages with zinc roofs, in lieu of the former houses'. He then proceeds as follows.

As to the mortality of the children, I believe the cause can be traced to the oily nature of their food, consisting chiefly of seabirds, which build in incredible quantities on the different islands forming the group. The fulmar, which is found in no other place in the United Kingdom, is a peculiarly oleaginous bird, containing in its stomach a considerable amount of clear pinkish oil . . . Though they have cows, potatoes and meal, this is their chief article of food, and thus the system becomes so impregnated with fatty matter that it gives a peculiar odour to their persons, and the touch of their skin is like velvet. The startling mortality of the children before the ninth or tenth day (which has not been over-rated), is caused by the strength of the mother's milk while nursing; and to prove this theory, a child being born during our stay, the mother was kept on cocoa, meat and biscuit, and the child throve well.[8] Those that survive infancy grow up strong, healthy men and women, in spite of their intermarrying so much among themselves. As to the dirty state of their dwellings, it never struck me they were worse than their neighbours' on the main islands, if so bad; and, in proof, the late Duke of Athole chose one of their cottages as his residence during a stormy night, instead of the manse.

Admiral Otter incidentally alludes to the frequent intermarriages of the St Kildans, which some persons have supposed may be calculated to produce the malady in question by having an unfavourable effect upon the offspring. If, however, these unions had any connection with the matter, it seems highly improbable that their injurious influence would terminate a few weeks after

8 This child was named 'Mary Jemima Otter', after the wife of the gallant admiral – its surname being Gillies.

the occurrence of the births, seeing that the children which survive that period usually turn out healthy and vigorous.

Such, then, are the various explanations that have been offered with regard to the frequent occurrence of the eight-day sickness in St Kilda. It does not appear that since 1862, when the present improved cottages were erected, there has been the slightest reduction in the number of fatal cases; and accordingly, we may reasonably conclude that a vitiated atmosphere is at least not the sole cause of the fatal malady. Doubtless, the insanitary conditions which pertained to the older habitations – now chiefly if not entirely used as cellars and byres – may have exercised a baneful influence upon infant life, and moreover, it is possible that these unfavourable conditions may have left a temporary mark on the constitutions of the adults of St Kilda; but I am disposed to acquiesce in Admiral Otter's views regarding the effect of the oily food of the sea-birds upon the mother's milk, and indirectly upon the health of her offspring.

A somewhat similar opinion is entertained by Miss Macleod, who considers that there is a tendency to inflammation among the islanders, owing to the strong and oily character of their ordinary food. Instead of both mother and child being judiciously starved, the moment the latter is born stimulants are administered. During Miss Macleod's recent sojourn on the island, she saw port-wine and cow's milk poured down the throat of an infant of one day old! She at once stopped the procedure, and the child survives in a thriving condition. Unfortunately there is no properly qualified nurse in St Kilda. On Miss Macleod suggesting that an experienced woman ought to be procured, an old man calmly said – 'If it's God's will that babies should die, nothing you can do will save them'![9] After her return to Dunvegan, Mrs Macleod (her sister-in-law) wrote to ask whether one of the St Kilda women would come to the castle, with the view of learning English, and

9 Mr Sands states that he 'heard more than one pious gentleman suggest that this distemper was probably a wise provision of Providence for preventing a redundant population on a rock where food was limited'.

then proceeding to Edinburgh to receive a thorough medical education; but the generous proposal was declined, on the ground that all the women were afraid to leave their sea-girt home. Miss Macleod contemplates another visit to St Kilda in the course of next spring, and hopes to succeed in persuading one of them to accompany her to Skye. *Apropos* to the treatment of infants, Mrs McVean states in her Reminiscences that a St Kilda mother never thinks of providing clothing for her babe, until she sees whether or not it will survive the critical eighth day. Meanwhile, it is swaddled in coarse home-made flannel; and Captain Thomas considers that, on these occasions, the usual tendency of the mother is to smother the infant with blankets and other wraps.

Another very remarkable malady which occasionally prevails among the inhabitants of St Kilda is a species of influenza, locally termed 'boat-cough', 'strangers' cold' (*cnatan na gall*), or 'the trouble'[10], by which the natives are almost always attacked shortly after the arrival of a vessel from the Outer Hebrides. They allege that the illness is most severe when the visitors come from Harris, and that they suffer less when the vessel hails from Glasgow or more distant ports. It is particularly referred to by both Martin and Macaulay, and also by most of the more recent writers on St Kilda, some of whom were eyewitnesses of its effects. Mr Wilson informs us that the Rev. Neil McKenzie confirmed the account of it which he had formerly read and disbelieved; and Mr Morgan gives some curious details of its character from actual observation. As already stated, about ten days before his visit to St Kilda in 1860, HMS *Porcupine*, commanded by Captain Otter, and with the late Duke of Athole and Mr Hall Maxwell on board, had visited the island; and a day or two after the departure of the vessel, 'the trouble' made its appearance – the entire population being more or less affected by it. The same thing occurred after the arrival of the factor's smack in 1876, and also on the landing of the Austrian crew in the present year. It usually begins with a cold sensation,

10 Sometimes called *cnatan na Heric*, or 'the Harris cold'.

pain and stiffness in the muscles of the jaw, aching in the head and bones, and great lassitude and depression – the ordinary symptoms of catarrh in an aggravated form – and is accompanied by a discharge from the nose, a rapid pulse, and a severe cough, which is particularly harassing during the night. The malady first attacks those persons who have come most closely into contact with the strangers, and then extends itself over the whole community. Mr Morgan saw an unfortunate little infant, not more than a fortnight old, 'grievously tormented with it'. The fatal cases of boat-cough, although not absolutely, are relatively, numerous – three of the sixty-eight deaths entered in the older register having been caused by the disorder. By some the seizure has been attributed to the circumstance of the inhabitants exposing themselves to cold, by rushing into the water to render assistance to strangers in landing on the island; but when we consider the hardships to which they are inured in the prosecution of their hazardous avocation of fowling, such an explanation cannot possibly be admitted. Others allege that the disease is consequent upon easterly winds, which, however, are the most unfavourable agencies for the approach of a vessel from the Hebrides. As already stated, a landing is most easily effected when the wind is contrary; and in the case of Martin's party, whose visit was followed by an attack, the sailors were obliged to have recourse to their oars. This solution is suggested in a letter quoted by Boswell in his *Life of Dr Johnson*, in which the writer states that an ingenious friend – the Rev. Mr Christian of Docking – considered the cause to be a natural one, under the erroneous impression that the situation of St Kilda rendered a north-east wind indispensably necessary before a stranger could land. Hence he concluded that the epidemic was caused by the wind, and not by the visitor.[11] Boswell also mentions

11 In a recent paper in *Land and Water*, descriptive of the cruise of the Herring Commissioners on board HMS *Jackal*, Mr Frank Buckland suggests the same explanation, being apparently unaware of the theory propounded by Mr Christian upwards of 100 years ago.

that the celebrated Dr John Campbell endeavoured to account for it on physical principles – to wit, from the effect of effluvia from human bodies. The great moralist himself appears to have been somewhat sceptical upon the subject. 'How can there be a physical effect,' he said, 'without a physical cause?' – jocularly adding, 'the arrival of a shipfull of strangers would kill them; for, if one stranger gives them one cold, two strangers must give them two colds, and so in proportion.' On its being mentioned that the truth of the fact is annually proved by Macleod's steward, on whose arrival all the inhabitants caught cold, he humorously answered: 'The steward always comes to demand something from them, and so they fall a-coughing!'[12]

Like the great lexicographer, Macculloch appears to have been utterly incredulous on the subject of the 'strangers' cough'. In hopes of hearing the whole island join in one universal 'chorus of sneezing', he watched with great anxiety; but no sneezing was heard, and none did cry, 'God bless him!' He then ironically says that the perfection of faith is to believe against our senses, and that although the event could scarcely be concealed in the limited number of pocket-handkerchiefs which the islanders possessed, nevertheless, nobody doubted that it was an actual fact. 'Everybody had witnessed it, from Martin to Macaulay; everybody believed it, from Macaulay to the present day; the whole island – including the minister's wife, then regent of St Kilda – was agreed upon it, and who, then, dared to doubt?' The doctor appears to have expected to witness an immediate visitation. 'Everybody looked at every other's nose; but not a drop of dew distilled, and not a sneeze consented to rouse St Kilda's echoes.' He proceeds to quiz the would-be philosophers who must find a cause for everything. 'It is all owing,' say some of these wise personages, 'to the east wind: "*causa pro non causa*"; because this is precisely the wind which prevents any boat from

12 Mr Trevelyan, in his *Life and Letters of Lord Macaulay*, refers to Dr Johnson's visit to Cawdor, and his interest in the minister's allusion to the 'boat-cough', in his *History of St Kilda*, which, he says, 'touched the superstitious vein in Johnson, who praised Macaulay for his magnanimity in venturing to chronicle so questionable a phenomenon.'

landing on the island.' Among other humorous solutions he suggests the idea of strangers being naturally welcomed by a sneeze instead of a kiss of peace, a trifling modification of the well-known salutation by noses in which certain nations indulge.

Some persons have maintained that the boat-cough is an annual epidemic; but Mr Morgan assures us that, within the short space of eight weeks, three several outbreaks have been known to follow the arrival of as many boats. While acknowledging that the origin of contagious diseases is involved in great obscurity, the same writer suggests that the usual isolation of the inhabitants – who are under exceptional conditions both as regards diet and occupation – when followed by sudden contact with strangers, may exercise an infectious influence on the more susceptible of their number. A curious confirmation of this opinion will be found in Mr Bates's interesting work, entitled *The Naturalist on the River Amazon*. Speaking of the gradual extinction of certain tribes friendly to the whites, who inhabit the country near Ega, he says

The principal cause of their decay in numbers seems to be a disease which always appears amongst them when a village is visited by people from the civilised settlements – a slow fever, accompanied by the symptoms of a common cold – '*de fluxo*', as the Brazilians term it, ending probably in consumption. The disorder has been known to break out when the visitors were entirely free from it – the simple contact of civilised men, in some mysterious way, being sufficient to create it.

A still more recent as well as a more strictly parallel illustration of the occurrence of the malady in question, in another part of the globe, is contained in the account of the *Cruise of* HMS *Galatea*, in 1867–68, where the following statement occurs: 'Tristan d'Acunha[13] is a remarkably healthy island; but it is a singular fact that any vessel touching there from St Helena invariably brings

13 See Note at end of chapter (p. 182).

with it a disease resembling influenza. St Kilda, off the west coast of Scotland, is known to be also similarly afflicted whenever a party lands amongst the people from any vessel.' With regard to St Kilda, *pace* Johnson and Macculloch, there can now be no doubt as to the fact of a visitation of influenza having hitherto been the apparent result of numerous visits from the outside world. Whatever may be the real cause of the mysterious ailment – whether it is produced by contagion, like certain other epidemic diseases, or by a feverish excitement arising from the contact of a higher with a lower civilisation – the actual occurrence of the distemper seems to be fully established, and the experiences of Ega and Tristan d'Acunha afford interesting illustrations of somewhat similar results in very different parts of the world.

Dysentery is another pretty frequent disease in St Kilda, and is supposed to be produced by severe intestinal irritation, arising from the continuous use of salted sea-fowl and coarse oatmeal, more especially the former. Seven of the sixty-eight deaths recorded by Mr McKenzie – two males and five females – are attributed to that disease, which, however, does not appear in the later register. Possibly some of the deaths tabulated under the heads of 'Unknown' or 'Not specified' may have been caused by dysentery.

In common with the Western Highlanders generally, the inhabitants of St Kilda enjoy a remarkable immunity from consumption and other tubercular diseases. Only two cases of deaths from consumption – both females advanced in life – appear among the 132 deaths embraced in the registers. Martin refers to the fact of the island being free from many diseases which are common in other parts of the world. 'The distemper,' he says, 'that most prevails here is a spotted fever, and that, too, confined to one tribe, to whom this disease is, as it were, become hereditary. Others are liable to fluxes, fevers, stitches and the spleen, for all which they have but very few remedies . . . The smallpox hath not been heard of in this place for several ages, except in one instance of two of the steward's retinue, who not having been well recovered of it, upon their arrival here infected one man only.' I have already referred to the smallpox epidemic of 1724, which proved so disastrous to the inhabitants. So far as I am aware, it has not appeared in St Kilda since that date.[14] Seventeen of the islanders, including all the children, were vaccinated – by Dr Webster of Dunvegan in June 1873, and the rest of the inhabitants about three months later by Dr Murchison of North Harris, who was conveyed to St Kilda in HMS *Jackal*, under the sanction of the authorities of the Admiralty. On the occasion of my visit to the island in July, three children were vaccinated by Dr McKellar of Obbe. Martin states that some thirteen years before he went to St Kilda, leprosy broke out among the islanders, and that two families were 'labouring under the disease' at the time of his visit. He considers that the malady was in a large measure to be ascribed to their 'gross feeding' on the fulmar and solan goose.[15]

'Of peculiar diseases or disorders', says Mr Muir, 'to which the people are liable, we did not hear much. Rheumatism, swellings, ulcers, eruptions, sore throats and other complaints of an inflammatory and cutaneous description, arising from frequent exposure and an unvaried diet, were, as might have been expected, common.' He considers, however, that both in their frequency and virulency these ailments are probably much abated from what they used to be, in consequence of the comfortable quality of the clothing already referred to. From the medical report furnished to Mr Macdiarmid by Staff Surgeon Scott of HMS *Flirt*, I extract the following statement.

The ailment *par excellence* is rheumatism, as might be expected from the exposed nature of their island home. This disease is

14 In one of the Faroe Islands, rarely visited by strangers, but containing 7782 inhabitants, there had been no measles for sixty-five years, till it was imported by a sick sailor in 1846, when 6,000 of the natives took the disease – *First Annual Report of the Massachusetts Board of Health*, 1870.
15 Some interesting particulars relative to the occurrence of leprosy in Scotland will be found in Chambers' *Domestic Annals*, i, 226.

common to both sexes, and in a number is attended with pain in the cardiac region, with irregular heart's action. Dyspepsia is also common; and it is noticeable that the teeth were in general short and square, as if they had been filed down. There were several cases of ear-disease, and there is a tendency to scrofula. One boy had disease of the bones of the leg . . . Colds and coughs are common enough, but no case of phthisis presented itself. We saw only two cases of skin-disease, and these were trifling, for Nature seemed to have endowed them with very clean, smooth, epidermic coverings.

After a reference to the eight-day sickness, the reporter adds: 'The children whom we saw were all healthy-looking. The medicines which would be of most use are those for cough and rheumatism; and for the latter, strong liniments would be the most appreciated.' In the preceding excerpt, dyspepsia is mentioned as a common ailment in St Kilda. An anonymous visitor to the island in August 1875 sent a short notice of his experiences to one of the Edinburgh newspapers, in which he specially referred to the prevalence of that disease, and attributed its occurrence to the constant use of dried fish. Mr Sands replied to the communication, stating that the islanders rarely partake of fish, and that he never heard of their being subject to dyspepsia. The same anonymous visitor mentions that the physician by whom his party was accompanied, had to prescribe for the various diseases consequent upon poor living and an utter ignorance of the laws of health, and that he left a large quantity of iodine and Gregory's mixture with the islanders. On the occasion of the visit of the *Dunara Castle* in July, we happened to have no fewer than five distinguished medical practitioners on board, most of whom, I believe, gave suitable advice to all the invalids, real or imaginary, who solicited their aid. Martin tells us that, in his day, the inhabitants 'never had a potion of physic given them in their lives, nor know they anything of phlebotomy'; but in modern times, they appear to have rather a weakness for medicine, of which the proprietor sends an annual supply, in the shape of castor oil, senna, salts and various tonics. Captain Thomas informs me that the doctor of the *Porcupine* once attended a sick man in St Kilda, for whom he prepared a few ordinary pills. The patient, however, objected to take so small a quantity of physic, on the ground that 'it was not a fit dose for a grown man'! A homeopathic chemist would make a poor living in St Kilda.

Judging from the statement of Sir Robert Moray, violent deaths must formerly have been much more frequent in St Kilda than in recent times. 'The men', he says, 'seldom grow old; and seldom was it ever known that any man died in his bed there, but was either drowned or broke his neck.' We have already seen that only four deaths appear in the records kept in the island since 1830, of which the cause is attributed to a 'fall over the rocks', while the only deaths from drowning were the eight that occurred in 1863, at the loss of the *Dargavel*, already referred to.

Mr Morgan contrasts the vital statistics of St Kilda with those of the Faroe Islands, in which the habits of life are, in many respects, very similar to those of the St Kildans. From the conclusions at which he arrives, it appears that notwithstanding their nauseous food and the open sewers in the immediate neighbourhood of their huts, the Danish islanders are the longest-lived community with which we are acquainted – their annual rate of mortality being only 12.5 in every thousand persons. In St Kilda, on the other hand, the death-rate, during the ten years ending 1840, amounted to very nearly sixty-one in every thousand, or nearly twice as high as that of the most unhealthy of the manufacturing districts in England. If the abnormal infantile mortality could only be checked, there seems to be no reason why the death-rate of St Kilda should not ultimately approximate to that of Faroe. It must be borne in mind that the present startling results do not afford an illustration of what certain modern philosophers would term 'the survival of the fittest'. The destroying angel finds his way to every cottage in the island within which an infant's voice is heard – the strong as well as the weak proving victims to the scourge.

Although in 1841 Mr Wilson found both sexes represented by three years beyond fourscore, in the persons of Finlay Macleod and Catherine Ferguson, the comparative longevity of the female population of St Kilda is a remarkable feature in their social condition. While the ages of the men rarely exceed sixty, the women not unfrequently reach the 'scriptural period'. Thus, at the census of 1861, although the males between twenty and sixty were slightly in excess of the females at the same age, the only persons above sixty were four females. At the last census, however, five males and only four females had passed the period of threescore years. Again, of the six deaths above sixty years of age in the registers pertaining to the twenty-one years ended 1876, one was that of a married male – his age being sixty-three, – while the five other cases were females, aged respectively seventy-five, eighty-three, eighty-four, eighty-six, and eighty-eight – all widows except the oldest – two McQueens, two McCrimmons, and one M'Kinnon. It has been very plausibly suggested that the shorter lives of the male population are the necessary consequence of their peculiar avocation. The St Kilda fowler is frequently suspended by a rope round his waist for several hours together, and the continued strain – both bodily and mental – not improbably induces congestion, and ultimately disease of some of the more important internal organs. With the view of checking such serious results, a leaf might be judiciously taken out of the book of the Faroe cragsmen, whose mode of fowling, as already mentioned, appears to be conducted on more scientific and safer principles than that which is adopted in St Kilda.

Note referred to at page 177

The Tristan d'Acunha group of islands, so named from the Portuguese navigator who discovered it early in the sixteenth century, lies in mid-ocean – lat. 37° 2′ 48″ S, long. 12° 18′ 30″ W – about 1300 miles south of St Helena and 1500 west of the Cape of Good Hope, nearly on a line between that Cape and Cape Horn, and is probably the most remote of human abodes.

Like the St Kilda group, it comprises three islands – viz, Tristan, and two smaller islands called Inaccessible and Nightingale, each being about twenty miles distant from Tristan. The main island, which is almost circular and about seven miles in diameter, consists of a huge volcanic rock, rising perpendicularly some 3,000 feet out of the sea, with a lofty cone on its summit ascending upwards of 5,000 feet more, making the entire height of the island above sea-level 8,300 feet! It is occupied by an interesting English colony, resembling in many respects the inhabitants of Pitcairn Island, to which reference has already been made. Temporarily occupied at different times by a few American sailors, it was formally taken possession of in the name of the British Government in 1817, the first 'governor' being William Glass, a corporal of artillery and a native of Kelso, in Roxburghshire. The original settlers were Glass and his wife (a Cape creole) and their two children, besides John Nankivel and Samuel Burnell, natives of Plymouth. In 1824, the population amounted to twenty-five, of whom only three were females; in 1836, to forty-two; and in 1852, to eighty-five, all English by association, but not by birth and parentage, being of the mulatto caste. At that date the island was visited by Captain Denham in HMS *Herald*, who considered that a more healthy place could not be found, none of the epidemical diseases having reached the settlers. Glass was then nearly seventy years of age, having, besides his wife, seven sons and eight daughters. In 1857, the Rev. W. F. Taylor, who had been sent to the island some years previously by the Society for the Propagation of the Gospel, went with about forty-five of the inhabitants – the majority being women, then greatly in excess of the men – to the Cape; and about the same time, five families went to the United States. Before that exodus, the population had increased to 112. When the island was visited by the *Galatea* in 1867, the population amounted to fifty-three, including seven unmarried girls, and the same number of eligible bachelors, none of whom, however, accepted the chaplain's offer to unite them in the holy bonds of matrimony! Seven years later (1874), HMS

Challenger found a population of eighty-four, the females being slightly in the majority – most of those who had left the island in 1857 and subsequently, having returned. From Mr Taylor's account of the island, published in 1856, it appears that in his opinion the settlement must be abandoned. He alludes to the total disappearance of trees, involving the prospect of a great scarcity of fuel, and the consequent want of shelter for both animals and vegetables against the heavy gales to which the island is exposed. Another evil to which he refers is the large excess of females (now apparently reduced), the boys being continually enticed away by the whale-ships which touch at the island. He also alludes to the small quantity of arable land, the great distance of the island from other places, and the consequent difficulty of finding a profitable market. 'I think', he says, 'it will be a happy day when this little lonely spot is once more left to those who probably always were, and now, in its present barren condition, certainly are its only fit inhabitants – the wild birds of the ocean.'

A graphic account of the *Challenger*'s visit to the Tristan group, including notices of the albatross, penguin and other sea-birds, will be found in two papers contributed by Sir Wyville Thomson to *Good Words* for 1874.

Education, Morals and Religion

The state of education in St Kilda has long been very far from satisfactory. At the time of Macaulay's visit in 1758, all the inhabitants of the island, 'except three or four smatterers', were perfectly illiterate. He gives the credit of the introduction of letters to the Rev. Alexander Buchan, who officiated as a catechist during the reign of Queen Anne, and who was afterwards sent, as already mentioned, by the Society for Propagating Christian Knowledge, in the capacity of an ordained minister. With the aid of some charitable persons in the Scottish metropolis, he was enabled to train up some Hirta boys at his school; and, according to Macaulay, the progress which they made was 'considerably greater than anything that has been done there during the incumbency of his successors'. He admits, however, that the aversion of the islanders to a foreign tongue, and the rarity of their intercourse with an English-speaking population, constituted a formidable barrier in the way of educational improvement.

Mrs McVean informs me that when her father went to the island in 1830, the people were deplorably ignorant Only one woman could read and write a little, and none of the females even knew how to hold a needle. Mr McKenzie started a daily school for the purpose of teaching reading, writing[1] and arithmetic; and

---

1 Martin alludes to the astonishment exhibited by the St Kildans when they witnessed the process of writing by some members of his party. 'They cannot conceive', he says, 'how it is possible for any mortal to express the conceptions of his mind in such black characters upon white paper.'

in the same class, three generations of the same family might occasionally be seen. He also instituted a Sunday-school, which all the inhabitants attended, their religious knowledge being then very deficient. Mrs McKenzie gave the women instruction in sewing, in order that they might themselves make the white calico frilled caps which they then wore, and for which they had formerly to pay the Harris women pretty heavily in 'kind'. Unfortunately, however, they knew not how to wash the head-dresses of which they were so proud. Their mode of proceeding was to carry their clothes to a pool of salt water, and to pound them with a wooden mallet, till they were almost beaten to shreds! They never could be brought to understand washing upon scientific principles, preferring to adhere to their own peculiar style.[2]

When Mr Grigor visited St Kilda in 1861, only two of the inhabitants – neither of whom were natives – could speak English. Two men, besides the catechist, who acted as registrar, were able to sign their names, which was the maximum of their calligraphic powers. The catechist gave instruction in Gaelic reading, and also to a small extent in writing, while his niece assisted him in his tuition, and taught the young women sewing and knitting. According to Macaulay, the language of the St Kildans is 'a very corrupt dialect of Gaelic, adulterated with a little mixture of the Norwegian tongue. They have many words and cant phrases, quite unintelligible to their neighbours. Their manner of pronouncing is attended with a very remarkable peculiarity; every man, woman, and child has an incorrigible lisping; not one of them is able to give their proper sounds to the liquid letters.' Dr

2 The Scotch appear to have indulged in more than one singular mode of washing. Even at the present day, the delicate susceptibilites of the English traveller are occasionally outraged, as he strolls along the banks of some clear-flowing country stream, by the startling discovery that the kilt is not confined to the persons of the sterner sex. In one of the editions of an amusing work, entitled *Letters from Scotland*, by an English officer of Engineers, the curious reader will find a graphic pictorial illustration of the process to which I have ventured to allude.

McDonald, on the other hand, informs us, from frequent conversations with the islanders, that their language is purely that of the Western Isles in general, and has no Scandinavian or other foreign mixtures, that can be regarded as peculiar to St Kilda. At present, only one of the islanders (a married woman from Ross-shire) understands English;[3] and in the various registers kept since 1856, all the native 'informants' sign by mark. All the adults are able to read the Gaelic Bible, and Mr Macdiarmid was informed that one or two of them could repeat the whole of the Psalms from memory.

They all [he says] have a pretty fair idea of numbers and dates in Gaelic, and know the value of the current coins . . . They are anxious, and desire very much to be educated in English and arithmetic, and many earnestly beseeched of me that a schoolmaster might be sent to them. It is my opinion that they would learn English very soon – the grown-up people as well as the young. They are very sharp and quick at picking up English names and words, though our captain's name (O'Rorke) proved rather a puzzler to them, and invariably stuck in their throats. Their keen, bright eyes bespeak an intellect easily susceptible of impression. Why should not a representation be made to the Highlands and Islands Committees of the Churches to give their attention to the matter, and get the St Kildans taught, at least, the simplest rudiments?

Mr Sands heard one man, who is reputed a scholar, mutter in Gaelic 'Units, tens, hundreds, thousands', before he ventured to decipher 1875. Others asked him the situation of Australia and California; and not having a map in his possession, he was obliged roughly to indicate the forms and relative position of the two countries by tearing up an old newspaper, and placing the pieces on the ground.

3 The wife of Neil McDonald, who came to visit her sister, servant to a former minister of St Kilda, and, as she herself expressed it, 'found a man'!

Like the island of Bernera, St Kilda forms part of the parish of Harris. Is no help to be looked for from that quarter? – is there no school board there? In the course of my recent wanderings among the various Western Islands, I encountered more than one 'palatial' edifice, in the form of a new schoolhouse, in the midst of a very limited population. Till a proper building is provided, the little church might be temporarily used in that capacity; and accordingly, all that is wanted, in the first instance, is a suitable pedagogue. It appears that the present minister was for a long time schoolmaster at Garve, in Ross-shire; and, as already mentioned, he acts as registrar of births, deaths and marriages. Failing a special instructor, he might be induced, by way of experiment, to act in the additional character of teacher,[4] with a small supplement to his present moderate allowance of eighty pounds per annum. Perhaps, however, if he has read the 'Deserted Village', he may philosophically regard himself as more than 'passing rich', thus obviating the necessity of anything in the shape of an 'augmentation'! Mr Macdiarmid specifies a few of the volumes of which his little library is composed – Smith's *Moral Sentiments*, Butler's *Fifteen Sermons*, Harvey's *Meditations*, the works of Dr John Owen, Baxter's *Call*, the select works of Dr Chalmers, and Sir John Herschel's *Astronomy* – all very solid and unexceptionable productions; but a sprinkling of lighter literature would probably help to brighten the atmosphere of his secluded study. With access to the priceless treasures of Shakespeare, Milton and Burns, Bunyan, Cervantes and Scott, he would have the chance of interspersing the uniform 'corn-fields' of his mind with a few patches of 'pleasure-ground'. His present intellectual isolation is a somewhat painful thought, and the advent of an English-speaking schoolmaster would prove a perfect godsend.

Even in more important islands than St Kilda, the all but exclusive maintenance of the Gaelic language – Professor Blackie

4 Even at present, the minister is believed to do a little in the way of teaching English.

notwithstanding – is much to be regretted. An intelligent and accomplished Lowlander, whose official duties imply a residence in one of the largest of the Western Islands, very recently informed me that, after a good many years' experience of the locality, he had been forced to the conclusion that the people among whom he lived were afflicted by two 'curses' – one of which I forbear to mention in the present connection, the other being the perpetuation of the Gaelic tongue. Probably, however, its knell has been sounded even in St Kilda; but the demise promises to be both slow and 'hard'. Apropos to Gaelic, the St Kildans are said to be devoted admirers of the queen, partly, it is supposed, from the belief which they entertain regarding her Majesty's liking for a Gaelic-speaking race. During Miss Macleod's late sojourn in the island, she was minutely interrogated as to the queen's personal appearance and other attributes. It is to be hoped that the news of a recent royal row, on a Sunday, upon the waters of Loch Maree, has not reached the distant shores of St Kilda!

In the matter of morals, in the ordinary sense of that term, the people of St Kilda have long cut a most respectable figure. When Macaulay wrote, drunkenness had not been introduced into the island; 'but the St Kildans,' he says, 'could be reconciled without any difficulty to spirituous liquors!' He then alludes to their 'violent passion for tobacco', already referred to, and specifies the various valuable commodities which they barter for the 'bewitching article'. In confirmation of Mr Grigor's statement, Mr Sands mentions that 'every family keeps a bottle of whisky in the house, but it is never used except as a medicine.' He attributes their abstinence, however, to their thrifty habits and the dearness of the liquor, rather than to any dislike to the latter or dread of its consequences. 'Still,' he adds, 'whatever may be the motive, the fact remains; the people are perfectly sober, and one is never disturbed by the drunken brawls which occur in places of greater material civilisation.' The annual bacchanalian indulgences mentioned by the 'High Dean of the Isles', to which I have already incidentally referred, are now a thing of the past. Neither Father Mathew nor the President of the Good Templars would find a field for their labours on the sea-girt isle.

Till very recently, the inhabitants of St Kilda appear to have been altogether free from the other dark stain on the moral escutcheon of Scotland, which a writer on the 'noble science' may be excused for describing as the 'bend-sinister', and of which we have all, unfortunately, heard so much during recent years. 'Impurities fashionable elsewhere,' says Macaulay, 'if committed here, are never unattended with infamy . . . Their morals are, and must be, purer than those of great and opulent societies, however much civilised.' Mr Wilson was informed by the minister (Mr McKenzie) that, on the whole, the people were a very moral race, and that many of them were under serious religious impressions. The first illegitimate birth occurs in the register for 1862, and since that date, as already indicated, there have been two other cases, of which one was of an aggravated kind. Without venturing to cast the slightest reflection on the reputation of the women, Captain Thomas considers the morality of the men to be, if possible, even more unimpeachable than that of the softer sex. The vast difference between the eastern and western counties of Scotland in respect to illegitimacy is now universally known. While in more than one of the former the ratio continues almost stationary at about sixteen per cent, in some of the latter, it is as low as from five to eight per cent. A satisfactory solution of the striking disparity has still to be found.

Notwithstanding their gradually increasing intercourse with the outside world, the people of St Kilda are still most creditably distinguished by the primitive character of their habits and the contentment of their lives. Martin compares the 'simplicity, purity, mutual love and cordial friendship' of the inhabitants of St Kilda to the condition of the people in the poet's 'golden age'. Besides declaring them to be free from care and covetousness, envy and dissimulation, ambition and pride, he describes them as 'altogether ignorant of the vices of foreigners, and governed by the dictates of reason and Christianity, as it was first delivered to them by those heroic souls, whose zeal moved them to undergo danger and trouble to plant religion in one of the remotest corners of the world. There is only this wanting to make them the happiest people in the habitable globe – namely, that they themselves do not know how happy they are, and how much they are above the avarice and slavery of the rest of mankind.' He might most appropriately have closed his panegyric with Virgil's well-known verse—

O fortunatos nimium, sua si bona norint!

Macaulay follows in a somewhat similar strain, and concludes his eulogy by stating that 'if all things are fairly weighed in the balance of unprejudiced reason, the St Kildans possess as great a share of true substantial happiness as any equal number of men elsewhere'. Half a century later, Macculloch paints, if possible, a still brighter picture.

If this island [he says] is not the Eutopia so long sought, where will it be found? Where is the land which has neither arms, money, law, physic, politics nor taxes? That land is St Kilda. War may rage all around, provided it be not with America, but the storm reaches it not. Neither *Times* nor *Courier* disturbs its judgments . . . No tax-gatherer's bill threatens on a church-door, the game-laws reach not gannets. Safe in its own whirl-winds and cradled in its own tempests, it heeds not the storms which shake the foundations of Europe; and acknowledging the dominion of Macleod and King George, is satisfied without inquiring whether George is the First or the Fourth of his name. Well may the pampered native of the happy Hirta refuse to change his situation. His slumbers are late, his labours are light, and his occupation is his amusement, since his sea-fowl constitute at once his food, his luxury, his game, his wealth, and his bed of down . . . His state is his city, and his city is his social circle; he has the liberty of his thoughts, his actions, and his kingdom, and all his world are his equals. His climate is mild and his island is green; and, like that of Calypso, the stranger who might corrupt him shuns its shores. If happiness is not a dweller in St Kilda, where shall it be sought?

The praises of the historians of St Kilda are eloquently re-echoed in Mallet's poem:

> Thrice happy land! though freezing on the verge
> Of Arctic skies, yet blameless still of arts
> That polish to deprave each softer clime,
> With simple nature, simple virtue, blessed!
> Beyond ambition's walk, where never war
> Upreared his sanguine standard, nor unsheathed
> For wealth or power the desolating sword;
> Where luxury, soft syren, who around
> To thousand nations deals her nectared cup
> Of pleasing bane, that soothes at once and kills,
> Is yet a name unknown: but calm content,
> That lives to reason, ancient faith, that binds
> The plain community of guileless hearts
> In love and union, innocence of ill
> Their guardian genius; these the powers that rule
> This little world, to all its sons secure,
> Man's happiest life; the soul serene and sound
> From passion's rage, the body from disease:
> Red on each cheek behold the rose of health;
> Firm in each sinew vigour's pliant spring,
> By temperance braced to peril and to pain,
> Amid the floods they stem, or on the steep
> Of upright rocks their straining steps surmount,
> For food or pastime: these light up their morn,
> And those their eve in slumber sweetly deep,
> Beneath the north, within the circling swell
> Of ocean's raging sound: but last and best

What avarice, what ambition, shall not know,
True liberty is theirs, the heaven-sent guest,
Who in the cave, or on the uncultured wild,
With independence dwells and peace of mind,
In youth, in age, their sun that never sets.

A later and more illustrious poet, in his well-known 'Ode on the Popular Superstitions of the Highlands', gives a shorter and still more beautiful description of the remote islanders—

But, oh, o'er all, forget not Kilda's race,
On whose bleak rocks, which brave the wasting tides,
Fair nature's daughter, virtue, yet abides.
Go, just as they, their blameless manners trace!
Then to my ear transmit some gentle song—
Of those whose lives are yet sincere and plain,
Their bounded walks the rugged cliffs along,
And all their prospect but the wintry main.
With sparing temperance at the needful time
They drain the scented spring; or, hunger-prest,
Along the Atlantic rock undreading climb,
And of its eggs despoil the solan's nest.
Thus blest in primal innocence they live,
Sufficed and happy with that frugal fare,
Which tasteful toil and hourly danger give.
Hard is their shallow soil, and bleak and bare;
Nor ever vernal bee was heard to murmur there.

Both Martin and Macaulay descant upon the disregard of money evinced by the St Kildans, who, according to the former, 'cannot distinguish a guinea from a sixpence'![5] 'Their riches', says

5 Macculloch tells a story of a Highlander accepting sixpence for a crystal for which he had asked a guinea, and when rated for his conduct, replying, 'Och! isn't a guinea and a sixpence the same thing to you?'

Macaulay, 'consist in their commodities. They have frequently heard of gold, without thirsting for it; they have not touched coin of any kind, I believe, before this age. They are now perhaps possessed of a score of shillings and some brass pence, more than will pay off the debt of their whole state.' Mr Muir, however, failed to discover the extreme simplicity and contempt of silver and gold to which the older authors refer, and goes the length of saying that 'in later times, money having become to some extent the medium of traffic, a thirst for it is now as keen in lonely St Kilda as it is in quarters where its acquisition is matter of hourly concern.' He refers to the bargaining that he had to go through before three or four of the islanders could be prevailed upon to accept a good day's wages for an hour's exhibition of their mode of descending the cliffs. 'They had *once* got as many pounds as we were offering shillings for doing the same thing for a Lady Somebody, and what was there to hinder us from giving a like sum?' No doubt exorbitant gratuities on such occasions are very apt to demoralise the persons on whom they are bestowed, and probably, as Mr Muir suggests, the lady in question was 'more wealthy than wise'; but the thoughtless stranger who opens his purse is not unfrequently more deserving of censure for his inconsiderate conduct than the unsophisticated islander in whose way the temptation is thrown. And, moreover, visitors to the island are still so comparatively few and far between, that one is disposed to hesitate before applying the rigid principles of political economy to the inhabitants of Hirta. When the *Porcupine* touched at St Kilda in 1860, several of the islanders went on board to see the wonders of the vessel; and when they appeared somewhat reluctant to go ashore, it turned out, upon inquiry, that they expected to be remunerated for their trouble! Some of them seriously expected that Captain Thomas would pay them for having allowed him to take their photographs. Whether this arose from selfishness or simplicity, may perhaps be somewhat open to question, although probably the Nairn mason employed by Captain Otter to construct a landing-place would have had very little doubt upon the subject – his estimate of the St Kildans being that they were 'the *most knowingist* people he had ever come across!' Even Martin, notwithstanding his very favourable estimate of the islanders, acknowledges that they are reputed to be 'very cunning'; and adds, that 'there is scarce any circumventing of them in traffic and bartering; the voice of one is the voice of all the rest, they being all of a piece, their common interest uniting them firmly together.' A purse of a few pounds was raised by the party in the *Dunara Castle*, on the occasion of my visit to the island, to compensate the cragsmen who illustrated the dangers of their calling; and at the suggestion of Captain Macdonald, the money was handed to the minister, with the view of his distributing it among them. Several of the visitors were presented with specimens of eggs and sea-birds; and the payments made for stockings, and other small articles knitted by the women, were very slightly in excess of an ordinary hosier's charge. The Highlanders on the mainland and elsewhere are supposed to have no particular aversion to English gold; and why the poor St Kildans should be expected to remain for ever beyond its influence, I am at a loss to comprehend. It will probably be time enough to preach a sermon against the weakness in question when a bank has been started on the shores of the distant isle.

If the inhabitants of Hirta are not altogether unacquainted with 'the root of all evil', the unanimous testimony that has been borne to their hospitality to strangers constitutes a very creditable feature in their character. I have already referred to the kindly treatment which Martin's party received from the islanders. In alluding to the virtue in question, Macaulay says that they are

> unfashionable enough to possess the virtue of hospitality in an eminent degree. In such remote places, the wise lessons of a parsimonious exactness have not hitherto been taught with any great success. To oblige the wealthy, to relieve the poor, to entertain the stranger and weary traveller – nay, to leave their doors open to every one, were heretofore the reigning maxims

there. The St Kildans retain much of this primitive spirit; they are remarkably generous and open-hearted.

During recent years, the hospitality of the natives of Hirta has been repeatedly exemplified. To say nothing of their invariable courtesy and kindness to casual visitors, we have seen that in more than one instance of enforced residence from shipwreck or other cause, the warm-hearted islanders have, for weeks and even months, shared their scarcity as well as their abundance with both foreigner and friend.

Macculloch refers to the blissful ignorance of the islanders respecting the doings of the outside world at the time of his visit to St Kilda, in the memorable summer of 1815.

They had imagined themselves at peace with Napoleon, and at peace they were. But while, good easy people, they dreamed in full security, Elba had appeared and vanished in the political lantern, the drama of the hundred days had been performed, and the curtain had descended at Waterloo over the fears and anxieties of all Europe; of all the world except St Kilda. But this news excited little emotion: it had no influence on the price of tobacco. The rebellion of former days had been a subject of far different interest to their ancestors; since of the only two powers they then knew in the world, their chief, Macleod, had declared war against King George.

The effects of their isolation have sometimes been amusingly illustrated on those rare occasions when they have ventured to cross the sea. Martin mentions the astonishment evinced by the local officer and others of the islanders, during a visit to Skye, on their witnessing the 'pomp and circumstance' of Macleod's family, which they regarded as 'equivalent to that of an imperial court'. They were also lost in admiration of his lady's elaborate costume, his riding-horses, glass windows and mirrors; and condemned, as 'vain and superfluous', the tapestry which covered the walls of his castle. The vast possessions of Macleod in Skye and elsewhere were a source of wonder to another islander on the occasion of a visit to Harris, while the altitude of the trees and the luxuriance of their foliage were quite beyond conception. On another occasion, a St Kilda man, after being fairly overcome by a pretty large dose of aqua vitae, was falling into a profound slumber which he imagined to be his last, expressed to his companions 'the great satisfaction he had in meeting with such an easy passage out of the world!' The same author describes the visit of a St Kildan to Glasgow, where he gazed with wonder at the lofty houses, stone pavements, and horse-drawn coaches – the mechanism and revolution of the wheels causing the most unbounded astonishment. But the venerable cathedral of St Mungo, as already incidentally mentioned, was the cause of his greatest surprise. He imagined that the pillars and arches were carved out of a huge rock, constituting the best 'caves' that he had ever seen! The patches of the ladies and the periwigs of the men appeared to his simple mind utterly ridiculous; while the vast number of the inhabitants, and the possibility of providing 'bread and ale' for such a multitude, filled him with amazement. 'He longed to see his native country again, and passionately wished it were blessed with ale, brandy, tobacco and iron, as Glasgow was!'

A good story is told of a St Kildan once landing during the night in the island of Scalpa, near the entrance to East Loch Tarbert. He wandered towards the lighthouse, and finding the door open, slowly ascended the long spiral staircase, which is supposed to have suggested the idea of Jacob's ladder, as he had never seen a stair before. On reaching the summit he opened the door of the light-room, and suddenly exchanged the outer darkness for the dazzling brilliancy of the inner chamber, where sat a venerable figure, with spectacles on nose, absorbed in the perusal of a newspaper. The astonishment was mutual; and after a brief pause, the unlooked-for visitor thus addressed the light-keeper, who appeared to him to be seated in awful majesty: 'Are you God

Almighty?' The immediate answer of the disturbed official was, '*Yes*! and who the devil are you?'

When Martin wrote, it would appear that, in common with the other Highlanders and Islanders of Scotland, at least some of the St Kildans professed to possess the gift of *taish* or second-sight.[6] Macculloch states that on the occasion of his visit in 1815, 'no inhabitant of St Kilda pretended to have been forewarned of our arrival. In fact,' he adds, 'it has undergone the fate of witch-craft; ceasing to be believed, it has ceased to exist . . . When witches were no longer burnt, witchcraft disappeared: since the second-sight has been limited to a doting old woman or a hypo-chondriacal tailor, it has become a subject for ridicule; and in matters of this nature, ridicule is death.' Mr McKenzie, however, mentions several recent instances of second-sight in an extract from his journal quoted by the author of *Sketches of St Kilda*; and his daughter, Mrs McVean, informs me that, in her infancy, the natives believed in the faculty, and used to say that they always knew when strangers were coming to the island, by 'hearing their footsteps shortly before they appeared'. At the same period, an old man professed to have seen 'most wonderful visions'.

The religious and ecclesiastical experiences of the St Kildans appear to have been of a somewhat checkered kind. In the early period of its history, the religion of the island has been described as 'a mixture of Druidism and Popery', and Macaulay conjectures that Christianity must have been introduced into the island by the Culdees, animated by the double motive of conversion and a passion for a solitary life. For at least some time prior to the date at which the Reformation reached the Western Isles, no resident priest of the Roman Catholic faith seems to have been attached to the island. 'The inhabitants of Hirta', says Buchanan, 'are

---

6 An account of the second-sight will be found in Martin's larger work relative to the Western Isles. See also a treatise on the same subject (1763) reprinted in *Miscellanea Scotica*, vol. iii, embracing an instance connected with St Kilda.

totally unacquainted with all arts, and more especially with religion. The proprietor of the island, after the summer solstice, sends thither his procurator, and in his company a priest, who is to baptize the children born during the preceding year. But, in the absence of a priest on that occasion, every one baptizes his own children.' I have already referred to the doings of Coll Keitach in St Kilda, in the year 1641, when he employed himself in giving the natives instruction in the Lord's Prayer, the Decalogue, and the Creed; and also to the extraordinary proceedings of Roderick the Impostor, towards the end of the seventeenth century. Martin's party, as we have seen, was accompanied by a clergyman, in the person of the Rev. John Campbell, minister of Harris, and one of the writers on St Kilda compares our author to 'another Knox', in consequence of his throwing down their altars and scourging their will-worship.[7] Martin describes the St Kildans as 'Christians, much of the primitive temper, neither inclined to enthusiasm nor to Popery. They swear not the common oaths that prevail in the world; when they refuse to give what is asked of them, they do it with a strong asseveration, which they express emphatically enough in their language to this purpose, "You are no more to have it than if God had forbid it"; and thus they express the highest degree of passion. They do not so much as name the devil once in their lifetimes.' In accordance with ancient custom, they leave off working from Saturday at noon till Monday morning. They believe in the Trinity, in a future state of happiness and misery,[8] in predestination, and in the embodiment of spirits: they use a set form of prayer in hoisting their sails, and begin all their labours with the name of God. In Martin's time, there were no fewer than three chapels on the island, called respectively Christ Church, St Columba's, and St Brianan's (or Brendan's), each with a churchyard attached, and about a quarter

---

7 His name – Martin Martin – might have suggested a comparison to another great religious reformer.

8 Flathannis, 'the Island of the Brave', and Ii bhròin, 'the Region of Sorrow'.

of a mile distant from each other. Not a vestige of these temples
remains, but their position is indicated in Martin's map. According
to Macaulay, the largest of these was Christ Church, which was
built of stone, without any cement – its length being twenty-four,
and its breadth fourteen feet. The temple of St Brendan was situated about a mile to the south-west of the village. It had 'an altar
within and some monkish cells without it'; and as these were
almost entire in 1758, our author concludes that the edifice must
have been of later date than either Christ Church or St Columba's
chapel, of which last he gives no details. In addition to the altar in
St Brendan's temple, there appear to have been no fewer than
four others in different parts of the island, one of which, situated
'on the top of a hill to the south-west', was dedicated to the god
of the seasons. On this altar the ancient St Kildans were in the
habit of offering propitiatory sacrifices, after the manner of the
pagans referred to by the Mantuan bard. Martin states that both
the old and the young islanders used to find their way to the
churchyard, every Sunday morning, to say the Lord's Prayer,
Creed and Ten Commandments, 'the chapel not being capacious
enough to receive them'.

In acknowledging Martin's attempted reformation, Buchan
asserts, from personal experience, that although the material
monuments of idolatry had been thrown down, 'yet the spiritual
ones which were erected in the hearts of the islanders were not
touched'. He then describes the circumstances under which he
was sent to St Kilda, as catechist, in 1705, by the Commission of
the General Assembly; the progress of his missionary efforts; and
his return to Edinburgh, after four years' residence in the island,
accompanied by two native boys, 'whom he had taught reading
and the principles of religion'. In the spring of the following
year (1710) he was ordained in the cathedral church of St Giles,
and shortly afterwards went to St Kilda to take the spiritual
oversight of the inhabitants, and to endeavour 'to root out the
pagan and Popish superstitious customs, so much yet in use
among that people'. From various 'charitable Christians', he

received money to assist in the erection of a manse, besides books and other useful gifts. In 1711, the Society for Propagating Christian Knowledge provided Mr Buchan with a salary of 300 merks (£16 13s 4d), to which a small addition was afterwards made. He leads us to understand that the islanders so thoroughly appreciated his ministrations that they would not allow him to go to Edinburgh 'anent his children', lest he should not return to St Kilda. After alluding to the kirk-session which he succeeded in constituting with a view to the exercise of discipline and the suppression of immorality, he expresses great anxiety relative to the future spiritual welfare of the island, and states that in order to meet the emergency, he 'is breeding his two sons at schools in Edinburgh, that if they ever be in a capacity, and do incline to the ministry, one of them may be employed in St Kilda; which is his sincere wish.' The worthy minister, after twenty-four years' residence in the lonely island, was cut off by fever in 1730,[9] and the fate of his surviving family is referred to in a previous chapter.

Mr Buchan's successor was the Rev. Roderick McLennan, a graduate of Aberdeen, from whom, as well as from his wife, poor Lady Grange experienced very great kindness, which 'helped to preserve her life and make it comfortable'. She pronounced Mr McLennan to be 'a serious and devout man, and very painfull in the discharge of his duties'. In 1743, he was appointed missionary in the Presbytery of Tongue; and since his time, none of his successors appear to have had a seat in the courts of the Church. In 1733, Mr Alexander Macleod, advocate, lodged in the hands of the Society for Propagating Christian Knowledge the sum of £333, 6s 8d, the interest of which was to be employed in support of the minister, catechist or missionary of St Kilda. Six years later, the directors increased the yearly payment to twenty-five pounds, and made arrangements for the patronage of the living being vested in the laird of Harris and his heirs male.

---

9 Mr Sands states that, according to the St Kildans, Buchan was killed by a bull.

When Macaulay visited St Kilda in 1758, he found the islanders very 'devout' in respect to their regular attendance at divine worship and their strict observance of the Lord's Day. 'Some of them, however,' he adds, 'are rather free of vices than possessed of virtues; dissimulation, or a low sort of cunning, and a trick of lying, are their predominant faults.' He also describes their apprehension of the Divine nature and perfections, as 'in some instances gross enough, though infinitely less so than those of many ancient and perhaps modern philosophers'. He refers to a belief in destiny, or an unavoidable resistless fate, as one of the strongest articles of their creed – fate and Providence at St Kilda being regarded as much the same thing; and then speculates on the 'metaphysical question' respecting the reconciliation of free will and predestination! He speaks of Buchan having displayed a much greater amount of zeal than his two immediate successors, and describes the 'fourth Protestant minister of St Kilda' (Donald McLeod), who held the cure at the time of his visit in 1758, as 'a man of sense, virtue and piety', but otherwise unfitted for the position on account of the precarious state of his health.

After McLennan's departure the succession of ministers was as follows.

1744 (?)	Alexander McLeod
1755	Donald McLeod
1774	Angus McLeod
1788	Lachlan McLeod
1830	Neil McKenzie

Lane Buchanan refers to the incumbent at the time of his visit (either Angus or Lachlan McLeod) as being 'illiterate', but discharging his duty to the best of his knowledge. He states that 'he studied his divinity from his father, who was a poor man that failed in his circumstances, being a farmer and mechanic in Uist, before he was clothed with the character of a minister and sent to officiate among those people, in which capacity he continued till his death opened the vacancy for his son, who was judged qualified to explain the English Bible into Gaelic'.

In the year 1821, in consideration of the Society for Propagating Christian Knowledge having agreed to double the yearly payment of twenty-five pounds, John Alexander Norman Macleod transferred his right of patronage to the Society, 'a special regard being still had to persons of the name of Macleod, in terms of the original mortification'[10]. Since that date, however, in the case of the only appointment that has been made, it will be observed that the bearer of another surname was selected. As already mentioned, St Kilda was four times visited by the Rev. Dr Macdonald of Urquhart – 'the apostle of the north' – between the years 1822 and 1830. On each of these occasions he remained for about a fortnight on the island. 'It grieves me to say,' he writes, 'and I took pains to ascertain the truth – that among the whole body I did not find a single individual who could be truly called a decidedly religious person.' He found, however, upon inquiry, that a few years before his first visit to the island, there was a young man of singular piety, who scarcely did anything else than read his Bible and pray, and who died at the early age of nineteen or twenty. The doctor told the islanders that, during his stay among them, he intended to preach every day, besides catechising and performing such other duties as might be necessary; and he appears to have been much pleased with the earnestness and docility which most of them displayed. Their gratitude to the worthy evangelist was evinced by various acts of kindness, including the presentation of a 'good fat wedder' at the conclusion of his second visit. In alluding to one of his discourses relative to the connection between faith and practice, Dr Macdonald says that, 'from the high ground he had occupied, he was afraid the people might veer towards Antinomianism (an extreme as dangerous if not more so than Arminianism); for he found that they could be led into any system, such was the confidence they put in their spiritual instructor'.

10 *Fasti Eccles. Scot.*, iii, 140.

On the occasion of Mr Wilson's visit to St Kilda, the spiritual oversight of the islanders was in the hands of Mr McKenzie, respecting whom he thus writes: 'The good minister is teacher and writing-master (literally prime minister) as well as priest, and seems to leave nothing untried to ameliorate the condition of his flock, whether by enlightening their spiritual darkness, improving their worldly fortunes,' or, as Dr Johnson would have said, raising them in the scale of thinking beings.' The same favourable testimony, is borne by the author of *Sketches of St Kilda*, who, in alluding to Mr McKenzie's self-denial and other good deeds, says: 'He is at this moment in Glasgow on an errand of mercy. It is well known the people never had a bed other than the earthen floor, or, what was little better, a cave in the earthen wall! never had a mill but the *brà*, or handmill, never had a stool or chair. Mr McKenzie induced them to erect better houses, came to Glasgow to plead for them, and, by the assistance of Dr Macleod of St Columba and other patriotic gentlemen, has the prospect of returning in a few days with beds, chairs, stools, mills, nay, even glass windows!' The same writer refers to the devotional character of the islanders, and, on the authority of Dr Macleod, mentions an instance of a St Kildan, on the occasion of a visit to the mainland, warmly asserting his constant trust in the Almighty. 'Elevated on his rock, suspended over a precipice, tossed on the wild ocean, a St Kilda man,' he said, 'can never forget his God – he hangs continually on His arm.' He also gives some interesting particulars regarding the religious services conducted at St Kilda by Drs Macleod and Dickson, when he visited the island in 1838.

The desirability of having the remote island erected into a parish has long been urged; but since the year after the Disruption the supervision of the spiritual wants of the St Kildans has been exercised by the Free Church – or, as Mr Sands expresses it, 'the swallows have allowed their nests to be taken from them by the sparrows!' As already stated, Mr Duncan Kennedy was appointed catechist in 1853; and on leaving the island towards the end of 1863, he was succeeded by the Rev. A. Cameron, who took his departure after a sojourn of about two years. Since October 1865, the Rev. John McKay, now about sixty years of age, has been the faithful bishop of St Kilda.

The stipend of the present minister is about eighty pounds, and it has been stated that the islanders annually contribute the sum of ten pounds to the 'Sustentation Fund' of the Free Church. In 1874, the contribution is said to have amounted to twenty pounds, which Mr Sands considers must have cost the islanders an enormous effort. 'Coupled with the unprofitable way in which their trade is conducted,' he says that it reminds him of the well-known passage in Joel – 'That which the palmerworm hath left hath the locust eaten.' The same writer speaks of the minister as

not only an earnest and honest man, but a kind-hearted one withal, whom those of any or of no persuasion would respect. There, posted like a sentinel on a rocky bank close to the sea, his whole aim is to keep the devil out of the island. Absorbed in this duty, he forgets the loneliness of his situation, and is deaf to the roaring of the waves that rage before his sentry-box during the long winter, and blind to the desolate aspect of the hills that tower steeply around, their lofty tops enveloped in drifting fogs. He is contented with plain fare and drinks none, is attentive to the infirm, and shares, in a stealthy way, what luxuries he has with them. Although an educated man, he has no books (?) and no newspapers to enliven his solitude. Who so anxious as he when the boats happened to be caught in a storm? Methinks I see him now, wandering restlessly on the shore, watching the waves outside the bay lashed into foam by the strong north wind, until the boats came round the rocky point . . . Although a bachelor, he is seldom to be seen without a rosy-cheeked urchin – a lamb of his flock – hanging on to his breeches-pocket and following him like a dog. Personally I am indebted to him for numberless acts of friendship – kindness continued from first to last. He pressed me to live in his house, and when, preferring freedom and ths bagpipes, I declined his invitation, he did his utmost to render me comfortable in my own quarters. Take him for all in all, the Free Kirk has few soldiers she has more reason to feel proud of.[11]

He elsewhere informs us that the islanders attend public worship three times every Sunday, and hold a prayer-meeting, which is conducted by the elders, every Wednesday night. They have also a thanksgiving service on the first Tuesday of every month for the preservation of the *Porcupine*, which was very nearly lost on the island in October 1860.

The Sunday [says Mr Sands] is indeed a day of intolerable gloom. At the sound of the bell, the whole flock hurry to church in single file, with dejected looks and eyes bent on the ground. They seem like a troop of the damned, whom Satan is driving to the bottomless pit. With no floor but mother earth, and with damp sticking to the walls like hoar-frost or feathers, the women sit in church for about six and a half hours every Sunday, with bare feet and legs, even in winter . . . All the men remain seated until the women have made their *exeunt* . . . No one visits another, or speaks above a whisper, on the Sabbath-day. I felt myself like an owl in the desert, and was fain to steal out in the dark to stretch my limbs with three steps and a turn before my domicile; for a long walk, or rather a climb, was evidently regarded as the height of iniquity. There is family

11 This eloquent panegyric is most unaccountably omitted from the second edition of Mr Sands' work, in which, however, there are several references to the minister of a somewhat less complimentary kind. In one place he speaks of him as having 'a disordered liver'; in another, he refers to his 'jealousy' and 'interference'; and in a third – in juxtaposition to a wretched caricature of the little pastor, which forms one of several additional illustrations – he indirectly describes him as 'a well-meaning but feeble-minded, irresolute, yet domineering fanatic!' Such, according to Mr Sands, is the minister of St Kilda in the year of grace 1877; while in 1876, he was earnest, honest and kind-hearted – a faithful sentinel – an educated man – although a bachelor, most tender to the young – friendly and kind to Mr Sands from first to last – and a soldier of whom the Free Kirk has great reason to feel proud. *Quantum mutatus ab illo Hectore!*

worship in every house every evening and morning, and every meal is preceded by a grace, nor will they take a drink of milk or water without uncovering the head.

A striking illustration of the extreme Sabbatarian views of the St Kildans was exhibited on the occasion of the gunboat *Flirt* carrying supplies to the island in the beginning of May 1877. The vessel reached St Kilda about half-past nine on a Saturday night, and the weather being fine and anchorage unsafe, efforts were at once made to land the provisions. The natives, however, headed by the minister, firmly refused to render the slightest assistance, on the ground that in doing so they would encroach on 'the Sabbath'; and all argument failed to overcome their religious scruples. They would rather trust to the weather continuing favourable till Monday morning. The captain endeavoured to land a few bags with the boats of the vessel, but was completely baffled by the violence of the surf. Accordingly, the only alternative was to wait patiently and 'wish' for Monday's dawn. Happily Providence was kind, and the supplies were duly conveyed to the shore in the course of Monday morning.

Considering the opinions that prevail in many of the larger islands, as well as in certain parts of the mainland, on the subject of Sabbath observance, it is hardly to be wondered at that the lonely inhabitants of St Kilda should still display the results of those unhappy influences which have unfortunately prevailed on the north side of the Tweed. It is pleasant, however, to find that sounder views are steadily extending over the length and breadth of Scotland; and if we only had a few more Norman Macleods, the spirit of our blessed religion would ultimately take the place which has so long been usurped by the letter. Of course, I am quite aware of the arguments founded upon 'Continental Sundays' and the 'thin end of the wedge'; but I am also aware of the extraordinary estimate which is still formed, in certain quarters, of the comparative heinousness of grossly immoral offences on the one hand, and of a so-called 'desecration of the *Sawbbath*' on the other. A good many years ago, Dr S—, a well-known and highly-esteemed clergyman of the Church of Scotland, had occasion to pay a visit of inspection to a northern parish, under the direction of the General Assembly. Immediately after his arrival, he was accosted by a member of the congregation, who informed him, in an excited tone, that he had a serious charge to make against the minister; and on being asked the nature of the accusation, the complainer said: 'Would you believe it, sir – he takes a waalk in his gairden on the Sawbbath?' Knowing something of the antecedents of the Highland Pharisee, the doctor quietly inquired whether or not it was the case that he had been cited before the kirk-session for 'discipline', on two different occasions. 'Deed ay, sir,' replied the consistent individual; 'but ye must remember that we are a' frail craturs!' 'Those who live in glass houses . . .' the reader knows the rest.

Music, Customs and Antiquities

Edgar Poe quotes from memory an idea which he found in an old English tale relative to the 'springheade and origine' of music, viz, 'the verie pleasaunte sounde which the trees of the forest do make when they growe'. In that view of the matter, it is difficult to conceive how the inhabitants of Hirta could ever have become amenable to the charms of the 'heavenly maid'; but more than one poet has indicated other sources of the divine science – the dawning morn, the twilight cloud, the depth of night, the sighing of a reed, and the gushing of a rill – from one or more of which the remote islanders doubtless derived their appreciation of music. Martin informs us that he found St Kildans of both sexes 'who have a genius for poetry, and are great admirers of music. The trump or Jewish harp', he adds, 'is all the musical instrument they have, which disposes them to dance mightily.' Elsewhere, however, he refers to the use of the bagpipe at their marriage festivals. In alluding to the use of the distaff by the women, he states that 'they sing and jest for diversion, and in their way understand poetry, and make rhymes in their language'. Macaulay bears still stronger testimony to the islanders' love of music.

> They are enthusiastically fond of it [he says] whether in the vocal or instrumental way: the very lowest tinklings of the latter throws them into ecstacy of joy. I have seen them dancing to a bad violin much to my satisfaction: even the old women in the isle act their part in the great assemblies, and the most agile dancers are here, as well as everywhere else, very

great favourites. They delight much in singing, and their voices are abundantly tuneful.[1] The women, while cutting down their barley in a field, or grinding their grain on their hand-mills in the house, are almost constantly employed in that way; and the men, if pulling at the oar, exert all the strength of their skill in animating the party, by chanting away some spirited songs adapted to the business in hand. The seamen of Athens practised the same custom.[2]

The same writer descants on the unpromising conditions of the seagirt isle for the votaries of Apollo and the nine sisters, but reminds his readers that the fogs of Baeotia and the mountains of Thrace have produced illustrious poets, and that it is easier to trace the Muses in the cold regions of the north than in sunnier climes. After specifying the subjects which have been handled by the bards of St Kilda in their odes – the beauty of their female favourites, the heroism of the men in climbing rocks and breasting the billows of the ocean, and 'the common topics of personal advantages and intellectual merit' – he proceeds to imagine the results of the residence of a great poetical genius amid the wonders of the romantic Ale – strange 'landskips', a boundless ocean, lofty precipices, mountains lost in the clouds, a countless variety of birds, 'monstrous sea-animals', a curious race of intelligent beings, noble cataracts, purling streams and crystal fountains, 'equal perhaps to those of Helicon and Castalia' – and comes to the satisfactory conclusion that such a gifted individual might very easily pursue, in the words of Milton,

Things unattempted yet in prose or rhyme!

1 In the notice of St Kilda in the *Edinburgh Encyclopaedia*, reference is made to the singing of the islanders while engaged in dancing, each of the party taking up the tune in succession, a practice which Dr McDonald states had gone greatly out of use upwards of fifty years ago, the violin having taken the place of vocal music
2 'Bragela listens to the winds of night, to hear the voice of thy rowers; to hear the song of the sea and the sound of thy distant harp' – Ossian's 'Fingal', book vi.

The author of 'Rasselas' takes a very different and somewhat matter-of-fact view. Speaking of St Kilda poetry, of which he had heard in the course of his tour, he observed that 'it must be very poor, because the inhabitants have very few images'. On Boswell remarking that a poetical genius may be shown in their combination, the Doctor replied: 'Sir, a man cannot make fire, but in proportion as he has fuel.' (In a literal sense, at least, this is painfully true at St Kilda!) 'He cannot coin guineas but in proportion as he has gold.'

Lane Buchanan refers to the delight which both the men and women took in singing. 'Their songs', he says, 'are wonderfully descriptive, and discover great strength of fancy.' As time wears on, however, another picture unfortunately begins to present itself, and a later visitor tells a different tale.

All the world [says Macculloch] has heard of St Kilda music and St Kilda poetry, just as all the world has heard of the musical and poetical genius of the Highlanders ... We were prepared to bring away some valuable relics; the staves were already ruled, the dragoman appointed; but alas! there was neither fiddle nor Jew's harp in the island, and it was not remembered when there had been either. The Muses, whom the Abbe Cartaud calls 'Jupiter's opera girls', seemed to have carried their functions to warmer regions. There was a day when he who had slept on the top of Concohan awoke a poet ... In the meantime, the poetry has followed the music; and thus common fame maintained its well-earned reputation.

The same writer devotes a good many pages of his earlier work to the subject of 'Highland Music', in which he makes the following allusion to St Kilda. 'Among other subjects', he says, 'which do not appear to have stood the test of examination, St Kilda has been celebrated for its music. That reputation, if it was ever well-founded, exists no longer; nor, at the time of my visit, did it appear that there was either a bagpipe or a violin in the island. The airs which are recorded as originating in this place are of a plaintive character; but they differ in no respect from the innumerable ancient compositions of this class which abound in the Highlands.' He classifies Highland music under the two grand heads of pibrochs and simple airs, the former being distinguished by a very irregular character without time or accent, and often scarcely embracing a determined melody, with a train of complicated and tasteless variations, adding confusion to the original air; while the latter are usually of a plaintive description, divisible into a regular number of accented bars, often in a minor key, and presenting very little variety. One peculiar characteristic of nearly all these simple airs is their adaptability to either slow or quick time, constituting, as they frequently do, the ordinary dance-music of the country, there being no essential difference between the reel and the pathetic air.

The 'Apostle of the North' incidentally alludes to the 'musical turn' of the St Kildans at the time of his second visit to the island in 1824; but a more recent writer confirms Macculloch's statement relative to the departure of a taste for music from the shores of St Kilda. 'At one period,' he says, 'they were fond of music, although the Jew's harp was the only instrument they possessed, and to its feeble twang they danced and were gay. None of them perform on any instrument now, and dancing is unknown.' In his notice of one of the oldest men on the island, still bearing the name of Donull Og, or *young* Donald, the same writer says that he may be seen daily, sitting on the low wall opposite his cottage, sewing clothes or making gins, and humming an *oran Hirtaich* or St Kildan song.

Donald McKinnon, the Obbe precentor, informed me that Finlay McLeod, like himself a native of St Kilda, who died about fifty years ago, composed an air – a species of *lilt* – which embraces no fewer than sixteen 'turns', and is very difficult to play. It received the name of 'The St Kilda Wedding' from Mr Angus McLeod, formerly a banker in Edinburgh, and son of one of the ministers of St Kilda. Christopher Macrae, an old piper in the same quarter, whom I also saw, plays the tune, but was unable to write the score. I understood McKinnon to say that the words by which the air is usually accompanied describe the performances of a skilful cragsman, and other exciting incidents.

On the occasion of his visit to St Kilda in 1838, Mr Maclean was much affected by the tremulous but musical voice of an old woman – Margaret McLeod by name – seated on a stone by the side of her cottage, and busily plying the spindle, as she sang an elegiac song or 'lament', composed by a sorrowing mother in memory of a favourite son, who met his death on the cliffs of Soa. As a tribute of respect to my esteemed friend, the professor of Greek in the University of Edinburgh, I subjoin the original words:

AIR – *McGregor's Lament*
Dh' fhag mi thall ann a' So'a,
Macan òg nach robh leumrach;
Thu bhi mach sa Gheo'-chumhann,
Gur aonail dubhach nad dheigh mi

Cha tig thu gud' mhàthair,
Ged is fail'neach a' leirsinn;
'Stu nach oladh le macaibh,
'Snach innseadh dhachaidh na breugan.

Dh' fhag thu d'fhuil air a chloich ud,
Rinn do chorpan a reubadh;
'S fuar do leaba fo'n tuinne,
Stu nad spurt aig na beistean!

Not many months ago, the following 'tolerably literal' translation of a St Kilda song appeared in the columns of the *Scotsman* newspaper, where it was stated to be at least as old as the middle of last century, and possibly much older. The contributor of the translation – Mr Alexander Stewart – first heard it sung some five-and-twenty years ago by one of the crew of the Revenue cruiser *Harriet*, a native of Lewis or Harris. He describes the air as one of the wildest and *eeriest* he ever listened to, 'the burden or refrain being manifestly an imitation, consciously or unconsciously, of the loud discordant clamour of a flock of sea-fowl over a shoal of fish.'

THE ST KILDA MAID'S SONG

Over the rocks, steadily, steadily;
    Down to the clefts with a shout and a shove, O!
Warily tend the rope, shifting it readily;
    Eagerly, actively, watch from above, O!
        Brave, O brave, my lover true, he's worth a maiden's love;
        (And the sea below is still as deep as the sky is high above!)

Sweet 'tis to sleep on a well-feathered pillow;
    Sweet from the embers the fulmar's red egg, O!
Bounteous our store from the rock and the billow;
    Fish and birds in good store, we need never to beg, O!
        Brave, O brave, etc.

Hark to the fulmar and guillemot screaming,
    Hark to the kittiwake, puffin and gull, O!
See the white wings of the solan goose gleaming;
    Steadily, men, on the rope gently pull, O!
        Brave, O brave, etc.

Deftly my love can hook torsc, ling and conger,
    The grey fish and hake with the net and the creel, O!
Far from our island be plague and be hunger;
    And sweet our last sleep in the quiet of the keel, O!
        Brave, O brave, etc.

Pull on the rope, men! pull it up steadily;
    There's a storm on the deep, see the skart claps his wings, O!
Cunningly guide the rope, shifting it readily;
      Welcome my true love, and all that he brings, O!
      Now God be praised, my lover's safe, he's worth
        a maiden's love;
        (And the sea below, etc.)

In the fourth volume of the *Scots Musical Museum*, I recently found a very sweet and plaintive air entitled 'St Kilda Day'. The words by which it is accompanied are said to be a translation, by the Rev. Andrew McDonald,[3] of a favourite Gaelic song sung by the natives of St Kilda to the air in the *Museum*, from which both words and music were reprinted by Mr Charles Stewart in his *Vocal Miscellany*, published in 1798. I venture to think that the introduction of the air will be generally appreciated. The disconsolate songstress appears to be in search of her lover, who, we may suppose, has met with an untimely end in the course of a fowling expedition. As in the poetical epistle from 'Matilda', referred to in a previous chapter, Mr McDonald's verses embrace some allusions not quite appropriate to the seagirt isle, which, so far as I am aware, can boast of neither 'waving ivy' nor 'twisted willow'.

St Kilda Song
Slow, with expression

By the stream so cool and clear,
And thro' he caves where
breezes languish,
Soothing still my tender anguish,
Hoping still to find my lover,
I have wander'd
far and near:
O where shall I the youth discover?

Sleeps he in your breezy shade
Ye rocks with moss and ivy waving,
On some bank where wild waves laving,

---

3 McDonald was the son of George Donald, gardener in Leith. Born in 1757, he studied at the University of Edinburgh, received deacon's orders in the Scottish Episcopal Church in 1775, when 'Mc' was prefixed to his surname, ultimately settled in London as a literary character, and died in 1790. The song is embraced in his *Miscellaneous Works*, 'including the *Tragedy of Vimonda* and those productions which have appeared under the signature of Matthew Bramble, Esq.' London, 1791.

Murmur through the twisted willow?
On that bank, O were I laid,
How soft should be my lover's pillow!

It would appear that, in recent times, all ordinary vocal music of a secular character has been in a great measure superseded by psalms and hymns. One of my fellow-passengers in the *Dunara Castle* was the bearer of some perfectly unobjectionable Gaelic song-books, and on his presenting them to the islanders, they were immediately submitted to the censorship of the minister, who decided that as they were 'neither psalms nor spiritual hymns', they could not be accepted! Even when I distributed my fairy tales and other picture-books among the children, I had a vision of the *index librorum prohibitorum*, but the 'holy father' of Hirta made no sign of disapproval.

In describing the Sunday services at St Kilda, Mr Macdiarmid says that 'the singing baffles description. Everybody sang at the top of his voice, and to his own tune; there was no attempt at harmony'. According to Mr Wilson, the Irish melodies are unknown to the islanders. 'Dancing,' he says, 'is also now regarded by them as a frivolous amusement, and has ceased to be practised even during their more joyous festivals, such as marriage or baptism.' Captain Thomas attributes these changes in their habits to the instruction of fanatical teachers, the result of which is merely the exchange of one superstition for another. 'One prominent instance,' he writes to me, 'is the belief that all secular music is vicious; and both in St Kilda and the Long Island, one of the ruling canons is that "it is easier for a camel to pass through the eye of a needle, than for a piper, etc." I have been told,' he says, 'that, in Uig, it was proposed by some of the ascetics to give church censure to a man who received his brother, who was a piper, into his house, but that the minister refused. An Established minister may play the accordion, but not the fiddle – a Free Churchman is restricted to the Jew's harp!' My correspondent's statement reminds me of an amusing story which is told of a Dissenting minister who was appointed to a charge in Paisley, and whose musical fame reached the town before he himself arrived. He had not been many hours in his new sphere of labour, when a female member of the congregation, who highly disapproved of his fiddling propensities, waited upon the divine and said, in a censorious tone, 'So I hear you play the violin!' 'Yes,' said the minister, seizing a huge violoncello which happened to be within his reach, 'and I will play you a tune.' Before the astonished *frondeur* could interpose an objection, he proceeded to discourse in most melodious strains, and after finishing an exquisite air, he asked her what she thought of it? 'Very bonnie,' she immediately replied, 'very bonnie; but then, you see, that's no the sinfu' *little* fiddle' – a fair example, by the way, of Scotch meta*phee*sics!

A few of the *customs* of the St Kildans have been incidentally mentioned in a previous chapter. In his description of Christ's Chapel, the site of which is occupied by the necropolis of the island, Martin mentions a brazen crucifix which lay upon the altar, not exceeding a foot in length, and the head bearing a crown. 'They hold it', he says, 'in great reverence, though they pay no kind of adoration or worship to it, nor do they either handle or see it, except upon the occasions of marriage, and swearing decisive oaths, which puts an end to all strife, and both these ceremonies are publicly performed.' He also mentions that the islanders observed the festivals of Christmas, Easter, Good Friday, St Columba's Day and All Saints, on the last of which 'they have an anniversary cavalcade, the number of their horses not exceeding eighteen; these they mount by turns, having neither saddle nor bridle of any kind, except a rope, which manages the horse only on one side. They ride from the shore to the house, and then after each man has performed his tour, the show is at an end.' Macaulay connects the St Kilda 'Derby' with Michaelmas, when, he informs us, 'the ablest horsemen among them ride their little high-mettled nags, like so many Numidians or old Britons, without saddles, stirrups, or bridles. Those who distinguish themselves in these races, are supremely happy in the rewards of honour and glory which they obtain, though strangers to the royal plates of the moderns, and the palm crowns of ancient times.' The nature of the ground could not have been very suitable, one would think, for rapid riding; but to this day the inhabitants of Siena, in North Italy, indulge in the ancient horse races of their ancestors – some of the steepest streets in the city being selected for the course. Macaulay gives a detailed account of the festivals of St Kilda, specifying New Year's Day and Michaelmas, in addition to those mentioned by Martin. It appears that the festival of St Columba was held on 16 June, although, according to the calendar, it falls upon the ninth – St Brendan's festival being observed on 27 May, instead of 16th, as in the calendar. He tells us that Brendan, in Gaelic *Brianin*, was an Irish saint, a contemporary of St Columba, and that a great number of churches were dedicated to his holiness in the Western Isles. On these two saints' days, all the milk of the commonwealth was delivered to the steward or his deputy with the view of its being equally distributed among every man, woman and child in the island, after the manner of the *agapae* or love-feasts of early times; and our author conjectures that the practice was probably introduced into St Kilda by the Culdees. On Christmas and New Year's Day, besides eating and drinking 'the best things their land affords', the islanders danced with great skill and agility, while a grave demeanour was the order of the day on Easter Sunday. The same writer informs us that 'till of late', it was the custom of the islanders to prepare in every family, on Michaelmas Day, an enormous cake, compounded of various ingredients. 'This cake belonged to the archangel, and had its name from him. Every one in each family, whether strangers or domestics, had his portion of this kind of shew-bread; and had, of course, some title to the friendship and protection of Michael.'

I have already referred to the altar on *Mulláchgeal*, where the ancient St Kildans offered sacrifices to the god of the seasons. Macaulay mentions a large stone, 'white and square', on the face of another hill between the village and the north-west side of the island, on which the islanders formerly poured libations of milk, every Sunday, to a 'good-humoured, sportive and placable deity', named in Gaelic *Grugach*, or the divinity with fine hair or long tresses – the Grannus of the Britons and the Apollo of Greece and Rome. A little above the Grugach stone, there appears to have been a small green plain, called by the St Kildans *Liani-nin-ore*, or 'the Plain of Spells', exorcisms or prayers, where they implored God's blessing on their cattle, and lustrated the animals with salt, water and fire, with the view of removing 'the power of fascinations, the malignity of elves, and the vengeance of every evil genius'[4]! Below the field of spells and lustrations was another fertile spot, which the natives declined to convert into arable ground, under the idea that it ought to be kept sacred, and that any encroachment upon it 'would be infallibly attended with the loss of their boat, or some other public calamity'. Although they had forgotten the name of the divinity to whom this piece of ground belonged, like the Athenians of old, they continued to worship the 'unknown god'.

Both Martin and Macaulay allude to the consecrated wells, already referred to, which were formerly held in great veneration. The latter specially mentions three – viz, *Tobirnimbuadh*, or the spring of diverse virtues, situated near the *Camper*, or crooked bay;[5] *Toberi Clerich*, or the clerk's well, below the village; and *Tobir Childa Chalda*, or 'Kilder's Fountain', from which the island is supposed to have derived its modern name. 'At every full tide the sea overflows the clerk's well, but how soon that ebbs away, nothing can be fresher or sweeter than the water.'

Martin gives a short account of what appears to have been a species of '*anachd*', or shinty, a game which the Scottish Highlanders have long enthusiastically practised. 'They use', he says, 'for their diversion short clubs and balls of wood. The sand is a fair field for this sport and exercise, in which they take great pleasure, and are very nimble at it. They play for some eggs, fowls, hooks, or tobacco; and so eager are they for victory, that they strip

---

4 See Tibullus, lib. ii, eleg. I.
5 More correctly derived, according to Captain Thomas, from *kambr*, the Norse for 'crest' or 'ridge'.

themselves to their shirts to obtain it. They use swimming and diving, and are very expert in both.' Curiously enough when Mr Wilson visited the island in 1841, not a single inhabitant could swim – 'A fact', he says, 'which at first surprised us; but on reflection it is evident that when any unfortunate catastrophe does take place, no human strength or skill in any art can save them from destruction.' No sports or amusements of any kind are now indulged in by the islanders, and even the introduction of a 'draught-board' is said to be interdicted by their present spiritual guide! An innocent 'rubber' would probably be regarded as highly immoral, on the ground that the 'picture-books' of the universal enemy, whom the St Kildans 'do not so much as once name' in the course of their lives, ought to be scrupulously eschewed by them; and accordingly, it is to be feared that they would not appreciate the genius of our great national poet, who did not hesitate to sing the 'horned Deil' under his various names and guises!

In his interesting little volume, entitled *Celtic Gleanings*, Dr McLauchlan makes the following statement, relative to the equivalent of the Saxon *mote* or council which still exists in St Kilda.

In the island of St Kilda, far out among the waves of the Atlantic, is a purely Celtic population, retaining many of the earlier customs of the race. They have never been brought into contact with our civil government, and they have no sheriffs, jails or policemen. Yet they have important causes to be decided: an annual division has to be made of their rocks for fowling; the birds caught on neighbouring islands have to be allocated; and disputes of various kinds among the community arranged. And how is this done? Just by means of the 'mod'. The men of the island, as often as needs be, meet in a certain spot, and there, as round the Indian council fire, settle the affairs of the nation.

He then refers to a visit which he had paid to St Kilda, along with some friends, when they entertained doubts as to how they could apportion among the islanders, without causing offence, the gifts which they carried with them. A reference to the 'mod' was at once suggested by one of the community whom they consulted, and in the course of half an hour the presents were divided without a murmur. On the occasion of one of Dr McDonald's visits to St Kilda, he held a sort of justice of peace court along with the steward and the Gaelic teacher, with the view of settling any differences that might happen to exist among the islanders; but he was pleased to find that there were none of any consequence, except one relating to a marriage, the result of which he does not indicate. Mr Sands alludes to the St Kilda 'parliament', or almost daily council of the men, for the discussion of business, in front of one of the houses. 'When the subject is exciting, the members talk with loud voices and all at one time; but when the question is once settled, they work together in perfect harmony. Shall we go to catch solan geese, or ling, or mend the boat today? are examples of the subjects that occupy the house. Sometimes disputes are settled by drawing lots.' The 'obstructives' of St Stephen's would do well to borrow a leaf from the book of these remote islanders!

When Martin visited St Kilda, there was but one steel and tinder-box in the entire commonwealth, 'The owner whereof', he says, 'fails not, upon every occasion of striking fire in the lesser isles, to go thither and exact three eggs, or one of the lesser fowls, from each man, as a reward for his service; this by them is called the "fire-penny", and this capitation is very uneasy to them.' Our author advised the natives to try the effect of their knives upon the 'chrystal', which abounded in the rocks, and on their finding that fire was the result of the collision, 'they were not a little astonished'; 'and by means of this discovery, the fire-penny tax came to an end. At the same period, the islanders had another impost, called the 'pot-penny' tax, which Martin pronounces to be 'much more reasonable' than the other. 'The pot is carried to the inferior isles for the public use, and is in hazard of being broken; so that the owners may justly exact on this score, since any may venture his pot when he pleases.'

As late as the end of the seventeenth century, it would appear
that the St Kildans married very young – the women as early as
thirteen or fourteen years of age; and Martin further informs us
that before entering into the holy bond, they

> are nice in examining the degrees of consanguinity . . . When
> any two of them have agreed to take one another for man and
> wife, the officer who presides over them summons all the
> inhabitants of both sexes to Christ's Chapel, where being
> assembled, he inquires publicly if there be any lawful impedi-
> ment why these parties should not be joined in the bond of
> matrimony? and if there be no objection to the contrary, he
> then inquires of the parties if they are resolved to live together
> in weal and woe. After their assent he declares them married
> persons, and then desires them to ratify this their solemn prom-
> ise in the presence of God and the people, in order to which
> the crucifix is tendered to them, and both put their right hands
> upon it, as the ceremony by which they swear fidelity one to
> another during their lifetime. Mr Campbell, the minister,
> married in this manner fifteen pairs of the inhabitants on the
> 17th of June (1697), who, immediately after their marriage,
> joined in a country-dance, having only a bagpipe for their
> music, which pleased them exceedingly.

He elsewhere gives a curious account of the mode in which a
youthful St Kilda wooer was expected, in former times, to
exhibit some proof of his courage, before securing the plighted
troth of the object of his affections. For that purpose he assembled his friends round the inner margin of 'the lover's stone',
resembling a 'door' in form, which occupies the very verge of a
perpendicular precipice, from twenty to thirty fathoms in height,
at the south-east corner of the island, the situation being indicated in Martin's map under the name of 'the mistress stone'.
Planting the left heel on its outer edge, and with the sole of the
foot entirely unsupported, he extended his right leg beyond the

other and grasped the foot with both hands. He continued in this ticklish position sufficiently long to satisfy the spectators of his pluck and devotion; and after the performance of the feat – a practical illustration of the proverb, 'Faint heart ne'er won fair lady' – he was accounted 'worthy of the finest mistress in the world'. Our author judiciously declined the grave proposal of one of the islanders that *he* should try this 'piece of gallantry' before his departure, on the ground that the result of the performance, in his case, would probably be the loss of both life and mistress at the same moment!

Mr Maclean quotes a long extract from the *Journal* of the Rev. Neil McKenzie relative to a modern marriage ceremony. The minister states that he was invited to the *reiteach* or agreement between the young couple, and on arrival at the house of the bride's father, he found all the men of the island reclining close to the outer wall, the female relatives being inside with the bride. A glass of spirits was handed round to each person to drink to the health of the contracting parties; and on the following Sunday, the banns were duly proclaimed 'for the first, second and third time'[6]. After various preparations, the young couple, accompanied by their nearest relations and a 'best man'[7] and 'bride's maid', attired in their best garments, found their way to the manse, on Monday afternoon, to be married, and to receive the cap which Mrs M'Kenzie was in the habit of presenting to the bride on such occasions. A considerable number of the villagers attended the 'marriage sermon',[8] immediately after which the parties went

6 Happily defined by Lord Chelmsford to be 'a suspension of the standing orders', in terms of which the banns ought to be proclaimed (*Anglicé*, published) on three several Sundays – See *Report of the Royal Commission on the Marriage Laws*, 1868, p. 94.
7 On the occasion of the late Duke of Athole's visit to St Kilda, already referred to, he acted in the capacity of 'best man' at a marriage, when, Mr Morgan informs us, the conventional wedding-cake formed an item in the feast, and which he 'wellnigh mistook for white-washed peat', an article which unfortunately does not exist in the island.
8 'The wedding, you know, is always before the sermon – which is one of the chief things wherein hanging and matrimony disagree' – Fielding.

'home'. In the course of the evening, the bride's brother, with a piece of white cotton cloth attached to each shoulder and the front of his bonnet, came to invite the minister to the 'marriage feast'. The viands consisted of mutton, barley-bannocks and cheese, there being 'neither soup nor drink of any kind'. From first to last, it appears to have been a very solemn business. Ignoring the advice of the immortal dramatist

> Prepare for mirth, for mirth becomes a feast

they seem more disposed to exemplify another of his statements of a somewhat different tone

> A man may weep upon his wedding-day!

Mr Grigor was present at the marriage of four couples on 15 July, 1861, there having been only one marriage for several years previously. Both men and women were very decently attired — the former in jackets and trousers and black silk neckerchiefs, and the latter in printed dresses, bonnets and shawls. The ceremony was performed in the church, but Mr Grigor left the island before the festivities took place. Since the 'Disruption', St Kilda has been frequently visited by clergymen, chiefly of the Free Church, from Harris, Skye, etc.; and indeed a year seldom passes without a parson presenting himself, and thus affording an opportunity for the due consummation of nuptial vows. On these occasions, also, the sacraments of Baptism and the Lord's Supper are usually celebrated. Captain Thomas informs me that at a comparatively recent date, when a clergyman happened to be in St Kilda, a certain bachelor cautiously considered the profit and loss of a proposed union, and at length intimated the result of his cogitations to another island swain by saying, 'If you will take my sister I will take yours!' The latter took the proposal to 'avizandum', and after giving due weight to the moral of the Gaelic lines, thus Englished:

Woe is me, if bad she be,
Woe is me to carry her;
She'll take her food and do no good,
I was a fool to marry her

he arrived at the conclusion that he would not be much worse by the exchange; and no fewer than three weddings was the practical result. The docile character of the women in St Kilda and in the Western Islands generally has been frequently remarked upon – 'grey mares' being very uncommon among them. The jocular pilot of the *Porcupine* told a group of St Kilda girls that, as there was a clergyman on board, they could all get married. Their answer was delightfully Delphic in its character – 'The lads know best!'

I have already referred to the civil or conjugal condition of the inhabitants of St Kilda at the three last censuses. Mr McKenzie's register embraces twenty-two marriages, the bride being in five cases the second wife. Fifteen marriages appear in the new register during the twenty-one years ended 1876, the ceremony having been performed in the last ten cases by the present minister, Mr McKay. In the case of these fifteen marriages, the maximum ages of the bridegrooms and brides respectively were forty-five and thirty-five, and the minimum ages twenty-one and seventeen. The average age of the men was slightly above twenty-eight, and of the women twenty-five – a very different state of matters from that described by Martin. I lately endeavoured, with the aid of the registers and the census enumeration books, to draw up some tabular statements illustrative of the intermarriages of the islanders, but the endless confusion produced by the constant recurrence of the same surnames – particularly Gillies, McDonald, and McKinnon – rendered my attempt comparatively worthless.

In alluding to the appearance of the St Kildans, Mr Muir says 'Notwithstanding that their blood must have greatly degenerated from a long course of intermarrying among themselves, they looked healthy and intelligent'; and subsequent inquiries seem to establish the fact that, contrary to the popular impression, the practice in question is not productive of either physical or mental deterioration. A good many years ago, Dr Arthur Mitchell, one of the Scottish Lunacy Commissioners, sent a series of queries to Mr McRaild, the factor of the late owner of the island, and also to Admiral Otter, on the subject of consanguineous marriages in St Kilda; and the purport of their replies – which agree in all important particulars – is given in his second paper on these unions in the *Edinburgh Medical Journal* for April 1865. In the case of not one of the fourteen married couples then in the island was the relationship between husband and wife that of full cousins or cousins-german. Not less, however, than five of the fourteen couples were second cousins. 'Of these five couples fifty-four children had been born, of whom thirty-seven died in early infancy, when only a few days old, leaving seventeen alive . . . Of the seventeen survivors it is distinctly stated that not one is either insane, imbecile, idiotic, blind, deaf, cripple, deformed, or in any way defective in body or mind.' As Admiral Otter remarks, 'It is certainly strange that though they marry so much amongst themselves, there is only one – a spinster – who is weak in intellect.' The inhabitants do not consider that a blood-relationship between the parents is injurious to the mental or bodily health of the offspring. I have already referred to Dr Mitchell's remarks respecting the connection between the enormous infantile mortality of St Kilda caused by *trismus nascentium*, and the increased fertility of the women. The average age of the fourteen wives was forty-three and a half, and the average number of children to a marriage nine; or ten, if we except the case of one couple without children. The same result is found in Iceland, and medical men have little difficulty in explaining the cause. 'What influence', says Dr Mitchell, 'this great infantile mortality may have on the surviving offspring, taken as illustrative of the effects of consanguine marriages, it is not easy to say.'

As I have already incidentally stated, the 'High Dean of the Isles' informs us that 'McCloyd of Herray, his stewart, sailes anes in the zeir to Hirta at midsummer, with some chaplaine to baptize bairnes ther, and if they want a chaplaine, they baptize their bairns themselfes.' According to Martin, 'the parent calls in the officer, or any of his neighbours, to baptize his child, and another to be sponsor or *gosti*. He that performs the minister's part being told what the child's name is to be, says, "A.B., I baptize thee to your father and mother, in the name of the Father, Son and Holy Ghost." Then the sponsor takes the child in his arms, as doth his wife as godmother, and ever after this there is a friendship between the parent and the sponsor, which is esteemed so sacred and inviolable, that no accident, how cross soever, is able to set them at variance; and it reconciles such as have been at enmity formerly.' So far as I am aware, the present procedure at baptism is in accordance with the ordinary practice observed on the mainland, the ceremony being performed either by the pastor of St Kilda or by a clerical visitor.

In olden times, when a death took place in St Kilda, the 'cry' went through the whole island, in order that all the inhabitants on the rocks or in the fields might cease from their labours, and return to their homes. A few days after the demise, the body was interred with due solemnity with the face towards the east; and after the burial, a 'snuff-mull' went round the mourners. Doleful songs, called 'laments', were composed on such occasions. Shortly before Martin's visit, on the news of Macleod's death reaching the island, the St Kildans 'abandoned their houses, mourning two days in the fields'.

Mr McKenzie, in his *Journal*, gives a detailed account of the modern course of procedure. On the occurrence of a death, the near relatives and friends, especially the females, weep and wail, and, like Rachel of old, 'refuse to be comforted'. In a short time, however, some of those who appear inconsolable, are 'nearly as cheerful as ever'. The body of the deceased is usually kept not more than three days in the house; and during that time the coffin is constructed, and a feast of bread and mutton prepared for the use of those who watch the corpse and the other mourners. 'The more sheep they kill, and the more barley they use, the more honour do they intend to confer on their deceased friend; and those who have lost many relatives have been much reduced by this foolish custom.' Accordingly, it would appear that the funeral extravagance of the mainland, recorded in Dean Ramsay's *Reminiscences*, has found its way to St Kilda! On the day of the burial, the coffin is tied upon two sticks or bearers, and carried 'in the course of the sun' – if necessary, through the corn. When the grave is filled up, the mourners sit down, at all seasons, and partake of the food which has been prepared for the occasion. Adults are interred in the afternoon, and children late in the evening. According to Mr Sands, the interment now takes place on the day of the death; and as deaths are comparatively rare, they occasion a general mourning, which lasts for a week, during which no work is performed. Mr Sands attended the funeral of a child. Prior to the interment, 'an elderly man offered up a long prayer in Gaelic, whilst the women chanted a monotonous tune in a low tone.' The cemetery, *Cill-Chriosd* or 'Christ's sepulture', occupies, as already stated, the site of Christ's Chapel, behind the village. It is surrounded by a stone wall, and the gate is carefully fastened with wooden pegs.

A recent volume of the *Proceedings of the Society of Scottish Antiquaries*[9] contains an interesting letter, dated 9 April, 1862, addressed to Captain Thomas by Miss Anne Kennedy (afterwards Mrs Ure), niece of the Rev. Duncan Kennedy, for ten years missionary in St Kilda. The letter embraces several curious traditions, which were communicated to the writer by Euphemia Macrimmon, at that time the oldest inhabitant, and probably the last *sennachie*, or verbal historian, of St Kilda. She died about seven years afterwards (31 May, 1869), at the age of eighty-eight – 'influenza' being entered in the register as the cause of her death. Among other 'stories', the letter embraces the following:

9 X, 702 (1874).

Before the forefathers of any of the present inhabitants came to the island, two men, named Dugan (Duncan) and Ferchar (Farquhar) Mor, while gathering heather on Oiseval, the most eastern hill of St Kilda, called aloud to the islanders – 'The wargalleys are in the Sound of Borrera; flee to the temple [Christ Church] – to the horns of the altar.' Alarmed by the warning, the injunction was forthwith obeyed, and the two men brought bundles of heather, which they placed and set fire to at the door of the church. All the St Kildans were burnt within the sacred walls, except a solitary woman, who escaped under cover of the smoke and took refuge in St Brendan's Chapel. Unknown to the two men, she came to the village by night, and stealthily carried off some corn, fire and a hand-mill, and thus preserved her life till the arrival of a boat at St Kilda. This boat was welcomed by Dugan and Ferchar, and soon afterwards the woman made her unexpected appearance and reported all that had occurred. The boatmen seized the two culprits, and put Ferchar on a stack beside Borrera, from which he jumped after the boat into the sea and was drowned, while they carried Dugan to Soa, and took the woman away with them, thus leaving St Kilda without a single inhabitant. It is not known how long it continued in that condition; but after a time, Dugan's bones were found in a cave in Soa, with a dirk stuck in the ground beside them! The cave bears the name of Dugan to the present day.[10]

Miss Kennedy's communication refers to the wreck of 'a son of the King of Lochlan'[11] on a rock to the west of St Kilda. He

10 Mr Maclean gives a slightly different version of the incident, which he refers to 'several hundred years ago'. He makes Duncan and Farquhar natives of *Lewis*, the invaders 'Sassenachs', and the boat the *birlin* of the owner's steward.

A somewhat similar occurrence, so far as the burning is concerned, took place in 1603, at the Church of Kilchrist, in Ross-shire, in connection with the long-standing feud between the Mackenzies and the Macdonalds of Glengarry – See Fraser's *Earls of Cromartie*, I, xxxii.

11 The Gaelic name for Scandinavia in general, and in a more limited sense for the peninsula of Jutland – See Ossian's *Fingal*, book i.

landed on the island in a small boat, and while drinking at a water-brook near the present church, the natives 'caught him by the back of the neck, and held his head down in the brook until he was drowned.' The rock on which he was wrecked still bears the name of *Sgeir Mac Righ Lochlain*, or the Rock of the son of the King of Lochlan.

The letter also alludes to the first Macdonald who went to St Kilda – one of two brothers who fled (from Uist?) after inflicting, as he supposed, a fatal blow on the head of the other. His son Donald, accompanied by John Macqueen, on their way to Oiseval, passed a *sithean*, or little green hillock – an abode of the fairies – in which they heard churning. Macqueen exclaimed, 'Ho, wife! give me a drink' – on which a woman came out, clothed in a green robe, and offered him some milk, which he declined. She then offered it to Donald, who drank it off, 'with God's blessing'. They proceeded to hunt sheep on the hill, where Macqueen fell over a precipice and was killed – as a punishment, it was believed, for his having refused the proffered beverage. Donald Macdonald is said to have died of smallpox in Harris, at an advanced age, about the year 1729; and on the assumption that his father, the refugee, died thirty years earlier, i.e. in 1699, and that he went to St Kilda in the prime of life, the date of his arrival there would probably not be before the middle of the seventeenth century. Captain Thomas conjectures that the tradition might possibly refer to Archibald (Gillespie) Dhu, who murdered his two legitimate brothers about the year 1506; but he acknowledges that such a view would not tally, in point of date, with the story relative to the death from smallpox in Harris, nor with Macaulay's statement that the Macdonalds of St Kilda claimed kinship with Clanranald of South Uist, seeing that Gillespie Dhu was of the clan Huisten of Slate. He considers that of the two clans formerly in St Kilda, Mac Ille Mhoirre ('Son of the Servant of Mary') is plainly Morison from Lewis, but can make no sense out of the other, *Mac Ille Rhiabhich*, which appears to mean 'the Son of the Servant of the Grizzly Man'.

A few words on the antiquities of the island must close the present chapter. In Martin's time, some of the inhabitants of St Kilda occupied, during the summer, the house of the Amazon or female warrior, now called *airidh mhòr*, situated on the southeast side of the valley or glen of the same name, although it was then believed to have been 'some hundred years old'.

> The whole [he says] is built of stone, without any wood, lime, earth or mortar to cement it, in form of a circle, pyramid-wise towards the top, having a vent in it, the fire being in the centre of the floor. The stones are long and thin which supplies the defect of wood. The body of this house contains not above nine persons sitting; there are three beds or low vaults that go off the side of the wall, a pillar betwixt each bed, which contain five men apiece. At the entry to one of these vaults is a stone standing upon one end fixed; upon this they say the Amazon ordinarily laid her helmet; there are two stones on the other side, upon which she is reported to have laid her sword.

This remarkable lady is said to have been addicted to the chase, and, in her time, 'all the space' between St Kilda and Harris was a continuous tract of dry land. Some years before the date of Martin's visit, a pair of large deer's horns were found about a foot under ground on the summit of one of the hills, also a wooden dish 'full of deer's grease'. Toland, in his *History of the Druids*, after noticing the building, almost in Martin's words, says that it is similar to 'Arthur's Oven' in Stirlingshire, and according to tradition, belonged to a Druidess. 'Just such another house', he adds, 'in all respects, but much larger, and grown over with a green sod on the outside, is in Borrera, an isle adjacent to St Kilda, and was the habitation of a Druid, who 'tis probable was not unacquainted with his neighbouring Druidess.' Mr Muir gives a detailed description of the Amazon's abode, which, he says, is scarcely distinguishable in its general appearance from any of the innumerable oblong cells or pyramids already referred to – the internal measurement of the structure being eleven feet by nine. He considers that this 'bee-hive' house was unquestionably designed for human habitation, and that it probably belongs to a time not much posterior to that of St Columba or his immediate followers. The third volume of the *Proceedings of the Society of Scottish Antiquaries* contains a joint paper on the subject by Mr Muir and Captain Thomas (16 March, 1859), accompanied by elevations and a ground-plan of the remarkable building, with some curious traditions which are supposed to relate to the Diana of St Kilda. It appears from a recent communication by Mr Sands to the same Society, that the ancient dwelling has been almost entirely destroyed by the removal of stones for the purpose of building *cleitan* or storehouses – another of many recent illustrations of the necessity of some such legislative measure as that of Sir John Lubbock for the preservation of historical relics.

As already mentioned, not a vestige now remains of the three chapels which existed in the time of Macaulay; but their respective sites are well known to the St Kildans, and are distinctly specified in Mr Muir's *Characteristics*. The occurrence of so many ecclesiastical buildings in St Kilda might be supposed to indicate a much larger population at some former period than is known to have existed during the last three hundred years. In alluding to the numerous remains of sanctity in the various Western Islands, Dr Johnson truly observes that 'these venerable fragments do not prove the people of former times to have been more numerous, but to have been more devout . . . The religion of the middle age is well known to have placed too much hope in lonely austerities. Voluntary solitude was the great art of propitiation, by which crimes were effaced, and conscience appeased; it is therefore not unlikely that oratories were often built in places where retirement was sure to have no disturbance.'

Miss Kennedy's letter refers to two underground structures, or 'Picts' houses', one of which was discovered in a hillock, about forty-four years ago, when the St Kildans were making a level space for the new houses then erected. It had croops in the wall and 'seems to have been a fairy's residence'! The other was discovered a few years afterwards above the present burial-ground, and is probably the subterranean dwelling which was explored by Mr Sands in July 1876, and described in his communication to the Society of Scottish Antiquaries already referred to. It was ascertained to measure twenty-five feet long by three feet eight inches wide, and about four feet in height. Among the *débris* on the floor 'numerous stone axes, knives and fragments of a lamp, as well as pieces of rude pottery', were found.[12] Mr Sands also refers to an 'old cellar 'at the back of the village, built of huge stones, and indicating an approximation to the principle of the arch. It is said to have been erected by one man in a single day, and the St Kildans point to this structure as a proof of the superior strength of their progenitors. Close to the burial-ground is a stone called the "Stone of Knowledge," which is said to have possessed magical qualities, in the way of conferring the gift of second-sight for a limited period on any one who stood upon it 'the first day of the quarter.'

Both Martin and Macaulay refer to an old ruinous fort on the southern side of the bay called the Dune, and the latter writer comments upon the natural protection against invasion afforded to the islanders by the proximity of the hill Osterveaul, immediately above the landing-place, from which 'it is very easy to

---

12 Some of these have been presented by Mr Sands to the Museum of the Society of Antiquaries, along with one of the wooden locks and keys already referred to, a distaff and spindle, portion of a hair-rope, and a spoon formed of the breast-bone of a solan goose, all comparatively lately in use at St Kilda. There is also in the museum a circular flattish stone (quartz?), two and a half inches in diameter, and half an inch thick, with the outer edge worn flat, found near the Amazon's dwelling, and presented about twenty years ago by Mr Thomas S. Muir. A pair of bronze shell-shaped brooches found at St Kilda, similar to the Islay specimens presented to the Society in 1788 by Mr Campbell of Ballinaby, are preserved in the Andersonian Museum, Glasgow, of which one is figured in a paper by Mr J. J. A. Worsae in the *Aarboger for Nordisk Oldkyndighed* for 1873. See communication by Mr Joseph Anderson on the 'Relics of the Viking Period' – *Proceedings of Society of Scottish Antiquaries*, x, 555.

..ischarge volleys of loose stones'. Macaulay tells us that the stones of which the fort was constructed were 'large and nearly square', indicating a knowledge of masonry not displayed by the St Kildans of the eighteenth century; and he has some learned speculations on the origin of the name – *Dun-Fir-Bholg*, or 'the Castle of the Men of the Leathern Bags'[13] – by which the structure was known. Mr Sands was unable to find any remains of the building, but he discovered the wall described by Wilson, which is still in good preservation, and seems to present the appearance of fortification. He also found the site of an ancient altar, from which, however, the stones used in its formation have been removed. Toland makes the following allusion to the St Kilda fort: 'Dún is a general Celtic word for all fortifications made on an eminence, and the eminences themselves are so called . . . There's none of the lesser isles but has one fort at least, and they are commonly in sight of each other. But the *Dún* in St Kilda (for so they call the old fort there) is about eighteen leagues distant from North Uist; but a large fire there would be visible at night, as the ascending smoke by day.'

I have already incidentally referred to the ancient dome-roofed house called *Tigh an Stallair* on the island of Borrera, a detailed account of which is given by Captain Thomas in his elaborate and interesting communication to the Society of Scottish Antiquaries, on 'Primitive Dwellings and Hypogea',[14] where he quotes the descriptions of Martin and Macaulay, as well as the circumstantial statement by Euphemia Macrimmon embraced in Miss Kennedy's letter. The building is supposed to have derived its name from a devout hermit called *Stallir*, or 'the man of the rocks'[15], and is considerably larger than the Amazon's dwelling, being, according to Macaulay, eighteen feet high, and containing four large wall-beds, or croops, roofed with strong lintels. The only apertures

---

13 According to others, 'the Castle of the Men of Quivers'.
14 *Proceedings of the Society of Antiquaries of Scotland*, vii, 153 (1867).
15 From *stal*, the Gaelic for 'a ledge in a cliff'.

were a low doorway on the side facing the sea, and a small hole in the top for the egress of smoke; and Euphemia Macrimmon remembered having seen stones in the structure 'on which there were writings'. Before the roof fell in, about thirty-five years ago, it was occasionally occupied by the St Kildans during their fowling expeditions. Besides the house of Stallir, it would appear that there formerly was an altar on Borrera, and also a temple or chapel built of hewn stones, which, like those of the Amazon's dwelling, were used by the St Kildans for constructing cleitan or storehouses.

The Future of St Kilda – Recent Newspaper Correspondence, etc.

During the past year, a large amount of correspondence has appeared in some of the leading Scottish journals relative to the present condition and future prospects of the inhabitants of St Kilda. As one of the writers in the *Courant* jocularly alleged, there was, at one time, an indication that the 'Eastern Question' would be eclipsed by the momentous considerations connected with the remotest of the Hebrides; and that, ere long, the words 'Western Question' would find a prominent place among the headings of the daily press! Meanwhile, however, a lull appears to have occurred; and accordingly, we are probably now in a better position to estimate the numerous suggestions that have been made respecting the natives of Hirta. One class of correspondents adopts the Gladstonian theory of sweeping the St Kildans, not, indeed, out of the world, but out of what has always been the world to them – to wit, their lonely rock. Others, again, consider that such procedure would be both unkind and impolitic, and advocate their continuance on their native shores, subject, however, to various modifications of existing circumstances. Lastly, a sort of intermediate plan has been propounded – thus making up the celebrated 'three courses' of the distinguished statesman to whom I have already referred – viz, the temporary removal of the inhabitants to the mainland, during the tempestuous months of winter, with the view of their returning to their native rock in the spring, to prosecute fowling and the other avocations to which they have so long been attached. With regard to the first and second of these proposals, I am disposed to prefer the second; but perhaps the last of the three expedients might at least be worth a trial, pending a gradual endeavour to accomplish the modification to which I have referred in connection with the second alternative. On the assumption that Mr Sands is correct in stating that the islanders are 'not unfrequently brought face to face with famine', an anonymous writer, in one of the Edinburgh newspapers, advocates the propriety of an effort being made to induce them to leave their isolated rock. Without basing his proposal on the 'famine' outcry, Sir William Baillie, in a letter addressed to the editor of the *Courant* in March last, also pronounces in favour of removal, suggesting that the proprietor might send well-equipped parties of fowlers to the island, at certain seasons of the year, for the purpose of procuring the feathers of the sea-fowl. The same proposal is made by Lady Baillie in the paper which she contributed to the *Church of Scotland Missionary Record* for January 1875, on the ground that such an arrangement 'would be the most humane and benevolent in the end, although the people might rebel against it in the first instance'. Those who incline to take this view will not have much sympathy with Dr Johnson's reflections on the evils resulting from Scottish emigration. 'In more fruitful countries,' he says, 'the removal of one only makes room for the succession of another: but in the Hebrides, the loss of an inhabitant leaves a lasting vacuity, for nobody born in other parts of the world will choose this country for his residence; and an island once depopulated will remain a desert, as long as the present facility of travel gives everyone who is discontented and unsettled the choice of his abode.'[1] We ought to bear in mind that the

---

1 In these later days, when the folly of the emigration mania appears to be all but universally admitted, the introduction of another passage from Dr Johnson's *Tour* will probably not be considered out of place. 'The great business of insular policy', he says, 'is now to keep the people in their own country. As the world has been let in upon them, they have heard of happier climates, and less arbitrary government; and if they are disgusted, have emissaries among them ready to offer them lands and houses, as a

circumstances of St Kilda are very different from those of such islands as Pitcairn or Tristan d'Acunha. Apart from other points of distinction, the history of the two solitary colonies of the Pacific and South Atlantic is a thing of yesterday compared with that of St Kilda; and accordingly, the influence of its local associations is proportionally much more powerful. If, again, we contrast the St Kildans with the inhabitants of the more accessible islands, and still more with the population of the mainland, I am inclined to think that the very fact of their isolation adds to the strength of the chain which binds them to their native rock. An Inverness-shire man shows comparatively little hesitation in transferring his 'household gods' to the adjoining county of Perth, from which he is only separated by an imaginary boundary. Even an inhabitant of the Long Island thinks nothing of transporting himself and his belongings to almost any portion of the mainland, with which his communication, if not frequent, is at least regular and continuous. But the natives of Hirta are in a very different position. With rare, though gradually increasing opportunities of intercourse with other parts of Scotland, they are necessarily much more ignorant of the ways of the outside world; and the natural result is an exceptionally strong attachment to their sea-girt isle.

> There's a strange something, which, without a brain,
> Fools feel, and which e'en wise men can't explain,
> Planted in man, to bind him to that earth,
> In dearest ties, from whence he drew his birth.

---

reward for deserting their chief and clan. Many have departed both from the main of Scotland and from the islands; and all that go may be considered as subjects lost to the British Crown; for a nation scattered in the boundless regions of America resembles rays diverging from a focus. All the rays remain, but the heat is gone. Their power consisted in their concentration: when they are dispersed, they have no effect. It may be thought that they are happier by the change; but they are not happy as a nation, for they are a nation no longer. As they contribute not to the prosperity of any community, they must want that security, that dignity, that happiness, whatever it be, which a prosperous community throws back upon individuals.'

It is pleasant to be able, once in a way, to agree with Mr Sands. In one of his letters he objects, for 'sentimental reasons', to a well-behaved and ancient community being scattered over the earth, and tells us that, although it is the fashion to sneer at sentiment (which I fear is too true), the great Napoleon declared that 'imagination (or sentiment) rules the world!' In another effusion he gives three reasons why the St Kildans should be allowed to remain on their native shores. 'First, because there is such a faculty in the human soul as *amor patriae*. Secondly, because there is plenty of food and materials for clothing. Thirdly, because the little commonwealth ought to be preserved as a curiosity, it being the only part of Scotland where drunkenness is unknown.' To all of these reasons I feel very much disposed to subscribe; indeed the first is practically a reiteration of what I have already said regarding the natural attachment of the islanders to their *natale solum*. The force of the second reason – so far at least as food is concerned – is amply confirmed by Macaulay, who states that 'if other countries are furnished with a variety of the luxuries, St Kilda possesses, in a remarkable degree, the necessaries of life.' After recapitulating the various sea-fowl which contribute to their 'plentiful repasts,' and referring to the abundance of bread, mutton, and fish with which they are blessed, he says: 'Upon the whole, in spite of hard usage and peculiar disadvantages, they feed more luxuriously, if that be a part of human felicity, than perhaps any small or great nation of slaves (?) upon the face of the whole earth.' While at Obb, on his way to the island, in the summer of 1876, Mr Sands came across two St Kilda women, who were yearning to be home again. 'They looked thin,' he says, 'and grumbled afterwards at the Harris fare, which consisted chiefly of tea and bread. No fulmars, no solan geese, no mutton. Ah! *àite bochd*.' With regard to the third and last reason, a sober colony is indeed a rare spectacle on the northern side of the Tweed; and so long as the threatened still (to be afterwards referred to) is kept away from the shores of Hirta, the disciples of Father Mathew will have reason to rejoice.

Before proceeding to consider a few of the principal suggestions that have recently been made regarding the modification of
existing arrangements and the introduction of various improvements into the social condition of the islanders, I deem it my duty
to refer to the crusade that has for some time been carried on
against the present owner of St Kilda.

The profession of theoretical philanthropist has long been a
favourite avocation with a certain class of individuals. Most sensible
people who have reached the meridian of life must have encountered the enthusiastic 'social reformer' who has made the important
discovery that it is a good deal easier to tell our neighbour how to
do his duty, than to fulfil the obligations which lie at our own door
– who is in the somewhat paradoxical condition of being both
long-sighted and short-sighted at the same time, and who seems to
have forgotten a very wholesome and authoritative injunction as to
the propriety of removing colossal 'beams' at home, before proceeding to deal with microscopic 'motes' abroad. But the man of
enlarged views and energetic character disdains to notice the ill-fed,
ill-clad, badly-housed denizens of the city slums, or the insanitary
and pestilential arrangements of the country village, and must,
forsooth, wend his way to some distant and untrodden shore,
where hitherto no murmur has been uttered and no complaint
made – where neither the enervating luxury of wealth, nor the
depressing cares of poverty, have ever been experienced, and where
the simple-minded inhabitants have been contented with their lot,
and somewhat jealous of proposed 'ameliorations'.

Some people, however, are uncharitable enough to suggest
that the real motive for the 'philanthropic' agitation and sentimental outcry respecting St Kilda is not the improvement of the
condition of the islanders, but the enforced transference of the
remote rock from the hands of its ancient owners to a 'limited
liability association', with some unvouched adventurer as 'manag-
ing director', having for its object the development of the vast
resources, and the realisation of fabulous dividends from the sale
of the precious produce of the sea-girt isle!

> A purchase which will bring them clear,
> Above the rent, four pounds a year.

Somewhere about seventy years ago, a grand improvement scheme appears to have been contemplated. After referring to the presentation of 'two stout boats' to the St Kildans by the then proprietor, with the view of their having regular communication with the Long Island, the author of the *Agriculture of the Hebrides* informs us that 'a young man of knowledge and enterprise from Edinburgh has taken a part of the lands in lease, and bound himself to build a good house, and to improve the island in various ways, especially by teaching the inhabitants the best mode of turning to account the staple production of the place, which is wild fowls and their feathers or down. Of these, large quantities were always exported, but not one-tenth of what might have been secured by the natives. They will now prosecute their labours with additional perseverance and success, having abundance of the requisite tools and the advantage of a ready market.' I cannot, however, find any record of the result of this wonderful project, which probably was never attempted to be carried into execution.

It is not very easy to gather from Mr Sands's book what first induced him to go to St Kilda; but judging from the tone of some of his letters in the Edinburgh newspapers during last spring, he appears to regard himself as the champion of the rights, and the exposer of the supposed wrongs, of the remote islanders. Indeed he distinctly informs the public that he was formally appointed *Fear-ionad*, or representative of the island, by the minister (alias 'domineering fanatic') and all the male population who were not too diffident to write their names;[2] and in the forthcoming edition of Oliver & Boyd's *Edinburgh Almanac*, we may expect to find a sixty-first representative for that part of her Majesty's dominions called Scotland – another 'friend of the people' – in the person of

---

2 See statement at p. 185 *supra*, relative to the calligraphic powers of the islanders.

John Sands, Esquire, MP for St Kilda.[3] In two of the letters now before me, which appeared in the columns of the *Scotsman*, the *Fear-ionad* makes the following among other grave charges.

1. 'The proprietors of St Kilda have never shown any interest whatever in the inhabitants.'

2. 'Macleod of Macleod has never been on the island at all, and he left the poor people without oatmeal last winter, after he had made them depend on his sending it.'

3. 'When it was suggested in the *Spectator* last year that a mail should be sent to the island, the proprietor was the only one who objected. He wants to keep the inhabitants chained to their rock, that his factor may feed upon their entrails!'

4. The owner's monopoly is 'a cunningly contrived infernal machine – the works of which are so carefully encased and concealed that it requires study and reflection to understand them . . . Macleod seems to triumph in this concealment. "How can you possibly know?" is his favourite phrase.'

In another letter, the champion speaks of St Kilda as 'Macleod's prison', and asserts that certain well-known Edinburgh citizens interested in St Kilda, who happened to take a different view from himself, 'did nothing but curry favour with the proprietor'. He elsewhere refers to the possibility of 'famine' being the result of the uncertain communication with the island, and charitably describes Macleod as 'the present arrogant and unsympathetic proprietor, who keeps the St Kildans in darkness and poverty, and has the power to starve them when he feels inclined'. To these sensational insinuations the owner of St Kilda made a dignified and satisfactory reply, which concludes as follows.

As it is the practice in these days for the British public to take up the cause of oppressed communities, I suppose I must not

3 An elaborate document, in the language of Paradise, purporting to be a mandate to 'Maighistir Sands' from the inhabitants of Hirta, will be found in the appendix to the second edition of *Out of the World, or Life in St Kilda*.

permit myself to deprecate uncalled for interference between me and my tenants, creating discomfort and suspicion when there is no cause for either; nor may I resent the injurious and wholly untrue charges brought against me and my agent. I must, I suppose, be content to defend myself by assuring both the gentlemen to whom I have referred[4] that they have, on insufficient information, stated what is not true. The few articles required by the people are supplied at a moderate advance on the cost price to meet the cost of carriage, and a fair price is allowed for the produce, which is sold sometimes at a loss and sometimes at a profit, as the market rises or falls. If the inhabitants of St Kilda can be enabled to buy and sell for themselves, I shall be very glad to be relieved of a very onerous and responsible duty; but the care of the people should not be taken out of the hands of their proper protector, unless there is some security that the change is not one of merely experimental sentimentality.

Most of Mr Sands's charges are repeated, along with some additional accusations, in the second edition of his book, which has reached me as these pages are passing through the press.[5] In alluding to the owner's 'monopoly', he says that 'his serfs – so long incarcerated and cruelly used – are obliged to deal with him on his own terms. It is true he has offered to allow them to go and trade where they choose; but he knows he might as well tell one who has been fettered until his limbs have lost all ability that he is at liberty to run, or bid the ostrich lift its wings and fly.' He elsewhere speaks of a 'threatening letter', which Macleod had written to his 'poor tenants' in October 1875, being accompanied by a subsequent communication indited after he had 'exposed the

4 Mr Sands and a speaker at one of the meetings in Edinburgh relative to the state of St Kilda.
5 Although bearing the date of '1878' on the title-page, the second edition of *Out of the World, or Life in St Kilda*, was actually published before 1 November, 1877.

condition of the island', in which 'Macleod seemed to come down a peg' and agreed to let the people go to Harris and conduct their own business; but it was evident from the tenor that he meant

> To keep the word of promise to the ear,
> And break it to the hope.

Again, he tells us that 'his heart boils with pity for the poor people, and with unutterable hatred for the coldhearted wretches who try to keep them in darkness and in prison'; and, in referring to the failure of the factor's smack to appear at the expected time, he says that 'Macleod's breach of contract on such a serious matter was little short of culpable homicide.' During a 'ninedays' visit' from a certain 'treacherous jade' rejoicing in the appellation of 'Fame', the noble-hearted *Fear-ionad* appears to have been overwhelmed with sympathetic letters 'from all parts of Great Britain' – from 'people of genuine benevolence', 'haters of oppression', and 'firms of cattle-dealers' – a batch of which he thought of sending to Macleod in order 'that they might amuse him'. He adds, however, that 'remembering the dog-in-the-manger aversion he has to any one interfering in the management of his rocky estate, I refrained for fear the perusal might throw him into a fit of apoplexy.' The elegant philippic is appropriately closed with a complacent statement, in which the author 'flatters himself that he has kindled a flame which Macleod and his friends will find some difficulty in extinguishing, no matter how many wet blankets and petticoats they may use!'

I have already said it is difficult to discover the motive which induced the *Fear-ionad* to espouse the cause of the contented islanders, who it seems must now be described in parliamentary language as his 'distressed constituents'. But light is thrown upon the mystery in the second edition of his *Life in St Kilda*. The Ormiston mission is at last explained. 'Often,' he says, 'when rambling amongst the stern rocks on the tops of the mountains, or sitting listening to the solemn sound of the waves upon the lonely shore, I felt as if I had had a Divine call to perform the work, and must proceed at any cost, and despite of any opposition. Providence often selects strange instruments, with which to execute His purposes – instruments that would seem altogether unsuitable to Doctors Begg and McLauchlan.'[6] Possibly, a good many people who take the trouble to think for themselves, and who do not believe every wild assertion that they come across in the daily newspapers, will feel disposed to concur in the opinion of the two reverend doctors as to the character of the 'instrument' in question.

If I am correct in my estimate of the motives which have prompted the ungenerous outcry against the proprietor of St Kilda, I hardly consider myself called upon to say a single word by way of defence or reply. Suffice it to state that since the island returned to its ancient owners about six years ago, they have taken a lively interest in its inhabitants; and Mr Macdiarmid informs us, as already mentioned, that 'they speak of their land-lord in the very best terms, and consider themselves very fortu-nate in being under his guardianship. I must say', he adds, 'that I did not hear one single word or expression implying want of confidence or distrust in his dealings with them. As one old woman put it in Gaelic, "It would be a *black* day for us the day we severed ourselves from Macleod's interest." ' It is quite true that Macleod has not yet set foot on his remote possession; but it ought to be borne in mind that his official duties confine him to London during five-sixths of every year, and I am led to under-stand that he has made more than one unsuccessful attempt to reach St Kilda. During the past summer, his energetic and warm-hearted sister spent upwards of a fortnight on the island, for the express purpose of making herself familiar with the social condi-tion of the inhabitants; and, as already stated, she contemplates a

6 Perhaps the 'strange instrument' is not aware that nearly a hundred years ago the Rev. John Lane Buchanan indulged in the same species of 'tall talk' – See p. 17, *supra*.

second visit in the course of next spring. In Macleod's own letter he fully explains the circumstances which prevented the smack from reaching the island at the appointed time.

With regard to the proposed mail, I am not aware that he ever offered any objection to the matter being taken up by the proper authorities; and as to the 'chains' and 'entrails', none of the passengers on board the *Dunara Castle* succeeded in discovering a vestige of either the one or the other. In respect to the alleged 'monopoly' – elegantly described by Mr Sands as 'a cunningly contrived infernal machine' – there is no mystery or concealment about either exports or imports; and the fair and reasonable principles by which both are regulated are frankly and intelligibly stated in the excerpt which I have given from the proprietor's reply.

Lastly, the ludicrous insinuations as to the possibility of 'famine' are hardly worthy of notice. During last winter, in consequence of a bad harvest and the unavoidable delay in the transmission of supplies, the islanders were for a few weeks compelled to place themselves on short allowances, so far as meal was concerned. But they had abundance of salted meat and fulmar 'brew'. 'Judging from outward appearance,' says Mr Macdiarmid, 'I cannot believe the St Kildans suffered much from want of food'; and after alluding to the large supply of cured mutton in the proprietor's storehouse, at the time of his visit in May last, he adds: 'There can be no doubt, had the St Kildans been in great want, they would have used this mutton, and been made quite welcome to it by Macleod.' Moreover, Mr Sands himself practically contradicts his own insinuations when he tells us that he was well supplied during the winter with mutton, potatoes and oatmeal; and the nine Austrian sailors informed him that as much meat was offered to each of them at every meal as would have served three ordinary men!

If it should be alleged that, in making the preceding observations, I have been confronting an unworthy foeman, I have merely to remark that they have been elicited by the reflection that the intelligent section of the community which draws a distinction between facts and assertions is unfortunately very limited, and by a belief in the truth of the saying that where a quantity of mud is vigorously thrown, some of it is apt to stick, especially if the projector is entirely ignored. That which is '*vox et praeterea nihil*' to a thinking few is gospel to an unthinking many.[7] Hence my sincere, if only *human* endeavour to examine the authenticity of the grave charges which have been so freely made under the influence of a 'Divine call', and I confidently leave the verdict in the hands of my readers. Perhaps the champion of the remote islanders, who, on his own admission, had a very limited acquaintance with the 'treacherous jade' already referred to, may yet prove a striking illustration of the lines of the old dramatist:

> Fame is swittest still when she goes laden
> With news of mischief—
> Thus are we Fortune's pastimes; one day live
> Advanced to heaven by the people's breath;
> The next, hurled down into th' abyss of death.

The cry of 'Highland persecution' is not a thing of yesterday. After referring to the 'systematic oppression' which is indicated in Martin's account of St Kilda, Macculloch says: 'The imaginary harsh conduct of Highland proprietors to their tenants, is not therefore a new grievance, as noisy people try now to make us believe.' Lane Buchanan throws the chief blame on the tacksman of his day, and not on the proprietor of the island, 'the imprudent part of whose conduct,' he says, 'lies in not placing the inhabitants under his own protection, as other tenants, and receiving his rents from themselves.' After enumerating a few of their 'grievances', he expresses his fear that 'to the end of time, these people will be at the mercy of some tacksman or other. Though the infamous pot-penny and fire-penny are dropt, as the people have got pots and flints of their own, yet there may be many other mean

7 How few think justly of the thinking few,
  How many never think who think they do!

practices exercised over these harmless people, without their having an opportunity of conveying those grievances to the ears of the public, with whom they can have little intercourse.' We have already seen that in alluding to the purchase of St Kilda, at the beginning of the present century, from its ancient possessors, the author of *Agriculture of the Hebrides* informs us that the new owner proves 'a blessing to the inhabitants', adding that 'they are no longer fleeced to the skin, or oppressed to downright beggary and starvation as formerly, but encouraged to industry, and amply rewarded for their labours by a humane and enlightened master'.

Fortunately, however, we have a bright side of the shield to present in contrast to these alleged blemishes and stains, and I venture to think that the witnesses to whom I am about to refer will be considered as infinitely more worthy of credence than any of the foregoing accusers. What says the Rev. Alexander Buchan, who, as we have already mentioned, spent nearly a quarter of a century in St Kilda?

None can subsist in this island [he states] without the favour and countenance of the laird of Macleod and the steward; and Mr Buchan gives thanks for the kindness he has had from the managers of that estate during the minority. And now that the representative of that ancient family is near the years of majority, it is not to be doubted but he will go on to encourage the promoting the knowledge of religion among that people, as his predecessor did. Not only the head of that family, but almost the whole name of Macleod have been assertors of the Protestant religion, and against Popery; and will give orders that Mr Buchan meet with all encncouragement in Hirta.

Some forty years later, the Macleod of the day is extolled by Pennant for his estimable qualities. After alluding to the antiquity of his descent, he says that

to all the milkiness of human nature usually concomitant with his early age, is added the sense and firmness of more

248

advanced life. He feels for the distresses of his people; and insensible of his own, with uncommon disinterestedness has relieved his tenants from their oppressive rents, and has received instead of the trash of gold, the treasure of warm affections, and unfeigned prayer . . . The noxious part of the feudal reign is abolished; the delegated rod of power is now no more. But let not the good part be lost with the bad; the tender relation that patriarchical government experiences should still be retained, and the mutual inclination to beneficence preserved.[8]

Such, he states, are the sentiments entertained by the laird of Macleod; and such, I have pleasure in adding, are the principles on which the present representative of the ancient house, as well as every member of his family, desires to act towards the tenants and retainers, whether in Skye or St Kilda, in spite of all the malevolent insinuations of the Sassenach, great or small.

He it is [says Robert Buchanan] who abuses the people for their laziness, points sneeringly at their poor houses, spits scorn on their wretchedly cultivated scraps of land; and he it is who, introducing the noble goad of greed, turns the ragged domestic virtues into well-dressed prostitutes, heartless and eager for hire. In the whole list of jobbers, excepting only the 'mean whites' of the Southern States of America, there are few paltrier fellows than the men who stand by Highland doors and interpret between ignorance and the great proprietors. They libel the race they do not understand, they deride the affections they are too base to cultivate, they rob and plunder, and would exterminate wholly, the rightful masters of the soil. They are the agents of 'civilisation' in such places as the Outer Hebrides; so that, if God does not help the civilised, it is tolerably clear that the devil will.

8 *Tour in Scotland*, ii, 338, 339.

With regard to reforms and improvements at St Kilda, various suggestions have been made, during the past year, of a more or less practicable character. The erection of a lighthouse, for example, has been seriously proposed; but every one who is conversant with the circumstances of the case appears to look upon such a scheme as entirely visionary. The geographical position of St Kilda has a totally different bearing upon the interests of mariners from that of Fair Isle, in Shetland. During Mr Sands's second sojourn of eight months on the island, he only saw some three or four sails. Fair Isle, on the other hand, lies in what may be termed an important ocean-highway; and in the course of the last few months, several valuable vessels have been wrecked upon its rocky shores. The proposed establishment of telegraphic communication with St Kilda may also be regarded, at least for the present, as purely Utopian, keeping in view that its distance from Harris or Uist is somewhere about fifty miles, and that the inhabitants amount to only seventy-six, and have no special desire to be kept *au courant* with the most recent proceedings in connection with Tichborne trials and Penge mysteries. A correspondent of the *Scotsman*, in a letter signed 'B.', and dated 9 March, 1877, suggests that, in addition to a lighthouse station, a meteorological observatory should be established, 'whence, especially in stormy seasons, the news of approach might be sent by secret submarine wire of many a disastrous gale. It might also become a valuable signal-station for our Atlantic squadron. The Committee of the Board of Trade have decided substantially that the area of weather work should be extended rather than otherwise. They are right; and St Kilda may be made useful to science, to commerce, and to the empire.'

Among other minor suggestions relative to St Kilda, the friends of the temperance movement have proposed the institution of a dipsomaniac establishment on its distant shores. Such philanthropic undertakings are known to be productive of no small advantage in certain other islands somewhat less remote than Hirta, and there seems to be no reason whatever why a branch establishment should not be tried on the lonely rock. The only possible objection that occurs to my mind is prompted by the recollection of a threat on the part of Mr Sands to introduce the 'light wine of the country' into St Kilda. In one of his many letters to the *Scotsman*, he says: 'If the government declines to send a mail to the island, I will go out myself and start a small still, by Jove! and compel them to send out a vessel!' A reformatory for refractory wives may perhaps also have occurred to some considerate individuals as a suitable institution for St Kilda, and no doubt the painful episode of poor Lady Grange is calculated to give rise to the idea. In the event of the inhabitants being removed from the island, the expediency of converting it into a penal settlement is perhaps worthy of consideration, now that our colonies naturally object to receive the criminal population of the mother country.

To a limited amount of postal communication no reasonable person will probably offer any objection. In these progressive days, any place that happens to be situated considerably more than 'ten leagues beyond man's life,' and whose inhabitants 'can have no note, unless the sun were post', is surely worthy of our practical sympathy. In the meantime, I venture to think that the proper authorities might be approached with the view of provision being made for at least two mail steamers in the course of each year – say, towards the beginning of April and October. In the event of such arrangement being carried into effect, a special agreement might be made to convey the proprietor's factor on these two occasions; and through the same medium, regular communication would be secured between the Registrar-General and the registrar of St Kilda. If it should be thought desirable to endeavour to make these steamers available for the conveyance of scientific men and ordinary tourists, one of the trips would probably require to take place during the summer months, unless, indeed, special provision should be made by the advancing enterprise of Messrs Cook and Sons! Of course a very essential preliminary to any such scheme would be the formation of a safe and substantial landing place, for the cost of which application would probably require to be made to the government. Increased means of communication would in all likelihood result in the introduction of new blood, which would no doubt materially improve the physical character of the islanders, and perhaps also be productive of other important consequences, more especially if Miss Macleod should succeed in her humane and judicious endeavour to secure the services of a qualified nurse.

Not many months ago, Mr Kinnaird, MP for Perth, communicated, at the request of a constituent, with the Board of Admiralty, on the subject of increased communication with St Kilda. Admiral Yelverton stated in reply that the question belonged rather to the Home Secretary's department; adding that 'it would be impossible for the Admiralty to undertake to keep up regular communication with outlying British islands, affording relief when necessary, unless a special grant of money is set apart for the purpose.' At one of the recent Edinburgh meetings relative to St Kilda, a resolution was unanimously adopted, which embraced 'respectful representation to the government, with a view to the establishment of a regular postal system on the island'. So far as I am aware, the result of the representation has not yet been made public.[9]

One or two additional boats of a suitable and superior construction, and a good supply of nets and lines, would be a great boon to the islanders, to whom greater encouragement ought to be given to induce them to prosecute fishing as an important source of profit; and the introduction of the appliances used by the Faroe fowlers, in lieu of the uncomfortable, not to say dangerous system of ordinary ropes, would also be a very desirable reform. Dr

---

9 Towards the beginning of the present year, a fortnightly postal communication with Fair Isle, in Shetland – wind and weather permitting – was established through the energetic action of Lord Beaconsfield and the Postmaster-General, consequent on a relative application about two years previously. It must be borne in mind, however, that Fair Isle lies in the direct line of the steamers plying between Kirkwall and Lerwick.

Angus Smith informs me that the St Kildans do not quite know their own minds as to the boats best adapted to their requirements. Mr James Young, FRS, in whose yacht Dr Smith visited the island in 1873, was requested to provide the inhabitants with a ten-ton boat; but before it was constructed, the minister (Mr McKay) wrote asking for one of smaller dimensions, which was duly transmitted from the Clyde. Immediately after it reached the island, a commotion was caused by Mr Sands on the plea of Mr Young's gift being unsuitable for the passage between St Kilda and the Long Island; and he himself raised a subscription to procure another craft, which was built at Ardrishaig, and conveyed by him to St Kilda in the summer of 1876, as fully described in the second edition of his book. Besides the supply of proper boats, the St Kildans seem to require some instruction in practical seamanship. Whatever they may have been in former times, they now appear to be very timid and unskilful sailors; and if the belles of Hirta could induce a few stalwart Orcadians to find their way to its shores, the result would no doubt be highly satisfactory in more ways than one.

Bearing in mind the consistent adherence on the part of Highland and insular Free Churchmen to the principles of a national establishment, the Endowment Committee of the Church of Scotland is no doubt keeping its eye upon the sea-girt isle; and perhaps the day is not far distant when the 'swallows' will peaceably resume possession of their former nests! Probably the most beneficial influence that could be brought to bear upon the St Kildans would be of an educational kind. Through the instrumentality of the Harris school board or otherwise, an energetic effort ought to be made to introduce a systematic course of instruction in English, with the view of the inhabitants enjoying the vast benefits which would inevitably ensue. At present, they are not only cut off from regular communication with the mainland, but in consequence of their ignorance of the language of the United Kingdom, they are debarred from the means of enlarging their minds and subverting their prejudices, by the perusal of

English literature. A recent number of *Chambers' Journal* – to which every English-speaking section of the globe owes such deep obligations – contains an admirable article, from the pen of the veteran senior editor, on the subject of 'The Gaelic Nuisance', to which I venture to call the attention of all who are interested in the future welfare of the inhabitants of St Kilda. The writer points to Galloway on the one hand, and to the Orkney and Shetland Islands on the other, as illustrative examples of the blessings which have flowed from the substitution of English for Gaelic and Norse respectively; and in the course of his remarks, he makes special allusion to St Kilda. Even after the entire abolition of Gaelic, Professor Blackie need have little fear as to the survival, for many a long day, of 'provincial peculiarities and local diversities', as well as 'marked individualism and a characteristic type', among the inhabitants of the Highlands and Islands of Scotland.

In a previous chapter I have referred to the want of peat and other kinds of fuel from which the islanders continue to suffer; and to the disastrous practice of stripping the precious turf as a substitute for the peat with which the inhabitants of Skye and the Long Island are so abundantly supplied. I have also mentioned the rarity of drift-wood, in consequence of the very small extent of the beach. Rare as it is, it is somewhat difficult to believe what Mr Sands states, that 'the Receiver of Wrecks at Stornoway claims the half of the flotsam and jetsam!' Surely a representation in the 'proper quarter' would put an end to so unreasonable a demand. Apart, however, from that special matter, the best mode of furnishing the remote islanders with proper fuel appears to be a question requiring immediate attention. As the bulk of the material is an important consideration, probably coal ought to be preferred to peat, as more lasting and cheaper in the end. A supply of the best kind of firelighters might perhaps also be occasionally transmitted.

At the Edinburgh meeting to which I have already referred, Mr Fletcher Menzies, Secretary to the Highland and Agricultural

Society, made a statement relative to the fund left, for behoof of the islanders in seasons of emergency, by a West Indian gentleman named Kelsall, in the year 1859. Originally amounting to upwards of £600, on various occasions payments have been made from it by the Society to meet the cost of supplying the St Kildans with boats, ropes, seed-corn, potatoes, and other commodities – the balance of the fund at present in hand being about £350. It is expressly provided that the money is not to benefit the proprietor; but, as Mr Menzies truly said, 'it is not very easy to benefit the inhabitants without in some way benefiting the proprietor.' It appears that the late owner of the island was extremely jealous of the interference of the Highland Society, on the ground that he considered himself able to look after his own people; but Mr Menzies indicated that no difficulty in regard to the administration of the fund would be raised by the present proprietor. In the second edition of his *Life in St Kilda*, Mr Sands comments, in severe terms, on the mode in which the Kelsall fund has been managed and applied, and makes various suggestions relative to its future disposal. He considers that the best plan would be to keep a store of bread-stuffs in the island, to be paid for out of this fund, and that 'the interest on the original sum (if the principal was invested, and not kept in a ram's horn) would have been more than sufficient to meet an emergency.'

At the same meeting, the Rev. Dr McLauchlan, who, besides having visited St Kilda, has communication with the inhabitants once every year, had the good sense to refer to the danger of destroying the independent spirit of the islanders by indiscriminate charity, and expressed a hope that some action would be taken to enable the people to help themselves. Such a course of procedure seems to be unusually necessary, if Dr Angus Smith is correct in his estimate of the islanders. 'We had proof', he says, 'that the St Kilda man is not loath to make demands. In this he differs from the Highlander, who is generally too proud and dignified, except perhaps when tourists may spoil him.' He elsewhere says: 'It would be a sad thing to do anything to make them feel dependent, or to pauperise them: we obtained too high an opinion of the people to wish them such an ending. They are evidently rising in the social scale, and their keenness made us believe that they would be quite a match for their fellow-men eastward.'

A recent writer in the *Courant*, in commenting on the Edinburgh St Kilda Committee assuming the guardianship of the islanders, suggests that they ought to have asked the Board of Supervision for the Relief of the Poor to allow their visiting inspector to proceed to the island, with the view of investigating the condition of the inhabitants. Without actually indicating an adverse opinion to the proposal, I confess that I am not sorry that there is still one little spot in the kingdom of Scotland which has not yet been embraced within the domain of pauperism; and until the Education Board of Harris has made an effort to supply the intellectual wants of the islanders, I, for one, am quite prepared to postpone the consideration of the question as to whether another Board of older standing in the same parish should take any steps to provide for the physical requirements of the inhabitants of Hirta.

In common with many others, Mr Fletcher Menzies considers that the main object to be aimed at in connection with St Kilda is the introduction of free trade; and with that view he suggests that the Long Island steamer (*Dunara Castle*) should call at least four times a year at the remote island. Each journey would imply a detour of only 140 miles, and arrangements could of course be made for the conveyance of the mails. Mr Sands informs us that he made an attempt to get the Commissioners of Northern Lights to act the part of the good Samaritan, on the ground that one of their steamers is in the habit of calling once a month at the lighthouse on one of the small islets beside the island of Monach, which is only thirty-four miles distant from St Kilda; but that Mr Duncan, the secretary – who seems to Mr Sands to be 'invested with extraordinary powers' – informed him that his request is not very likely to be complied with.

A good many years ago, a capacious boat was supplied to the islanders by a few gentlemen connected with the Highland Society, in order that they might have an opportunity of carrying on trade with the Long Island. Unfortunately, however, as already stated, it was lost in and shortly afterwards a boat of smaller dimensions was sent to St Kilda by the Society. Probably, for such a purpose, the craft ought not to be less than from nine to ten tons. Others have suggested that a smack should be kept at some suitable place in Harris, with the view of plying to and from St Kilda in favourable weather. Apropos to that recommendation, Mr Sands states that the inhabitants of Harris and those of St Kilda 'have no great respect for each other'. They are said to speak of each other in no very respectful terms; and when a Harris child is naughty, its mother invariably threatens to send it to Hirta! Possibly, however, a more friendly feeling would spring up between the two islands if intercourse were to become more frequent. Mr Macdiarmid suggests the establishment of a shop or store in St Kilda, which he thinks might be presided over by the wife of Neil McDonald, already referred to as a woman of education and intelligence.

Mr Sands refers to the large profit obtained by the proprietor's factor on all the imports, and to the comparatively small price which, on the other hand, he pays for feathers, cloth, and other articles exported, to which reference has been made in a preceding chapter. Various important circumstances, however, must be taken into account, if we wish to arrive at a just conclusion. The position of matters is very fairly stated by Dr Angus Smith, who writes as follows.

We cannot expect a landlord, or any business man, to send out a vessel with goods to be sold at the price at which they are sold in the nearer towns. It costs fifteen pounds, we were told, to send out a small schooner of eighty tons from Skye. Neither can we expect the business man to give for the produce as much as he could give at a nearer port. On the other hand, no landlord can make much of the island, and to be a constant giver is more than we can demand of him. But ninepence a head for feeding sheep seems very low. It is, I am told, from two to five shillings in Scotland. Even allowing the sheep in St Kilda to be very small, the price is low. The price for a cow feeding will bear the same remark. Again, it is easy to calculate thirty pounds as divided among seventy-two people, the schooner going twice in the year. It is eight shillings and fourpence a head. Even this may be reduced by having all their marketing done once a year, if this is possible, leaving only four shillings and twopence caused by disadvantage of position.

Upwards of a hundred years ago, in referring to the small amount of internal commerce in the Western Islands, Dr Johnson remarked that hardly anything, at that period, had 'a known or settled rate', and that 'the price of things brought in or carried out had to be considered as that of a foreign market'. He further states, in illustration of the common error which regards money and wealth as similar terms, that 'when Lesley, two hundred years ago, related so punctiliously that a hundred hen-eggs, new-laid, were sold in the islands for a penny, he supposed that no inference could possibly follow but that eggs were in great abundance. Posterity has since grown wiser; and having learned that nominal and real value may differ, they now tell no such stories, lest the foreigner should happen to collect not that eggs are many, but that pence are few.'

In one of his contributions to the *Ayr Observer*, Mr W. M. Wilson makes some very sensible remarks on the alleged grievances of the St Kildans.

> Their social condition [he says] is much higher than that of the Hebrideans generally, from whom we hear no complaints, and for whom we hear no mawkish and maudlin sympathy. They are well housed, well clad, and well fed, and live natural and

comfortable lives . . . If they *wish* to trade to Harris, they *can* trade to Harris. If their present boats are not seaworthy, they have resources available to procure a suitable smack. If Mr Mackenzie, the factor, can bring Dunvegan to St Kilda, they can carry St Kilda to Dunvegan. That Macleod does not grind the face of St Kilda might at least be presumed, in the first place, from his own character and the character of Miss Macleod, as well as from the character of his factor, Mr Mackenzie, and the spirit and character of the islanders themselves. They are not pigeon-livered. They do not 'lack gall to make oppression bitter', were it practised. They have sense enough to feel it, and wit and courage enough to devise and secure redress, were there any grievance to be redressed. But there is none.

He then alludes to the concurrent testimony of Mr Macdiarmid (already referred to), Captain Macdonald of the *Vigilant*, the Rev. Roderick McDonald of South Uist, and the captain and purser of the *Dunara Castle*, relative to the comparatively satisfactory condition of the islanders. The captain of the *Vigilant* considers that there is not a more comfortable set of people between Kintyre and Cape Wrath, or from the Butt of Lewis to Barra Head, than the St Kildans. The genial old minister of South Uist, formerly pastor of Harris, has paid several visits to the island, and knows the people well. He agrees with Captain Macdonald, and warmly protests that it is due to truth and honesty, as well as to Macleod of Macleod, that the aspersions on his character should be exposed and condemned. Captain McEwan and Mr Donald of the *Dunara* are thoroughly familiar with the Inner and Outer Hebrides, and entertain the same opinion regarding the inhabitants of the most distant isle. Lastly, Mr Wilson fairly asks

Shall any one gainsay the corroborative testimony of the clergy, and lawyers, and doctors, and civil engineers, and artists, and merchants, and travellers – the passengers of the

259

Dunara Castle, who spent that Monday in July last upon the island of St Kilda? They landed with minds open to truth. They observed, for themselves, the St Kildans, their appearance and character, and social economy. Some of them, acquainted with Gaelic, entered freely into personal communication with the islanders, and had their confidence. And these visitors left St Kilda with the intelligent conviction that presumption, probability, experience, and fact, were all in favour of Macleod of Macleod; and that never was public agitation more delusive and mischievous than that based upon the fictitious oppression and misery of the poor islanders of St Kilda!

I have already incidentally referred to the great modification, if not the absolute decay, of the feudal system. That day has probably passed away for ever wherein we shall witness that mutual attachment which prevailed when the chieftain reigned in the hearts of his clan, while they bore his exactions without a murmur, and followed his fortunes without a call. The 'times are altered'. The commercial spirit of the age has substituted money for men, and the lawyer's contract for personal affection; and it is somewhat difficult for the most humane of masters to counteract the natural results. In many parts of the kingdom, however, a legitimate reverence for the past still influences a not inconsiderable section of our countrymen, even in the humblest ranks of life. The prestige of birth, when accompanied by honourable conduct and personal worth, can still accomplish some things that mere wealth signally fails to achieve. In that respect, the representative of the ancient owners of St Kilda has an advantage over even the best-intentioned 'men of yesterday', who now occupy the domains of many a historic race; but in addition to his 'blood' and his time-honoured appellation, he has also that 'good name' which is better than 'precious ointment'. On the grounds already indicated, I feel satisfied that the inhabitants of Hirta have no just reason to desire a more considerate patron than their present lord,

who might apply, with some slight modifications, the honest
Gonzalo's description of the insular republic, in the *Tempest*, to
the circumstances and condition of his lonely rock:

> I' the commonwealth I would by contraries
> Execute all things: for no kind of traffic
> Would I admit; no name of magistrate;
> Letters should not be known; no use of service,
> Of riches or of poverty; no contract, succession,
> Bourn, bound of land, tilth, vineyard, none;
> No use of metal, corn, or wine, or oil;
> No occupation; all men idle, all;
> And women too, but innocent and pure:
> No sovereignty . . .
> All things in common nature should produce
> Without sweat or endeavour: treason, felony,
> Sword, pike, knife, gun, or need of any engine,
> Would I not have; but nature should bring forth,
> Of its own kind, all foison, all abundance,
> To feed my innocent people . . .
> I would with such perfection govern, sir,
> To excel the golden age.

Addendum

As the last sheet is passing through the press, I am informed by Mr A. B. Stewart of Ascog Hall, Bute, that, accompanied by the Earl of Dunmore, he visited St Kilda in his yacht in the beginning of last September – his father having formed one of the party which embraced Doctors Dickson and Macleod in 1838, and being still remembered by some of the oldest islanders. Mr Stewart also informs me that Lord Dunmore, as the proprietor of South Harris, is the superior of St Kilda, the annual feu-duty for which amounts to the formidable sum of one shilling sterling!

My attention has been called to a little volume, published in 1825, and said to be uncommonly rare, of the existence of which I was not previously aware, entitled *A Critical Examination of Dr Macculloch's Work on the Highlands and Western Isles of Scotland*, attributed to James Browne, Advocate, LLD, author of the *History of the Highlands and Highland Clans*, and celebrated for his bloodless duel with Charles McLaren of the *Scotsman*. According to the writer of the *Scottish Nation*, he was 'always remarkable for his tendency to strong statement'; and notwithstanding his criticisms, I feel disposed to adhere to my remarks on Macculloch as an author.

THE END